A Work In Progress

A Work In Progress

Cover design: Charlotte Adlam

Published independently by Gethin J Nadin & Benefex Limited.

First printing October 2022.

References are listed at the end of this book.

ISBN: 9798842846337

22 23 24 25 26 10 9 8 7 6 5 4 3 2

A Work In Progress

A Work In Progress

Unlocking Wellbeing to Create More Sustainable
and Resilient Organisations

By Gethin Nadin

Published by

www.hellobenefex.com

A Work In Progress

Global Praise for 'A Work In Progress'

"Gethin's status as a wellbeing evangelist, well before it moved more into the mainstream, makes 'A Work In Progress' the must-have bible for leaders looking to drive genuine employee-centred change by putting wellbeing front and centre of how businesses operate"
- Marc Weedon, Senior Director (HR) International, Zuora

"A Work in Progress has two important features - the nature of the word 'progress' and a progression to more human-centred work; and the elegant way this book unfolds through facts, philosophy, and practical application of what matters to human beings at work. A must-read that brings all you need into one literary place. A much needed AND brilliant piece of work"
- Perry Timms, Author, TEDx speaker, HR's Most Influential & Chief Energy Officer at PTHR

"This book is HR's North Star for cultivating sustainable, inclusive wellbeing in a complex world. Coupling rich evidence with best practice, Gethin Nadin urges organisations to stop using nonsensical, surface-level approaches and start uncovering the root causes of employee unhappiness"
- Becky Norman, Editor, HR Zone

"In a post-pandemic world, employers face a new level of complexity in the wellbeing and engagement space. Gethin's narrative gives both the new and the advanced reader opportunities to navigate these vast topics with a balanced perspective of theory and business reality, enabling all to consider their strategies and build a more inclusive approach"

- Dr Andrea Kilgour, HR Director, Consumer Service, BT Group

"This book is essential reading for anyone interested in employee wellbeing. Gethin's insight and passion for the subject shine through on every page. This is a must read for HR leaders everywhere"

- Kevin Green, Chief People Officer First Bus, & Author of the bestseller Competitive People Strategy

"This book could not have come at a better time. Whether you know a lot or a little about wellbeing, Nadin has written a brilliantly inspiring, compelling, thoughtful, and incisive account of what workplace wellbeing is - and more importantly what it isn't. For me, A Work In Progress will become the Rosetta Stone for organisations seeking to move from 'do no harm' to 'we must do better"

- Chris Taylor, Host of the Oven Ready HR Podcast

"This book will challenge how you think of, and address employee wellbeing at your organization, providing thought-provoking questions and considerations to help you successfully navigate in this increasingly important area. For anyone who wants to better understand and improve wellbeing at their company, this is THE book for you!"

- Debra Corey, Author, Speaker, Consultant & Chief Pay it Forward Officer at DebCo HR

"I loved this book! My life is hectic, combining my executive HR leadership role, non-exec roles and family and books have in recent years become my escape route. They have to be easy to read and give me quick provocative thoughts and ideas. I rarely find a non-fiction book that does this, but Gethin's book is practical and provocative. This book will give you many of the answers you need to respond effectively to post-pandemic employee demand and in doing so, become an employer that cares"

- Jacqui Summons, Chief People Officer, EMIS Health

.

About the Author

Gethin Nadin BSc MBPsS FRSA

Chief Innovation Officer, Benefex

Gethin is a multi-award-winning psychologist and bestselling HR author who has been helping some of the world's largest brands to improve the employee experience and wellbeing of their people for more than two decades. The last 11 years of his career have been spent working as part of the senior leadership team at Benefex, where Gethin leads thought leadership and consults with organisations on employee experience and employee wellbeing.

As a frequent writer on various HR issues and the future of work, Gethin has been featured in Forbes, The Guardian, The Sun, LinkedIn News, The Huffington Post and The Financial Times, as well as all major global HR publications. Gethin is twice listed as one of the world's Top Global Employee Experience Influencers, has been named an HR Influencer five times, and was awarded Inspiring Workplaces 'Inspiring Leader 2021'.

Gethin is a regular conference speaker and awards judge, a HR Zone Culture Pioneer Ambassador, ex-Chair of Wellbeing at the UK Government-backed Engage for Success movement, is a wellbeing advisor to Investors In People, a member of the British Psychological Society and a Fellow at the Royal Society for Arts, Manufactures and Commerce (RSA). Gethin was also a key stakeholder in establishing employee wellbeing KPIs for the Rail Safety Standards Board in 2021.

In 2017, Gethin published his first book 'A World of Good: Lessons From Around the World in Improving the Employee Experience', which reached the top of the Amazon HR bestseller list. The book has become highly regarded in the HR world; it appears in more than 15 'must read' book lists for HR professionals, is quoted in academic literature and was inducted into the British Library. A World of Good has sold thousands of copies worldwide and maintains a 4.7 out of 5-star rating with hundreds of reviews across Goodreads and Amazon. As a result of its impact, the book was awarded the Lotus Award for Culture in 2019.

Amid the global Coronavirus pandemic, Gethin was invited to co-author his "second book", 'Das Menschliche Büro - The Human(e) Office'. This book was a collaboration between leading academics and workplace professionals from Europe, published by Springer in Germany.

As Chief Innovation Officer at Benefex, Gethin ensures innovation remains a core part of the proposition across employee experience, benefits, recognition, and wellbeing.

This book is kindly published by Benefex, the company behind OneHub, the award-winning employee experience platform. Supporting employee benefits, wellbeing, recognition, and communications for over 1.5 million employees in 650 organisations across 70 countries. Benefex has won over 50 awards for delivering consumer-grade employee experiences to global organisations, including AstraZeneca, Bank of America, BT, Centrica, Capita, Diageo, EDF, Just Eat, Liberty Global, Ocado, Philips, Salesforce, and Snowflake.

Find out more about Benefex at **www.hellobenefex.com**

A Work In Progress

Dedications

This book is dedicated to the Founder and CEO of Benefex, Matt-Macri-Waller. But also to everyone who has ever worked at this fantastic company. Benefex has given me a space to grow and thrive for half of my working life. It's an organisation led by people who genuinely care about others. It's been the privilege of my life to be a part of that team for so long.

This book is also dedicated to Elizabeth Eyre, Benefex's Content Manager. My last conversation with Elizabeth was about her wanting to edit and proof this book. Elizabeth sadly passed away in July 2022 before she could do that. This book is published in her memory.

A Work In Progress

Preface

"An old skeleton, a lot of steps and a global pandemic."

In the UK, there is a place called Cheddar Gorge in the Mendip Hills. This gorge has become famous for the discovery of Britain's oldest complete human skeleton in 1903. The whole of Cheddar Gorge is considered one of the top natural wonders of the United Kingdom and a pinpoint for early humans in the country. I think this link to early humans can tell us a bit about wellbeing at work. A set of 274 steps lead up the side of the gorge, formerly known as "Jacobs Ladder". They used to be named after the biblical ladder to heaven featured in a dream Jacob had in the Book of Genesis. However, in 2007, the steps were renamed to the imaginatively titled '274 Steps' after officials decided that most visitors didn't understand the biblical reference. But it's a sign at the top of the steps that shaped my thinking on employee wellbeing many years ago.

At the start and various points on your way up the 274 steps, signs indicate the different geologic periods from earth's creation at the first step to the present day at the last. As you ascend the steps, you pass through the Cenozoic period to the more familiar Cretaceous and Jurassic, all the way to the present day – the Holocene period. At the very top, a sign tells you that if you were to lay just one single piece of paper on the top of the last step, that would represent human life on earth since its creation. It's such a minuscule amount compared to the almost 300 steps you've just climbed that it's tough to fathom. Just like the idea that Cleopatra lived closer to the creation of the iPhone than she did to the construction of the pyramids of Gizeh. To me, these examples illustrate that in the grand scheme of things, humans have not been around for long, and we also haven't evolved much either. As a result, I don't think our wellbeing requirements have grown that much too.

An example of how much our needs haven't evolved is other people's role in our wellbeing. Humans have always needed other people to maintain wellbeing for thousands of years. Since early humans first walked the earth, we have been required to find a place as part of a functioning and successful group just to be well. Cooperating led to more remarkable survival and less harm for our ancestors - and the same plays out today in the modern workforce. Over the last few years, researchers have continued to prove our colleagues' role in our health and happiness[1]. Employees who benefit from a positive working environment and supportive colleagues have a better home life. Work is the start of something called a 'gain spiral', in which the benefits of a supportive relationship with a colleague start to transfer to our home lives and shared with our partner and family. Effectively this means we take the love we feel from work and move that to home, and vice versa. The link can be so strong that suddenly it makes complete sense that not only would an employer want to create a better work environment that supports wellbeing, but they would also want an employee's home life to do that as well. A happy and healthy home community and a happy and healthy work community become mutually beneficial.

In my "second book", 'The Human(e) Office' I wrote about the importance of community at work for our wellbeing in a post-pandemic world. When the Coronavirus pandemic and the advance of remote working pulled us apart from each other, feelings of loneliness and separation harmed our wellbeing. When burnout thrived during the pandemic, our social capital helped us be more resilient to it. So strong is this connection to other people that tending to the relationships in our lives was the number one reason people live longer, according to one large study by Harvard[2]. Yet I rarely see a wellbeing product or strategy that shows the benefits of creating better communities at work to support wellbeing. The reason for this, I think, is that our approach to wellbeing has become highly commodified.

Hundreds of thousands of wellbeing apps are available in the various global app stores, and wellbeing solutions have become big business. The global wellbeing market is estimated to be worth more than $1.5 trillion[3]. While apps and technology have a part to play, I don't think it's the panacea that was promised, and quite often, these approaches to wellbeing miss some of the fundamentally human things we need to thrive.

This is why I have written this book – the evidence largely isn't being followed by the market selling us wellbeing. Towards the end of the pandemic, the wellbeing market began to struggle with engagement as employees realised that when it came to the crunch, many widespread wellbeing solutions were materially ineffective at supporting them through one of the most challenging points of their careers. When the physical and emotional threat of the pandemic hung over them, employees realised that many 'perks' and wellbeing initiatives didn't support them in the way they needed them to.

At the time of writing this book, the UK's Department for Transport has announced that 11 local authorities have received more than £12 million to fund a pilot of 'social prescriptions'[4]. This means that shortly, doctors will start prescribing walking and cycling to help improve mental and physical health in the UK. Think about that for a moment; we are trialling encouraging people to do more of the things that we have been doing for centuries. The bicycle was invented 200 years ago, and humans have been walking upright for the last 3.6 million years. I guess the more things change, the more they stay the same.

The pandemic changed everything.

When the Covid-19 virus made its way across the world in early 2020, it began to change almost every part of work. It often seemed like any strategies or plans we had as employers needed to be ripped up, as the next few years were like nothing we had planned for. But it also changed wellbeing. It changed our collective attitudes toward our wellbeing, and it advanced employers' views of their role in wellbeing. As someone with (hopefully) an advanced understanding of wellbeing at work, it created the busiest time in my professional career. So prominent and influential was the pandemic on wellbeing that I think it almost reset employers' very understanding of not just how they develop workplace wellbeing but how they understand the role of the people working for them.

One fascinating study highlights just how important an event like the pandemic can be to our health and happiness. The study tried to examine the history of our joy on this earth by analysing texts from millions of fiction and non-fiction books and newspapers published over the last 200 years[5]. Using sentiment analysis, researchers measured how frequently positive words like "love" or "happiness" appeared in texts when compared to negative words like "death" or "anger". Written text from four Western countries (the UK, US, Italy, and Germany) was studied. What the researchers call 'The National Valence Index' was used to compute the relative levels of happiness or unhappiness by looking at texts from any given year.

The researchers found that large-scale events like the Civil war, the Great Depression, the Korean War, the Second World War, etc., significantly impacted our happiness across all countries studied. This becomes important for us to understand as it explains part of the challenge employers have when trying to improve employee wellbeing in a post-pandemic world.

Any attempt to improve employee wellbeing or happiness over the coming years will be more challenging than it has been in living memory. The majority of the workforce has now lived through several wide-scale, generation-defining events that have obstructed their happiness and wellbeing. For employers in 2022, this means they are starting from a position of trying to lift their people out of one of the largest slumps in happiness we have ever seen before they even get a chance to move their wellbeing back up to pre-pandemic levels. I think this begins with ensuring we, as employers, aren't creating problems for our people.

> *"Understanding our psychological past can help us to better envision a positive psychological future"*
> - Thomas Hills, Chanuki Illushka Seresinhe, Daniel Sgori and Eugenio Proto

Work must become the solution, not the problem.

At the time of writing this book, we are spending a lot of our life at work. Gallup suggests we spend, on average, 81,396 hours a year working[6]. The only thing we do in our lives that takes up more time than working is sleeping. So, while employer-led wellbeing is a new concept to many, with work taking up so much of our lives, I think we are at the start of wellbeing support finding its home far more commonly in the workplace than it is elsewhere – and that is a significant shift in what we all thought wellbeing at work was going to be. It's moved the dial away from ensuring people are present and productive and instead moved it towards ensuring that work is a force for good in our lives and doesn't make us unhappier or unhealthier.

In 2016, work-related diseases and injuries were responsible for the deaths of almost two million people worldwide[7]. Air pollution, ergonomic risk factors and noise at work, all contributed to millions of instances of fatalities on the job. But the critical risk exposure continues to be long working hours – linked to almost 750,000 deaths. Alongside long hours, around one in three global employees now say they are constantly struggling with fatigue and poor mental health because of the job they do[8]. Added to this is the growing evidence of the effects of job control and good mental health on mortality rates, and we start to see that wellbeing at work is no longer just about gym memberships and health insurance – it's about redesigning our organisations to protect better and serve the people working for us. It's about getting back to the tribe and the fire of what matters to us as humans.

But wellbeing has also become a way for us to create organisations that people *want* to come and work for. Globally, 40 percent of workers say they might leave their job soon. In India, that figure goes as high as 66 percent[9]. Across six countries assessed by McKinsey, every region showed a consistently high desire to work for a better organisation. So perhaps more than ever, we have to think more carefully about why someone would come and work for us. This is especially true as almost three-quarters of respondents told McKinsey that they felt it wouldn't be difficult to find a job elsewhere[10].

Pay aside, among the top motivating factors that keep people in their jobs at the moment are meaningful work, flexibility, and of course, wellbeing. More than a third of those who have quit their jobs between April 2021 and April 2022 say "uncaring leaders" was the top reason they left. Wellbeing now ranks consistently in the top four things that would encourage an employee to come and work for you. That's a huge - and marked change from pre-pandemic requirements. The way you treat and care for your people is now one of the main reasons why they'll choose to work for you in the first place.

Navigating your organisation with wellbeing as your compass.

What you'll discover throughout this book is that the latest research and thinking on employee wellbeing doesn't stray too far from the needs of early human. The things we wanted back then aren't much different to the things we want (and need) today. While our bodies and brains got slightly smaller, our health and wellbeing requirements remained essentially the same. The world and work have evolved significantly around us over the last 200 years, and yet it seems we are desperately trying to get back to the way things used to be.

The good news here is that I think it's entirely within every employer's power to change and adapt to these new employee requirements. You have far more control of the churn of your employees than you realise. In their 2022 Global HR Research Report,

Betterworks found that employees are more likely to be running away from old cultures than running towards new ones. Seventy-two percent say they are leaving a workplace rather than looking for a new one[11]. This means we can fix this – we can create an environment and experience that they *want* to stay in. I hope this book will give you the ideas to create the conditions that not only make people want to stay working with you but also attracts new, talented people too.

My aim is for this book to challenge the very well-marketed idea of what wellbeing is. I hope it will encourage you to look at your organisation and the way you treat your people differently. And most of all, I hope it inspires you to want to make a difference in your world. I want every organisation to use wellbeing as a way of navigating their organisation. I want us all to always hold our wellbeing strategy in one hand so that every decision we make is made with due consideration to how it will affect our people.

For employers wishing to understand and improve employee wellbeing, this book will give you the insight, provocation, and measurements of success that I think have been missing from an industry that has tried its best to sell us a false idea of wellbeing is for so many years. While it is in no way an exhaustive list, I've pulled together evidence and data from more than 500 studies, a group of global wellbeing and workplace experts, and my own meandering experience from the last 20 years. For those organisations that commit to making wellbeing support integral to everything they do, I genuinely believe they will attract the best and brightest employees, the most loyal customers and even the best investors and shareholders.

In 2022, your commitment to employee wellbeing is now a key determinant of your organisation's future success[12]. Thank you for including this book on your journey – I hope it remains a good travel companion for some time to come.

"To be an employer is a privilege. Employers have a moral obligation to ensure their people are taken care of. I believe care and kindness at work may be the most vital keys to the riddle of what makes a successful organisation"

Gethin Nadin, London, 13th October 2022

Foreword

Dr Paul Litchfield, OBE, CBE

Paul is currently independent Chief Medical Adviser to both ITV and Compass Group, having previously been Chief Medical Officer at BT. He has promoted better mental health and wellbeing in the workplace for more than 30 years and has worked with multiple international agencies to advance that agenda. Paul was founding Chair of the UK's What Works Centre for Wellbeing and co-chairs the National Forum for Health & Wellbeing in the Workplace. He has been awarded both the OBE and the CBE for his services to occupational health and wellbeing.

The world of work is changing quickly, and those changes have been accelerated by the pandemic. What we do, how we do it and where we do it have altered radically, and so have people's expectations of what work should offer. Labour is in short supply, and good people are at a premium – employers that apply 20th-century thinking to the employment relationship will end up paying unaffordable salaries and still won't keep their people.

Focusing on the wellbeing of the workforce is not a "nice to do", it's a business imperative. For more than a decade, the evidence base has been growing to show that placing employee wellbeing at the heart of the people proposition delivers hard benefits. Laboratory experiments and real-world studies conducted by economists, psychologists and a range of other academics show consistent improvements in absenteeism, productivity, customer satisfaction, profitability, and other business measures of 10 – 15 percent. In many ways, those findings are intuitive; happy people are more likely to come to work and to perform better when they are there.

Benefits are all very well, but they are of limited value to a business if the costs are prohibitive. Some organisations "gold plate" their offering, and others simply waste money by focussing on superficial, short-term initiatives – the "fruit and Pilates" approach to wellbeing. None of that is necessary because the What Works Centre for Wellbeing has developed with business an uncomplicated model for the drivers of wellbeing along with guidance on measurement. The drivers (health, security, relationships, environment, and purpose) can all be influenced by simple, affordable workplace measures, but the key is giving equal weight to activities targeted on the individual and the organisation.

Adopting a wellbeing approach within an organisation can be transformational. Looking at the people agenda through a wellbeing lens alters the perspective on many policies and procedures. The synergies (and sometimes conflicts) between isolated activities in reward, recruitment, organisational design, learning and talent, as well as health and safety, become apparent and can be aligned, so the whole is greater than the sum of its parts. Organisations that embrace the concept and execute it effectively will not only have happier, healthier workers but are also likely to survive and prosper through the turbulent years ahead.

Gethin has pulled together his extensive experience in consulting on wellbeing with large global employers, as well as the latest thinking and research in workplace wellbeing, to create a compelling handbook for any employer wishing to make a real commitment to employee wellbeing.

Dr Paul Litchfield, OBE, CBE

A Work In Progress

Contributors

The creation of this book was driven by the thousands of hours I spent consulting with large global employers, speaking at conferences and writing for the media on all thing's employee wellbeing. I'm incredibly grateful to every organisation that chooses to work with Benefex and the wider Zellis group, and who have allowed us to help them shape their wellbeing strategies.

Thank you to all the guest experts who gave their time to contribute leading ideas and opinions to this book. Scattered throughout 'A Work In Progress' you'll find the best advice from leading global voices in employee wellbeing to ensure you get a balanced view- not just that of the author.

Thank you also to all of those who pre-read the book before its release and gave early reviews, the Benefex marketing team for their support in organising the press launch and their ongoing help to market the book, and the many organisations who are supporting this book and spreading the word.

Finally, thanks to *you* for buying and reading this book. It's a huge privilege to have a platform that allows me to have a voice, which wouldn't happen if it weren't for people like you.

A Work In Progress

A Work In Progress

Contents

Introduction

Despite the growing interest and investment in workplace wellbeing, I'm not entirely sure this book would have been read by many if it hadn't had been for the global Coronavirus pandemic. Although I've been speaking, researching, and consulting on employee wellbeing for years, it's only since the pandemic took hold that most employers have started to pay closer attention to workplace wellbeing. I think the pandemic likely advanced the adoption of workplace wellbeing by ten years or more. While many of the most progressive organisations already had wellbeing leads and dedicated wellbeing budgets, the crisis forced the masses to confront and admit their role in employee wellbeing for the first time.

But as well as employers realising the role they had to play, a perfect storm of the pandemic, a challenging economic environment, and the cost-of-living crisis all led to stress among the world's employees reaching an all-time high. Global wellbeing was hit very hard by the pandemic. Half of us are now likely to say we experienced "a lot of daily stress" yesterday[13], and just 33 percent of global employees say they are 'thriving' when it comes to their wellbeing[14] - a figure that drops to just 11 percent in parts of Asia. Part of the reason we were hit so hard was that we were ill-prepared for the pandemic. Our financial resilience was low, most employers didn't know how to facilitate remote mass working, and wellbeing support from the state and most employers was either non-existent or in its infancy.

The world wasn't prepared for poorer mental health.

Before the pandemic, we were already failing people's wellbeing in almost every advanced economy. The world simply wasn't prepared for an event that would test and exacerbate our poor wellbeing as the pandemic did. Before 2020, global data on mental health conditions and overall wellbeing were bleak; mental health conditions contributed to 25 percent of lived years with disability worldwide; depression was a leading cause of disability, affecting 264 million people. Even for young people, a lack of state support, funding for and awareness of mental health was ensuring adults were entering the workforce already struggling. Around half of all mental health conditions start before working age, and suicide is the leading cause of death for younger employees[15].

Fast forward to the midst of the pandemic, and the global prevalence of mental health among the public was higher than expected. Data from 32 countries and half a million participants showed that our collective mental health got much, much worse because of the pandemic. The global prevalence during the pandemic was 28 percent for depression, 26.9 percent for anxiety, 24.1 percent for post-traumatic stress symptoms, 36.5 percent for stress, 50 percent for psychological distress and 27.6 percent for sleep problems[16]. Almost half of employees say their mental health got worse because of the pandemic[17]. Even Google searches for 'anxiety at work' were up by 89 percent [18]. Covid-19 walked back almost all of the very small advances we had made in supporting people's mental health.

Globally, mental health is one of the most neglected areas of health. This was true before the pandemic started and has been growing in significance in the time since it began to end. The numbers are pretty staggering; according to the World Health Organization (WHO), by 2020, nearly one billion people were living with a mental disorder. Yet in low-income countries, more than 75 percent of people with a mental disorder don't receive any treatment[19]. Governments spend on average only two percent of their health budgets on mental health and just one in five of us think the state health system prioritises mental health to the same extent as physical health[20]. As a result, treatment coverage for mental health is extremely low. People simply aren't getting the treatment they need. Only 48 percent of countries have a mental health policy - the WHO target was 80 percent by the time this book was published.

But we have another problem when your people look towards the state for support – trust in Governments and health systems is falling. In almost every country, trust in the state-provided healthcare has worsened during the pandemic[21]. In the UK, the public is generally quite pessimistic about the standards of care provided by the NHS with almost half believing standards will worsen in the future. More than two-thirds of Brits also think the standard of social care has gotten worse in recent years, too[22]. This is a considerable shift downwards from research conducted before the pandemic, where public views on the quality and standard of UK care were much more positive. So, where does this leave us? Globally, state-run healthcare tends to be stretched and underfunded, so over time, I think the public has begun to see a new role for the employer to provide where the state isn't.

In the UK, auto-enrolment for pensions took the responsibility of funding retirement away from the state and put it onto the employer. In the US, most people's healthcare is now tied to their jobs, and in France, obligatory health contributions are partly funded by the employer. So, this may be just part of a growing trend to raise the employer's role in supporting our wellbeing and a move away from the state.

Employee wellbeing: a problem for employers.

But just as a vast array of political and Governmental decisions directly affect our wellbeing as members of society, the decisions our employers make every day can also play a pivotal role in how well we are too. I think the lack of investment in, and attention paid to our wellbeing by the state is part of why employee wellbeing has - maybe unfairly - fallen on the shoulders of employers. But we also have evidence of the enormous financial toll poor wellbeing has on employers. Neglected mental health costs US businesses between $80 and $100 million yearly. Globally, the economy loses around $1 trillion each year to lost productivity due to poor wellbeing[23]. So, for employers, there has perhaps been no other option but to intervene to protect the organisation from rising costs.

During the height of the pandemic in 2021, the average employee took three-and-a-half days off due to poor mental health. That was up from 2019 and is now costing UK businesses more than £45 billion a year[24] - a rise of 16 percent since 2016. Around a third of the UK, workforce took time off due to poor mental health in 2021, with more than 60 percent of absences lasting longer than five days. But in addition to those that take time off to deal with their poor wellbeing, part of the reason why the cost to employers is now so high is because of those who continue to turn up to work while struggling.

Poor wellbeing at work is a major cause of low productivity and human error. Increased sickness directly impacts performance. A significant rise in mental-health-related 'presenteeism', where employees work when they are not at their most productive has been highlighted by Deloitte[25]. So again, we see that employers appear to have no option but to make bigger commitments to employee wellbeing; as people continue to struggle, so do organisations that employ them. We are not only making up for the lack of state support, but employers are trying to protect their own interests by making a bigger commitment to employee wellbeing.

While modern data makes the financial reasons why employers should care about wellbeing quite obvious, it doesn't tell us how this relationship began. It seems an almost odd situation we find ourselves in that wellbeing is somewhat tied to our jobs. In the US, more than 175 million people get health coverage through their workplace; how we go to this point is quite interesting and I think yet again, shows us that looking back at history can tell us a lot about how we get ahead in the future.

How health insurance at work in the US started is likely the same reason why wellbeing will become tied even closer to the workplace in the future. As the US came out of the Great Depression, hiring ramped up. With so many workers still overseas, it became a very competitive job market, so wages began to climb and the fight for talent raged. Sounds familiar, doesn't it? While this all happened in the US in the 1940s, as I write this book today in the UK, there are two jobs available for every job seeker, so employers are working harder than ever to attract the most talented people. Back in the 1940s, to protect the economy, the National War Labor Board stopped employers from competitively raising wages by introducing a wage cap. But health insurance was exempt from this cap and the IRS decided that employer contributions to health insurance premiums were tax-free. So to attract the best and brightest, employers began to offer health insurance on top of wages. In 1939 just 8 million Americans had health insurance, but by 1952, 92 million did. I think this was the start of a 70-year relationship our wellbeing has had with the workplace. The pandemic is influencing us just the same as the Great Depression did; by forcing employers to offer more over and above pay to support the lives of their people and attract the best people.

Employee wellbeing: a new requirement for employees.

It's very clear that wellbeing has become a new imperative for employers, but it's important to note it has shot

7

up the requirement list for employees too. For most employees, an organisation that "cares about employee wellbeing" is now the number one most desirable to work for[26]. Our global research at Benefex found that just under half of employees say their expectations of how their employers support their wellbeing have increased since the pandemic began[27]. A massive 92 percent of employees across the UK, US, Singapore, and India told us that a "commitment to employee wellbeing" was now *the* most important factor when selecting a new employer.

But employee requirements and employer actions aren't matching up. Three-quarters of younger workers admit to leaving a job for mental health reasons[28]. Yet while 60 percent of employees say they have experienced poor emotional wellbeing at work, close to 60 percent of them say they haven't felt able to talk about this in the workplace. Even for the 40 percent who did feel they could talk about their poor emotional wellbeing at work, less than half described talking about it with their manager as a "positive experience". We are pushing wellbeing at work, but it feels like in many cases we still aren't ready to culturally receive it - and that has to change – quickly.

The last few years have given many industries a challenging hiring environment. 'The Great Resignation' is fuelling employee confidence in walking away from those employers that aren't taking care of their wellbeing. CNBC report that "workers are quitting their jobs to put themselves first"[29], with one in four ready to quit their job over poor mental health in 2022[30]. It is blindly obvious that employee wellbeing is now a top priority for workers. But it's also obvious that employers are still struggling to understand wellbeing and know what actions to take to make a material difference to their people. Employers want to mitigate losses, and employees want to be looked after more, but both parties are still coming to terms with exactly how they do this.

According to the US Department of Health and Human Services, around 75 percent of healthcare costs originate from preventable illnesses and chronic conditions. This puts employers in a uniquely effective position to positively impact the wellbeing of their people[31]. Employers are now more primed than ever to step up. The huge evolution workplace wellbeing has gone through over the last few years has led to most large global employers now taking a more activist role in employee wellbeing and I hope this is one of the reasons why you've picked up this book.

Guest Expert View: Paul Devoy

CEO, Investors In People

Paul has been the CEO of Investors in People since 2017, when he led the buyout of the organisation from the UK Government, to become a Community Interest Company (CIC). As a CIC, they are all about purpose, not profit. Their purpose? To Make Work Better.

Since 1991 Investors In People have supported over 50,000 employers to Make Work Better for more than 11 million people all over the world - and they are just getting started. When people are happy and healthy, feel engaged and trusted, it leads to higher levels of productivity and wellbeing, which in turn leads to increases in business performance and greater societal impact.

———————

"I wish I could write them a prescription for a better boss". That's what a GP said to me when discussing wellbeing in the workplace. The same GP estimated that of the people that came into his surgery with a mental health problem, 80 percent were work-related and most of his patient's issues were related to their relationship with their line manager. It's no surprise then, that according to the Chartered Institute of Management, there are over two million 'accidental managers' in the UK. That's people who have been put into management positions without having had the proper training to do the role.

My view is that organisations look at wellbeing through the wrong end of the telescope. The 'dolly mixture' of wellbeing solutions provided by employers are often designed to address the symptoms and not the root cause of poor wellbeing. Unless your employees are well managed and experience a culture that is positive and helps them thrive, wellbeing solutions are at best, going to ameliorate the symptoms or, more likely, have little to no effect at all.

So what do you do about it? The first thing to say is that this piece is not about beating up line managers. Being a manager of people is one of the most difficult jobs you can do. The modern manager has to deal with a range of complexities the likes of which we have never seen before. We have a mental health epidemic, the way we design work has been turned upside down due to the pandemic and we have five generations in the workplace at the same time. Those are just three examples. There are many more I could list.

We need to invest in our managers. By that, I don't mean sending everyone on a two-week management course (although that is not a bad thing). We need to be providing ongoing development and support. It should start before someone even becomes a manager. That means identifying the people whom you believe have management potential and developing them to go into the role, not training them once they get there. This development should continue throughout their career, whether that be through coaching, mentoring, peer-to-support networks, and yes, of course, training.

It amazes me that this is some sort of change in thinking. In many other professions, you have to demonstrate your Continual Professional Development to continue to perform the role. But with management, we think it is something people can just pick up as you go along. This has a negative double whammy on both our productivity as a nation (which is low compared to our competitor nations) and on the wellbeing of your people.

When you travel on a plane, the emergency protocol is to put your own oxygen mask on before you look after anyone else.

Unless we invest in and support our managers, they won't be in the best place to support their teams.

When we developed our 'We invest in wellbeing' accreditation, it was to both hold employers accountable for having a wellbeing strategy that encompasses a focus on their employees' physical, social, and psychological wellbeing – whilst also celebrating the achievements of these employers for their commitments to such areas and ensuring they had the tools, processes and support they needed to improve and continue to support their people.

We have been making work better for over 30 years, supporting over 11 million people across the world. As the importance of wellbeing has never been more prevalent, it's time for more employers to hold themselves accountable, and demonstrate their commitment to wellbeing is more than just a fruit bowl.

I believe this book will become a tome for organisations wanting to make wellbeing a priority.

Throughout this book, we will look at what the evidence says; what are the most effective ways employers can design the employee experience with wellbeing in mind, and what is the best advice from decades of reading, researching, and consulting with large employers on wellbeing. Whether you are a large global employer, a small regional one, and regardless of industry or resources available, this book will give you all the knowledge and insight you need, to give your people what *they* need.

Chapter 1
Defining Wellbeing

Over the last decade, there has been a gradual, but fundamental shifting of our attitudes to the way we treat and look after each other in society. Governments have begun reassessing what a successful country looks like; one that is measured less by Gross Domestic Product (GDP) and more by the happiness and wellbeing of its people. This new way of thinking is now driving progress in many parts of the world.

The World Economic Forum (WEF) has warned that there is a "crisis of inaction" when it comes to people's wellbeing and suggests the Coronavirus pandemic acerbated the problem significantly. WEF has been calling on countries to do more to support people's wellbeing for us to advance our societies and economies with people's wellbeing in mind. As a result, wellbeing has surged dramatically up the political agenda over the last four years (and notably during the pandemic). UK health ministers agreed in 2021 to create the Comprehensive Mental Health Action Plan, which will guide their work through to 2030 and include goals and targets to track progress. And a slew of other Governments have committed to act on poor wellbeing by announcing new policies and programmes as well as changing legislation.

In 2019, New Zealand's Government, led by Prime Minister Jacinda Ardern revealed a national budget aimed at tackling some of the country's biggest wellbeing problems. The 'Wellbeing Budget' prioritised five main areas: mental health, supporting the aspirations of the Māori and Pasifika populations, transforming the economy, child wellbeing and building a productive nation. A large part of this strategy was the acknowledgement that not only was people's wellbeing vital to the country's success, but it also had to involve many different aspects of our lives covering the economy, access to healthcare, education, community, and many others.

Similarly, in the UK, the 2022 Scottish Budget led by First Minister Nicola Sturgeon, included a raft of wellbeing initiatives. Scotland believes quite strongly that wellbeing must sit at the core of the country's pandemic recovery. The Scottish budget included record levels of funding for health and social care, but also a huge investment in mental health, tackling poverty, further investment in social security, education, early learning, climate change, physical exercise, woodland creation, and affordable housing.

In a speech at the National Economic Forum in 2021, Scottish Finance Secretary Kate Forbes said:

"Putting Wellbeing at the heart of everything we do, the wellbeing of the economy, the wellbeing of the environment and the wellbeing of people is not just morally the right thing to do but it also unlocks the creativity and the confidence that we need, which in turn will help businesses to innovate, to grow and to make them more globally competitive."

- Kate Forbes, Scottish Finance Secretary

Scotland and New Zealand's holistic view of people's wellbeing is something we will revisit in this book and is important to our understanding of modern workplace wellbeing. Countries like these illustrate just how important wellbeing is to our future. However, I still think we are struggling as a society with creating the right conditions for us to begin to improve our wellbeing.

Have we eroded the stigma of talking about wellbeing?

As a result of Government and media attention, and the pandemic itself, cultural understanding of mental health has risen substantially. The pandemic provided us with a common human wellbeing experience that did a great deal to erode the stigmas that existed when talking about wellbeing issues like mental health and money. The pandemic and its universal struggle gave us a licence to openly grapple with wellbeing and talk about it like we had never done before. A recent poll by the American Psychiatric Association found that one-quarter of Americans made their New Year's resolution in 2022 to improve their mental health[32]. As a result of the erosion of the stigma, 90 percent of Brits now think mental health has a higher public profile than five years ago[33]. However, the latest data shows that there is still much work to be done on how we talk about wellbeing at work if we are to successfully define and improve it.

The language we use to discuss mental health matters. At Benefex, we use the term 'emotional wellbeing' to refer to mental health. This is because the stigma attached to mental health (and specifically the word 'mental') still exists. Despite the significant attention given by celebrities and the media to remove the stigma of mental health, around half of employees still say they've called in sick pretending to be suffering from a physical illness in order to hide their mental health problems[13]. More than 8 out of 10 employees with a mental health condition say they have hidden their problem from their employer[14]. This is a big issue for those who own wellbeing within an organisation – we can't change or improve wellbeing if our people still aren't willing to discuss it with us.

New research is showing us that even subtle changes to how we talk and use words regarding mental health and mental illness can affect our levels of tolerance. For example, one study found that people showed less tolerance towards someone rereferred to as "mentally ill" when compared to someone referred to as "a person with mental illness"[15]. Small changes in how we talk about our mental health will help to create environments that are more inclusive of those with problems. By choosing emotional wellbeing as a pillar that encapsulates mental health, we are not just focusing on serious ill health, but are also including how we can help employees with resilience, self-awareness and having the skills and resources to manage life's ups and downs. It's about helping employees to thrive and be happy, not just the absence of illness. That's important for us to think about when we are attempting to define wellbeing at work.

Less than half of employees believe their organisation does enough to create a culture that supports them with their mental health[21]. Worryingly, of those that do ask their employer for help, more than 10 percent say they faced disciplinary action or demotion after being open about their wellbeing. However, attitudes do still appear to be shifting, resulting in our people being far more comfortable admitting, talking, and dealing with their wellbeing more than they have ever been.

Most employees believe the pandemic has lessened the stigma of wellbeing at work. Over half of UK workers feel more comfortable than ever in requesting time off or discussing wellbeing with their co-workers[34]. Our research at Benefex found that 80 percent of employers report their staff are disclosing more wellbeing issues at work[35]. However, global attitudes aren't changing at the same pace. Looking outside of the UK and the US, the data reveals that for global employers, changing attitudes throw up a big problem with how we define and describe workplace wellbeing.

Global attitudes to mental health.

Of all the countries surveyed by Ipsos on attitudes to mental health, Brits were most likely to agree that mental illness is "an illness like any other"[36]. However, while 88 percent of people living in Britain and Sweden think it's ok for someone with a history of poor mental health to hold a position in public office. Just 24 percent of Russians do - making it one of the least tolerant countries. People in Japan, Brazil and Peru are least likely to agree that mental illness is "an illness like any other", and most people in South Korea and Japan *don't* think we should be developing a more tolerant attitude towards people with poor mental health.

For those organisations who have a global remit for employee wellbeing, these vastly different attitudes to wellbeing will play a part in how you define and develop your strategy. One in five Indian employees may suffer from depression in their lifetime (equivalent to 200 million people), but only 10-12 percent of these will seek help[37]. The reason is that more than a quarter of Indian employees say they have a fear of people perceiving their mental illness as meaning they are prone to violence. Similarly, in Arab households where a relative has a mental illness, one study found the family will associate fear, embarrassment, and disgrace with their situation[38]. In Japan, a "weakness of personality" is often considered the cause of mental illness[39]. These cultural stigmas mean how we define wellbeing at a global level has to consider that not every region is starting from the same place, with the same level of societal progression.

While the erosion of the stigma of poor wellbeing at work and in society is progressing, it's very much being driven by a few select regions. This poses a problem for an employer whose organisation crosses different cultures and territories. Not only because feelings of shame can exacerbate poor wellbeing[40], but thrusting Westernised attitudes onto other regions can negatively impact engagement in workplace wellbeing initiatives[41]. But regardless of how eroded the stigma is in your region, what is clear from the pandemic is that we have fundamentally started to change what wellbeing at work means and how we define it has to change with that too.

Moving from 'do no harm', to 'do better'.

Almost every person now agrees that wellbeing is important[42]. But one of the myths the wellbeing industry has drilled into us for years is that it is our individual issue to overcome. Historically we have been told that stress and exhaustion at work is 'normal'. We were sold the idea that we take two weeks' vacation in the sun to recuperate from a stressful year at work, with little thought given to why we needed the break in the first place. I think this has been a misdirection – wellbeing at work isn't about how we recover from the negative impact work can have on us, but instead, it's how the workplace becomes better at supporting us through life. Time away from work should be to recharge and refresh, not to lessen the effects of overwork and stress. Wellbeing at work should lift us up, not just repair damage. Work must be a positive force in the lives of its people. But for many, they are still grappling with the "do no harm" element of the phrase "moving from do no harm to do better". When we consider how we define wellbeing at work, we have to admit the old ways work has been harming our wellbeing.

Though data is scarce, it seems suicides related to workplace issues are rising. In the US in 2013 (the last time the data was available), around 300 employees took their own lives - a 12 percent increase from the year before. In the UK, work-related suicides are on the rise too[43]. Excessive workloads, insecure contracts, intense work, and interpersonal relationships appears to be the leading causes. In the US, work is now technically the fifth largest cause of death[44].

Over the years, the media has picked up on this growing issue - even when formal data is hard to find. In 2019, four members of the same UK ambulance trust took their own lives because of harassment and bullying[45]. In 2021, at least five members of the crew of the USS George Washington took their own lives as they struggled with working conditions[46]. Overworked and tired Californian firefighters are still battling with suicide in 2022[47]. But the most famous media story of suicide at work began in 2009. Just over ten years ago, multiple members of staff at France Telecom took their own lives because of "overwork" and "management by terror" as one employee's suicide note read[48]. In a now landmark ruling, a French court found that several executives at France Telecom fostered an environment that harmed employee wellbeing. The court felt this so strongly that it sent three of France Telecom's executives to prison.

In his book 'Dying for a Paycheck', author Jeffrey Pfeffer says that the way we run modern organisations is harming employee wellbeing. The book makes the links between diabetes, cardiovascular disease, and many other high profile medical conditions and how many are driven by stress - stress that in many cases is caused by work. In addition, he quotes the work of Professor Nuria Chinchilla from the IESE Business School who coined the term "social pollution"; the idea that working hours and employer demands are causing the breakup of marriages, harming children's up-bringing, and disrupting family life.

What won't fix the sometimes-devastating effect of work on our lives is the continuation of self-prescribing wellbeing initiatives to overcome issues caused by the organisation. While burnout was a feature of the pandemic, it was also the latest evidence we have that employee wellbeing is as much about how we structure our organisations, than it is how we help our employees out. When we seek to define wellbeing at work, we must consider the role that work itself plays in it.

Wellbeing is not self-care.

Even outside of the extreme examples mentioned above, as employees, we have been led to believe that wellbeing is a way to counteract the negative impact work can have on us. More than half of Americans say their work stresses them out and 69 percent say they turn to "unhealthy" coping mechanisms to deal with that stress[49]. Americans say they feel relaxed for just forty minutes a day[50]. So rather than explore why our people are stressed and anxious at work, we respond by putting tools in place to help them or send them away to find ways to destress for themselves.

We must get to grips with the idea that it is not solely our employees' job to fix stress that their job causes them. I think this is workplace wellbeing 101, yet it's not the way many have defined workplace wellbeing in the past. We have treated the symptoms of poor wellbeing, not the causes. The way we tend to think about workplace wellbeing, has been mostly focused on urgent hazards and risks, resulting in businesses responding to, rather than avoiding, poor employee health. Pandemic burnout gave us an almost perfect case study of how this thinking has played out recently. Almost half of the working population is now at risk of burnout at work[51], with one in four globally reporting experiencing burnout symptoms[52]. Yet in some case, the way of dealing with this burnout tells a story of the best intentions managed in the incorrect way.

In August 2021, Nike gave its head office employees a week's paid time off to "take time to unwind, destress and spend time with your loved ones". Nike was concerned that their employees were, or were on the verge of, burning out. Yet leaked employee surveys from Nike revealed that their employees said leaders "didn't inspire confidence" and were "burning out their best resources"[53]. In my view, this kind of paid time off (while no doubt appreciated by staff) wasn't solving the problem of burnout but instead sticking a plaster over the top of it.

Comparable stories emerged from other large employers. In June 2021, dating app Bumble gave almost all workers a paid week off to recover from burnout… but only after they had "correctly intuited our collective burnout"[54]. Similarly, LinkedIn found that pandemic related burnout had increased in their company, so they gave employees an additional paid week off[55]. But the evidence says that burnout is more likely to be caused by the way we build organisations than by the amount of time we spend at work. While mandatory time off may undoubtedly benefit some employees, it is unlikely to address the issues that are obviously in need of attention. On its own, employee burnout is unlikely to be reversed with paid time off. These employers should have looked at the reasons *why* burnout was happening, rather than just reacting to the immediate threat.

"We should be finding out why cars are crashing, rather than continuing to pull our people from the wreckage"
- Gethin Nadin

While I'm sure the gesture is good to the employees who have the time off, when we're talking about stress and burnout that are already in the lives of those who work at these organisations, I can't help but think the reasons will still be present when they return.

Employee workload, insufficient resources, toxic behaviour[56], position ambiguity, job expectations, and organisational structure are the key drivers of employee burnout, according to a study done by Cheng et al in 2014 and shared with me by Birkbeck University[57]. Uncertain expectations, dysfunctional interactions, a lack of social support, and a loss of control are all listed by the Mayo Clinic too. Yet how often do things like workload, position ambiguity and role expectations feature in our definition of wellbeing?

There is clearly a disconnect between employer efforts and rising wellbeing issues like burnout. On average, there is around a 20 percent gap between what employees are struggling with and what their employer thinks they are struggling with[58]. Grand wellbeing gestures from the likes of Bumble, LinkedIn and Nike seek to remind us that part of the problem with workplace wellbeing is that we still haven't properly defined it in a way that works for the employee.

Guest Expert View: Dan Cave

Multiple-award-winning HR, Work &
Business editor and journalist

Dan Cave is both an award-winning editor and award-winning journalist, who has covered HR, leadership, work, business, technology, workplace inequalities, homelessness, culture, and community issues across his career thus far.

Dan is currently freelance and has had work in international dailies and renowned culture magazines, as well as the business press. Dan has also reported from one of the most press censored countries in the world. Dan is an advocate for, and mentor to, working class and under-represented individuals wanting to work in media and journalism.

———————————

At both the start and peaks of the pandemic, I was the editor of an HR news publisher. As such March 2020 is still very clear for me: it's when our team decided (in suddenly virtual editorial meetings) to create standalone coronavirus sections for our sites, write Covid-19 people practice playbooks to give our audiences the information they desperately and instantly needed, and launch a weekly update newsletter on how the disease was overhauling HR practice.

All these actions were a response to pandemic-sparked reader interest. Although the HR press can often lead conversations around evolving subjects we only, for better or worse, reflect, and then create, based on demand. And that early pandemic demand, at least according to our website traffic and reader response, and the fact that mainstream and national press were also putting HR and wellbeing topics centre stage, was around one topic in particular: employee wellbeing. Therefore, we ratcheted up reporting in this area.

Seemingly, this demand was the result of the overwhelming majority of HR practitioners looking for a way to ensure they could keep their people as safe and well as possible (health-wise, mentally, and financially), keep their organisations and operations going, and that they made no people practice, legal, or publicly visible missteps.

This anxiety about doing right regards employee wellbeing, and being seen to do right, could also be seen in the popularly of Googled terms from the same period. Searches for "keeping staff safe", "employee wellbeing", and the meditation app "Headspace" all rocketed. On the flip side, page views on reports about companies that were perceived as not doing enough regarding their duty of care towards staff were huge. In a very grim way, stories on Wetherspoons,

Charlie Mullins and Alan Sugar ensured site engagement targets were met; driven, in part at least, by worried practitioners not wanting to get it wrong.

Yet, the fact that page views on wellbeing articles were high was not solely the result of the pandemic. Yes, the pandemic required the HR function to know about new wellbeing pivots, provisions, and strategies but it also highlighted and then exacerbated the poor state of employee wellbeing prior to the pandemic. Some of this is the result of paucity of provision from state institutions but also the result of mismatches between expectations from the workforce and what employers were providing in care, as well as work demands on employees.

Although there was a cost to this poor state of wellbeing before the pandemic, a difficult labour market, reconstituted employee-employer dynamics, and the so-called Great Resignation has truly made it a key issue (if it wasn't already) for employers. And whilst there are still no guarantees over whether this will spark employers into, in a total manner, reconceiving their approach to wellbeing, what is fairly certain is that – on a backdrop in which a cost-of-living crisis, rocketing inflation, a looming recession, an ongoing housing crisis, increasingly threadbare state healthcare provision, simmering population-wide mental health problems, and continued arguments over what wellbeing actually is – there will be ongoing demand for the most up-to-date information on this subject and what that means for employers as crises evolve and contexts changes.

For HR and business journalists, it means the subject will, without a doubt, continue to take up a significant amount of time in their day jobs going forward. That is why this book will no doubt become such a valuable resource for many employers.

Finding a definition for wellbeing at work.

At time of writing this book, a single, standardised definition of wellbeing does not exist in the literature. I believe historic attempts at defining wellbeing have been a description, rather than a definition of workplace wellbeing, as they tended to focus on the dimensions of wellbeing, rather than wellbeing itself. In addition, a big challenge to defining wellbeing is that a comprehensive list of things that impact our wellbeing would result in significant overlap; there is a very definitive symbiotic relationship between all areas of our wellbeing. Our social background, personality, relationships, and life events all impact our wellbeing. Social background is particularly interesting when trying to define wellbeing because any definition can be impacted by a variety of things such as gender, age, socio-economic status, cultural background, skin colour, neurodiversity etc. All of these factors add significant barriers to creating a universally agreed definition of wellbeing, let alone a specific definition for wellbeing at work.

While it's obvious that experts have been challenged in their attempts to define wellbeing, I fully understand and appreciate the need for employers to get closer to a definition that will allow them to act and measure improvements. Definitions will also help you to send a clear message to your organisation that will go far in helping you to remove the stigma and engrain wellbeing in your culture.

In this book I won't seek to define workplace wellbeing directly myself, as I believe it still remains subjective for both the employer and employee. But I will attempt to surface the most interesting definitions I have come across that I hope will help you to make your own definition. I think a very good starting point is to consider the definition of wellbeing put forward by Dodge, Daly, Huyton, and Sanders (2012)[59].

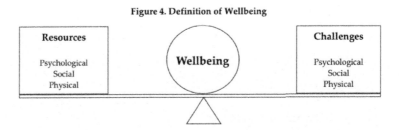

Figure 4. Definition of Wellbeing

Fig. 1. Definition of Wellbeing, Dodge, Daly, Huyton, and Sanders (2012)

Dodge et al believe that their 'seesaw' represents the drive of an individual to return to a set point for wellbeing, as well as our individual need for equilibrium. The elements that impact this equilibrium tip the seesaw from one side to another, which illustrates the flowing and ever-changing nature of our wellbeing. One thing this definition offers up that I like, is that our employees are constantly balancing the resources available to them with the challenges that life and work throw up. It acknowledges that from one day to the next, our resources change and when the balance of these challenges don't meet with our ability to handle them, problems arise. In a workplace context, this means that employers can begin to consider what resources they can provide their people and what challenges they can hope to support. And this is critical - because I think good employee wellbeing at work can be found more in the micro, everyday things we do as employers.

When we look at what the consensus of research appears to agree makes us happy and healthy in life, there is common set of dimensions that largely follow the OECD's list:

- **Income and wealth**
- **Work and job quality**
- **Housing**
- **Health**
- **Knowledge and skills**
- **Environment quality**
- **Subjective wellbeing**
- **Safety**
- **Work life balance**
- **Social connections**
- **Civil engagement**

Very similar dimensions can be found across other sources including the UK Office for National Statistics[60], the World Health Organization[61], the World Economic Forum[62] and the International Organization for Standardization (ISO)[63]. ISO is a well-respected worldwide federation of national standards bodies. In 2021, ISO produced new guidance on the management of psychosocial risks and promoting wellbeing at work. One of the first modern frameworks of its kind, and one that's very useful for employers to keep in mind when they are defining wellbeing at work because its all-compassing.

This new ISO guidance is aimed at preventing work-related stress or injury and to promote safer workplaces. The guidance is designed to encourage employers to take preventative measures to better support employee mental health and general wellbeing at work. As well as physical risks like musculoskeletal disorders, diabetes and cardiovascular disease, the guidance now covers more modem thinking on factors that impact employee wellbeing such as job satisfaction, financial security, social interaction, inclusion, recognition, and personal growth. Areas already covered within our Strategic Framework for employee wellbeing at Benefex for some years before the ISO standards were published.

Non-traditional areas of wellbeing that employers should be aware of that are contained in this guidance include:

- **Roles and expectations**
- **Job control and autonomy**
- **Job demands**
- **Organisational change management**
- **Remote and isolated work**
- **Workload and work pace**
- **Working hours and schedule**

- **Job security**
- **Interpersonal relationships**
- **Leadership**
- **Culture**
- **Recognition and reward**
- **Support**
- **Work/life balance**

By making yourself familiar with the psycho-social risks within your organisation, you will be able to demonstrate the far-reaching impact your wellbeing strategy can have. Across the ISO and OECD definitions, what we are generally looking at here are quality of life indicators. How does the workplace include (not exclude) people, how do we give our people a voice, how do we facilitate autonomy, do we help to improve health and financial literacy at work, how do we provide a safe environment for our people, how we reward and recognise efforts etc.

"The experience of health, happiness, and prosperity. It includes having good mental health, high life satisfaction, a sense of meaning or purpose, and ability to manage stress"

- Psychology Today

Psychologists' definition.

Alongside these dimensions and the 'seesaw' definition, we should also consider the view of psychology. Psychology Today defines wellbeing as "the experience of health, happiness, and prosperity. It includes having good mental health, high life satisfaction, a sense of meaning or purpose, and ability to manage stress"[64]. But to me, it seems a bit more than that. Where most of the research appears to define wellbeing through a lens of happiness and life satisfaction, it misses out the idea that you can be happy and unwell or that you can be free of disease and poor mental health yet still be sad or unfulfilled.

In addition, many other factors appear to affect the wellbeing of the population; the country you are born into, for example. Nordic countries tend to have above-average levels of wellbeing, and eastern European countries score lower than average[65]. Level of education also appears to have an impact on wellbeing[66], as does income[67]. So, the definitions set out by the likes of the OECD and ISO play a part, but I think only alongside the psychological definition.

From the research I've read, it seems appropriate that in a post-pandemic world, we also seek to redefine wellbeing with the idea that events and challenges can quickly impact us. The pandemic was a turning point for wellbeing at work; a significant threat to employee wellbeing was being driven by something entirely out of the employer's and employees' control. It turned out that many of the ways we sought to improve wellbeing at work failed because they hadn't been designed with an event like this in mind.

Opening up our definition wider than external influences and specific employer actions can help our definition appeal more widely to our people. In their definition of wellbeing and happiness, psychologists look at the combination of hedonic balance, life satisfaction and eudaimonia.

- **Hedonic balance:** Derived from the philosophy of ethical hedonism, hedonic wellbeing refers to pleasure and satisfaction. Generally, the balance of positive and negative emotions in an employee.
- **Life satisfaction**: An employee's judgement of their own life (including the things they care about). Work, basic needs, comfort, activism etc. Generally, this is how much employees like the life they lead.
- **Eudaimonia:** A sense of autonomy, mastery, purpose, and connectedness, removing the stigma surrounding certain health conditions. One of the oldest definitions of happiness and wellbeing, eudaimonia focuses on a process of an employee fulfilling or realising their potential etc.

Let's consider these three elements from psychology and add to them the resources available to us and how all of these are influenced by society and our diversity. I think we get close to a definition that I'm happy with. That being said, for HR, reward, and benefits teams, categorising the resources available to employees can be helpful, so at Benefex, we have also arranged them into high-level pillars of wellbeing to work alongside the models described previously in this chapter.

Although wellbeing covers a complex set of issues, we believe five common and important elements should form the foundations of any effective wellbeing strategy. Employers will have their own focus areas and may drill down into more detail in some of these areas. Either way, we believe it is important to establish your own elements of wellbeing and ensure the focus is on long-term preventative and short-term responsive measures. Pillars may seem a fairly basic approach, but they help break down wellbeing into smaller, more digestible pieces. Pillars also make navigating the wellbeing market far easier as they tend to follow similar categorisations of products and services.

In addition to the central pillars, at Benefex, we have also identified the common employer objectives and employee outcomes these wellbeing pillars seek to achieve. These have been based on the hundreds of hours spent running wellbeing workshops with global employers and taking a behavioural science approach to wellbeing.

Benefex's five pillars of wellbeing.

Across the five pillars of wellbeing I created for Benefex, I ask employers to consider how they provide resources, as defined earlier in this chapter. Whether these are employee benefits, company policy, third-party tools, or anything else offered in the workplace. We then ask employers to consider each resource in terms of its maturity:

- **Short-term responsive**
- _or_ **Long-term preventative**

We believe that by getting employers to think of all their wellbeing initiatives, we can help them achieve the balance that is so important to the 'seesaw' definition. For example, does offering health insurance benefit the employee in the short term (i.e., in a period of crisis or immediate need) or does it help them to change behaviour in the long term? (build better awareness of their health). We aim to ensure the resources and initiatives an employer makes available to their people are carefully balanced, not only across each pillar of wellbeing but also that they support employees in crisis, as well as encourage them to make decisions today that will benefit them in the future. Here are the pillars I created for Benefex:

1. Financial wellbeing

"Ensuring employees feel confident in and have a sense of control over their finances."

In the 2020 Risks that Matter survey by the OECD, young people across 25 countries were asked about their worries. Almost two in three reported concerns about their finances as their top wellbeing concern[68]. Over the years, the poverty risk has been slowly shifting away from older people and toward younger ones. By the time the pandemic hit, things had got worse. Employees were twice as likely to run out of money by the end of the month by early 2021 as they were before the pandemic, and over half of UK households reported going into debt because of it[69]. Younger workers are now officially under more financial hardship than *any* other generation since records began[70]. Let that sink in.

According to the Office for National Statistics (ONS), despite the greatest threat to our collective physical health that we ever saw, employees' primary worry during the pandemic was their financial wellbeing. According to YouGov's key banking insights, half of British people believe Covid-19 has raised their cost of living[71]. According to Step Change's

January 2022 research, one in every three people are now having trouble keeping up with their expenses and credit obligations - which is double what it was before the pandemic[72].

At the time of writing this book, more than 70 percent of employees say they are anxious about money, and it is harming their work[73]. A recent poll by Morgan Stanley found that 64 percent of employees feel financial stress is hurting their ability to accomplish their jobs[74] - this figure jumps to a massive 70 percent among younger employees. It's clear to me that for employers and employees, any definition of wellbeing *must* pay close attention to financial wellbeing as a starting point.

Fig. 2. Common financial wellbeing objectives and outcomes (Benefex, 2020)

2. Emotional wellbeing

"A positive sense of wellbeing which enables employees to meet the demands of everyday life"

Almost every area of wellbeing is interdependent. But emotional wellbeing almost certainly sits at the centre. Research shows that when we are under emotional distress, we become more vulnerable to physical illness[6]. In the US, poor emotional wellbeing has been linked with an increased risk of heart disease[7]. In the UK, those people who do the most physical activity are almost 20 percent less likely to get depression than those who do the least[8]. Even other areas of physical wellbeing impact our emotional wellbeing, such as sleep and nutrition. Sleep problems have been known to increase the risk of developing certain mental health issues[9], and high levels of emotional wellbeing are reported by those people who eat more fruit and vegetables[10].

There is a cyclical relationship that exists between financial and emotional wellbeing too. One in five people with a mental health condition are in problem debt – three and a half times the rate among those without mental health problems[11]. Half of those in problem debt also have a mental health condition. Financial concerns are now the top reason why employees say they are kept awake at night[12]. For me, this puts emotional wellbeing as the second priority in defining wellbeing at work.

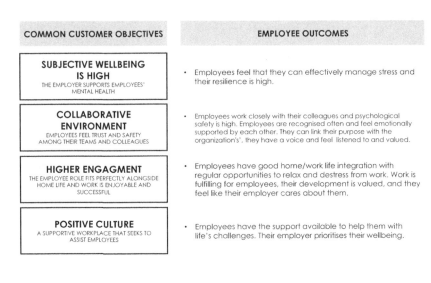

Fig. 3. Common emotional wellbeing objectives and outcomes (Benefex, 2020)

3. Physical wellbeing

"Employees' ability to improve their bodies through healthy behaviours, habits and the absence of disease"

When we talk about physical wellbeing at work, we are talking about a lot more than just exercise. What we eat, our relationship with food, the quality of our sleep, and our resilience to disease and illness all play a part. But in addition, so does our mental health.

In 1909, Sigmund Freud delivered five lectures at Clark University in Worcester, Massachusetts. He explained to the audience the foundations of psychoanalysis and how mental and physical wellbeing are not only alike but that they have a profound impact on each other. When our physical health declines, it can significantly impact our emotional wellbeing, and conversely, a decline in mental health can manifest itself physically.

Our physical wellbeing is our ability to maintain a healthy quality of life. It includes the daily lifestyle choices we all make and our ability to maintain good health and avoid sickness. Diet, health literacy, physical activity, nutrition, rest etc. should all form part of your physical wellbeing strategy. The World Obesity Atlas 2022 predicts that one billion people globally will be living with obesity by 2030[75]. In addition, people are sleeping less[76] and adult generations today are less healthy than their counterparts of previous generations[77]. For these reasons, physical health becomes our next priority in defining wellbeing at work.

COMMON CUSTOMER OBJECTIVES	EMPLOYEE OUTCOMES
ENGAGED FULLY IN OWN HEALTH IMPROVED HEALTH LITERACY, UNDERSTANDING OF ECOPSYCHOLOGY ETC.	• Employees have high levels of health literacy and an understanding of what impacts their physical wellbeing. Health hygiene is high and supported by employee benefits.
MAINTAINING A HEALTHY BODY EMPLOYEES UNDERSTAND HOW TO LOWER RISK OF SERIOUS ILLNESS AND UNDERSTAND MUSCULOSKELETAL RISKS	• Employees engage in regular physical activity and take steps to prevent damage to their bodies. Employees understand the important part nutrition and a balanced diet play to wellbeing.
PREVENTATIVE APPROACH PHYSICAL HEALTH, FREE FROM ILLNESS IS MAINTAINED BY INSURANCES, SCREENING AND ADDITIONAL SUPPORT	• Employees engage in preventative medical care by proactively maintaining their mind and bodies through regular check ups, screening and other preventative measures.
TAKING TIME TO RELAX EMPLOYEES COMMIT TO REGULAR OPPORTUNITIES TO RELAX, SLEEP, MEDITATE ETC	• Employees engage in good quality sleep and find regular opportunities to relax away from work. Employees understand the value of people to building resilience and calming stress.

Fig. 4. Common physical wellbeing objectives and outcomes (Benefex, 2020)

4. Community wellbeing

"How connected your people feel to their family, friends, colleagues, the environment, and their wider community."

Generally, the term 'community wellbeing' describes how people live or work together in a community and, at a larger scale, how those communities can facilitate the wellbeing of their members. Within a workplace context, our community wellbeing is the collection of people we work with and can also include those that interact with us at work, like customers and suppliers.

The combination of how we feel about the social connections we have at work, the recognition we receive, inter-generational relationships, the cultural and political conditions, sustainability, inequality, and psychological safety are among the factors that make up our community wellbeing. How we give back to our community also plays a vital role too. Using local suppliers, volunteering, altruism, and being able to help and support our colleagues increases a workplace's community wellbeing.

Our community wellbeing relies heavily on the quality of social support we get from our colleagues that help us feel like we are part of something. Our emotional attachment to work is driven by how far we feel we can participate and if we feel like we have a voice and opinions that are listened to. A strong sense of community at work can be cultivated by a wider commitment to initiatives that encourage employees to spend time together, to socialise and improve psychological safety. When employers do this well, the results can be impressive.

Community wellbeing at work is critical because people say they are feeling less connected to the people they work with[78], lonelier in their lives[79] and have a strong desire to build better communities. The altruism trend is on the up too[80]. People are keener than ever to give back, rebuild their communities and spend more social time with others.

Think back to the start of this book and the vital role other people played in our evolution from early humans to now. Community wellbeing is the next critical pillar in our definition.

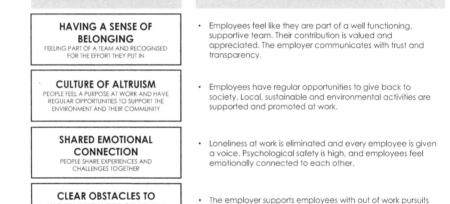

COMMON CUSTOMER OBJECTIVES	EMPLOYEE OUTCOMES
HAVING A SENSE OF BELONGING FEELING PART OF A TEAM AND RECOGNISED FOR THE EFFORT THEY PUT IN	• Employees feel like they are part of a well functioning, supportive team. Their contribution is valued and appreciated. The employer communicates with trust and transparency.
CULTURE OF ALTRUISM PEOPLE FEEL A PURPOSE AT WORK AND HAVE REGULAR OPPORTUNITIES TO SUPPORT THE ENVIRONMENT AND THEIR COMMUNITY	• Employees have regular opportunities to give back to society. Local, sustainable and environmental activities are supported and promoted at work.
SHARED EMOTIONAL CONNECTION PEOPLE SHARE EXPERIENCES AND CHALLENGES TOGETHER	• Loneliness at work is eliminated and every employee is given a voice. Psychological safety is high, and employees feel emotionally connected to each other.
CLEAR OBSTACLES TO WORK-LIFE INTERGRATION GIVES EMPLOYEES THE CHANCE TO DO WHAT THEY LOVE WITH WHO THEY LOVE	• The employer supports employees with out of work pursuits and places a high value on time away from work with family and friends.

Fig. 5. Common community wellbeing objectives and outcomes (Benefex, 2020)

5. Leisure wellbeing

"The satisfaction in the leisure elements of employees' lives that improve subjective wellbeing."

Not something we would often consider part of a workplace wellbeing strategy, but time away from work doing the things we love is critical to sustaining positive wellbeing. As we witnessed throughout the pandemic, removing opportunities to socialise and decompress from work significantly harmed mental health. The imposition of lockdowns in Australia was associated with adverse changes in overall population mental health[81], with similar results being found across the US[82], the UK[83] and China[84].

The opportunities we have in life to decompress and destress from work impact our overall wellbeing. Even the seemingly unimportant can have a positive impact. For example, going to the cinema has been found to improve the mental health of hospital patients[85]. Aerobic exercise like cycling has proved often to be great for our wellbeing[86]. Both bikes and cinema tickets are common features of employee benefit schemes yet aren't always discussed as part of a wellbeing strategy.

Modern research also emphasises the importance of vacations on our wellbeing. Those who travel frequently tend to have greater life satisfaction[87]. In one study, over 20 years, women who went on vacation regularly were less prone to getting a heart attack than those who took less leave[88]. So, leisure wellbeing is the final pillar in our definition of wellbeing at work.

COMMON CUSTOMER OBJECTIVES	EMPLOYEE OUTCOMES
LIFE SATISFACTION SUBJECTIVE WELLBEING AND QUALITY OF LIFE ARE IMPROVED	• The workplace supports the building of confidence and self esteem. Work enhances employee wellbeing and is a positive experience. Work supports employee's fulfillment.
RELIEF FROM TENSION AND FATIGUE PEOPLE ARE EMPOWERED TO PURSUE CULTURAL, SPIRITUAL AND RELIGIOUS ACTIVITIES	• Stress reduction is achieved through the value placed on leisure activities in being able to disconnect and re-energize from work
IMPROVED PHYSICAL AND EMOTIONAL WELLBEING SEES RECREATION AS IMPORTANT TO WELLBEING AND RESILIENCE	• Leisure time to improve physical and emotional wellbeing is encouraged. Time spent outdoors and in nature to restore energy and relax is encouraged.
BUILDS UNITY GIVES EMPLOYEES THE CHANCE TO PRIORITISE OUT OF WORK RELATIONSHIPS	• The workplace promotes friendships and sees family time as a priority.

Fig. 6. Common leisure wellbeing objectives and outcomes (Benefex, 2020)

Heritability of wellbeing.

An important note to make when we seek to define wellbeing at work is that each employee will have a general level of happiness (or what psychologists call 'subjective wellbeing') determined by their genes. At least in theories put forward and suggested by many experts (even those looking at the happiness of chimpanzees![89]).

"Genetics play a significant role in the development of our sense of subjective wellbeing."

- Abhishek Gupta, University of Connecticut

The role of genetics in our wellbeing may not be well researched, but what has been discovered can't be ignored. Some studies have suggested that as much as 70 percent of our happiness results from our heterogeneity, while others put this closer to 40 percent [90]. But as well as environmental factors, our genetics do appear to play a part in our wellbeing.

A 2020 review of the existing literature concluded "overwhelmingly that genetics play a significant role in the development of our sense of subjective wellbeing"[91]. Some historic studies looked at identical twins who grew up apart with no shared environmental influences or experiences and found that they were more similar regarding their wellbeing than fraternal twins who grew up together; the happiness of the identical twins was rated almost the same[92]. This is relevant for employers because we must get comfortable with the idea that our responsibility and influence over the wellbeing of our people is limited.

There are 102 known ways different DNA arrangements can increase our risk of depression[93]. Even with the world's most progressive and advanced approaches to workplace wellbeing, we will still have employees who are almost pre-dispositioned to struggle with their wellbeing – and that's critical to how we understand wellbeing at work.

Of more than 150 studies looking at the causes of poor mental health, almost every single one found associations between at least one socio-economic or economic characteristic and poor mental health[94] WHO states that many common mental disorders are shaped by the social, economic, and physical environment[95]. There is a bidirectional causal relationship between things like poverty and exclusion and mental ill health. Even before employees start working for you, their wellbeing may already be defined by their genetic and life experiences. So strong is this heritability that our DNA has even been found to predetermine how likely we were to follow Covid-19 lockdown rules[96].

Researchers from Edinburgh University have recently confirmed this theory in one study where they found that the love of alcohol can be found in the genes as DNA "helps to determine your preferred tipple"[97]. Study author Professor Jim Wilson told The Sun newspaper that "some people are absolutely born with genes that will make them like the taste of alcohol. More than that, we even found genes that gave preferences for specific drinks like white wine, beer, or whisky". The study involved more than 160,000 Brits and found that genes meant someone was more likely to drink or smoke too much. The implications of studies like these on workplace wellbeing strategies is huge. There were 8,974 deaths related to alcohol in the UK in 2020 (an 18.6 percent increase from 2019)[98]. According to The Lancet, alcohol-related liver disease accounts for 60 percent of all liver disease in the UK, and there has been an increase in alcohol-related hospital admissions over the last few years[99].

I estimate that around half of our mental health can be modified by lifestyle changes or behaviour changes that an employer can influence. When we seek to define wellbeing at work, we must take genetic and environmental factors into account. This is important because it not only helps us to fully understand that we can't fix or even support every employee, all the time.

A landmark new study published in August 2022 found that globally, nearly half of all deaths due to cancer can be attributed to preventable risk factors including the main leading risks: smoking, drinking, and having a high body mass index[100]. One of the study's authors Dr. Chris Murray, Director of the Institute for Health Metrics and Evaluation at the University of Washington wrote in the study:

"To our knowledge, this study represents the largest effort to date to determine the global burden of cancer attributable to risk factors, and it contributes to a growing body of evidence aimed at estimating the risk-attributable burden for specific cancers nationally, internationally and globally"
- Dr. Chris Murray, Director, Institute of Health Metrics and Evaluation, University of Washington

This study (funded by the Bill and Melinda Gates Foundation) reviewed cancer deaths and disability spanning the decade from 2010 to 2019, across 204 countries. The study clearly delineates the importance of a preventative approach to cancer by changing lifestyles. For employers, this is significant too because cancer remains one of the three big causes of workplace income protection claims, accounting for 59 percent globally[101]. Cancer is now the second leading cause of death in the US[102] and people are far less likely to be screened for cancer if they don't have employer-funded health insurance[103]. Employers and employees can both benefit when workplace wellbeing strategies are designed around modifying and improving health behaviours and encouraging healthier lifestyles.

 Guest Expert View: Arti Kashyap-Aynsley

Global Head of Health & Wellbeing at Ocado Group

Arti Kashyap-Aynsley started her career as a Chartered Accountant, whilst also embarking on a 15-plus year journey in the Professional Services Sector. She has worked between audit, tax, and advisory services, spending the largest chunk of her career as a Management Consulting, focusing on large scale Finance Transformation programmes.

Working and travelling the globe opened Arti's eyes to the impacts of what our working lives can have on our overall wellbeing. Therefore, with the experience she gained in her career, she decided to pivot into wellbeing, where she first worked with Deloitte Consulting in the UK, to design, develop and deliver on a comprehensive wellbeing strategy. By being able to create positive change, Arti was inspired to continue to grow in this field and is now the Global Wellbeing Leader for Ocado Group.

Outside of her day to day working life Arti is a qualified life coach, as well as an Advisor and Director to various organisations from both a strategic and responsible business standpoint.

———————————

If you type in the phrase "wellbeing definition" in google you get over a million hits in just a blink of an eye. The basic idea that follows out of all of those hits is that at its core wellbeing is really a state of being that looks and feels comfortable, happy, and healthy. But all of those words are so subjective, and the variations between what that means for one person over the next varies - especially as you layer in other considerations such as gender, ethnicity, socioeconomic background, ability, sexual orientation, etc.

The growing importance of diversity and inclusion in the workplace is valid and necessary as we evolve as a society, but what cannot be negated is the connection between inclusion and wellbeing. To feel included is to feel comfortable being yourself and accepted for who you are - irrespective of how you may define yourself. But in the absence of that inclusivity, what is impacted? Your wellbeing. So how can we look at one without the other? How can we not connect our relevant leaders in these spaces, the strategic focus that they take and the actions that they impart?

And the truth is, it doesn't stop there. If we look at the definition once again - those subjective words that come up are impacted by every aspect of our day-to-day work and outside of work environments. Therefore to address wellbeing in the workplace is to understand that it is connected to every aspect of the employee experience as well as the culture of the organisation, and cannot just be looked at in a silo, within a benefits function or as just something that "HR" manages.

Connecting wellbeing to the strategic focus of the organisation, having a united narrative and approach across connected topics, and embedding wellbeing into the employee experience are all fundamental to the success of any approach to health & wellbeing. And is one that creates a clear image and understanding by stakeholders (be it investors, employees, etc.) of the true commitment that the organisation has to its employees.

Chapter 2

Preparing Your Strategy

Before we delve into the evidence of what is needed to best support employee wellbeing in the workplace, and now that we have an outline of a definition, let's look at some common ways successful organisations have established an effective wellbeing strategy.

Assessing existing support.

Before designing and developing any wellbeing strategy, every organisation must assess their workforce in a way explicitly tailored to understanding their people's mindset and beliefs regarding wellbeing. This data is paramount to inform the design and extent of any wellbeing intervention – especially within those organisations that may be looking at wellbeing for the first time.

One of the first things employers should consider is how they can either evaluate the current wellbeing of their workforce or what areas of wellbeing their employees need most. For global employers, this should initially be focused on territories or countries that can be grouped where it makes sense. For example, UK and US challenges often appear the same. Global wellbeing strategies are often biased towards where in the world decisions are made, so try to focus on a wellbeing strategy that is biased towards where the strategy is going to be implemented.

Surveying employees directly across your different regions will help you assess the current climate regarding how a program might be received and what information employees are willing to share. It will also give you a view of what areas of wellbeing are most pressing worldwide. A helpful resource is The Center for Disease Control and Prevention (CDC), which provides guidance on designing an employee survey, including examples of survey topic areas[104].

If you are a global employer, you should consider creating country wellbeing champions that can help them build a better picture of what life is like in each region. This will help you accommodate the words countries use to describe the same things. Pay rise, raise or salary hike, for example. So, consider what wellbeing terms are familiar in your regions but may not be international. This exercise will also help you spot any cultural challenges when designing a strategy, especially when discussing mental health and financial wellbeing where societal stigmas still exist.

Employers should also identify key issues that their industry/sector face. Some industries have a much higher prevalence of poor mental health than others, for example. Find out what these wellbeing challenges are and ensure they are accounted for in your workplace assessment. Typically, retail manufacturing and food and beverage industries in the US have some of the highest rates of mental health issues[105]. In the UK, the construction industry frequently tops the list of industries with the highest volume of poor mental health among its workers[106].

Similarly, different regions have different rates of mental health due to varying levels of state support. For example, Sweden ranks among one of the world's best countries for good mental health[107], and countries like Nigeria, Shanghai and Italy are consistently low too. Yet, China and the US tend to be among the worst countries for their prevalence of mental health conditions like depression[108].

Guest Expert View: Daniel Chan

Global Workplace & Wellbeing Lead

Originally trained as a nurse, Daniel has worked in various roles throughout his career, both in the public and corporate sectors. In his current role, he leads on the future of work and employee wellbeing globally. Before this, Daniel lived in

Hong Kong, working in and around APAC, consulting internally and externally with multinational corporations on their health and wellness strategy and delivery.

———————————

Having worked in the wellbeing space globally for over 15 years, I have seen this landscape change from the services that should be offered to an approach taken to support employees in the workplace. During this time, my views and attitudes have shifted to meet the ever-changing needs but have also been influenced by global events.

We have now moved away from just focusing on one area of support, and I believe we need to take a holistic view, providing a personalised approach wherever possible. Wellbeing is not a one-size-fits-all solution, as we are all individuals, each with different needs. Although this can seem daunting and challenging when it comes to the workplace, there are some key priorities that have always been consistent when I look to prepare a wellbeing strategy:

1. Listen to your employees

They *are* the lifeline of your organisation and the ones that you are looking to support. We can sometimes forget this and go with what we think is best, rather than what is best for them.

2. Use available data

Data is essential to really understand your populations. It provides a clear sense of what is important and can help determine where to invest and the impact it can have.

3. Be innovative

Try new things, be open to change and have a flexible approach. What you think in the beginning will likely be different from your result.

Overall, make it simple, as overcomplicating processes will only overwhelm people and likely cause them more anxiety and distress.

In my most recent position, we use the data from our employee surveys, listen and understand what our employees are asking for. A framework is then developed with initiatives based on those findings. Following this, we saw an increase in our engagement scores around wellbeing and more positive employee sentiment.

I have seen many things that don't work when it comes to wellbeing, but one that many corporations tend to do is replicate what others are doing - only to see it fail. This is usually because it does not fit their people. Every workplace is different - from the value proposition to the culture. If you've done things in the past somewhere and have had a good response, make sure you look to adapt to make it fit and work for your current workplace, rather than create a carbon copy.

Workplace wellbeing can be intimidating for those trying to deliver the strategy and those it is trying to support. Pause and take the time and think about the delivery, goals, and outcomes you want to achieve, as it's not a sprint but more of a marathon.

Employee wellbeing and the employee value proposition.

Google searches for "wellbeing", investment in wellbeing companies and sales of wellbeing products and services have all boomed over the last few years. As a result, employees are far more likely to agree that their employer has responsibility over how they feel physically and mentally than they did in 2019. This means that wellbeing has evolved into a critical part of the Employee Value Proposition (EVP) for both employees and employers.

One of the primary reasons why organisations like the United Nations, The World Health Organization and The World Economic Forum are pushing Governments to do more is the mountain of evidence[109] that society is better off when its people are happy and well. Investing in people's wellbeing generates returns for us as individuals, our communities, our economies, and our businesses. Employee wellbeing has now become critical to sustaining economic and talent competitiveness.

Almost 100 percent of HR leaders told Benefex that employee experience has become more critical during the pandemic, and employee wellbeing is the primary driver for this increased focus on employee experience[110]. But as we discovered at the start of this book, a generational shift in attitudes toward wellbeing at work is being driven by employees too, which in my view, has now made wellbeing the most significant part of the Employee Value Proposition. Why an employee will come and work for you is now driven by the support you will provide, how well you may care for them and an assessment of how they think you'll support them when their next wellbeing challenge comes along. So it's no surprise that two-fifths of employers say they are re-evaluating their EVP 110 with wellbeing in mind on the back of the pandemic.

An EVP designed around wellbeing.

What was traditionally a balance of the rewards an employee gets for working for you, the EVP has begun a new evolution. No longer the "deal" you get in exchange for your skills and time, the EVP must now show how it can support people's lives. It's now so influential that three-quarters of employees say they are considering moving jobs for better wellbeing support[111]. So, before creating your wellbeing strategy, you have to look at your EVP and find out what wellbeing means to how you sell yourself to people.

For decades, employers have tried to modernise the EVP to support the organisation, like investing in more digital tools and upskilling. But these efforts haven't significantly moved the dial for employees. I think many organisations have failed in their attempts to redesign the EVP because they've done so almost entirely from the view of the employer, not the employee. When we consider what our people might need from us in 2022 and beyond, we realise wellbeing's role.

The pandemic held a mirror up to the organisation for millions of employees, who weren't happy with what they saw in many cases. So, when you think about how you support wellbeing as part of your EVP, be clear on your answers to the following questions:

- **What does your company offer to support a struggling employee?** Life throws up a variety of stressors; how are you there for your people when it counts? From a day off sick to long-term ill health, divorce, debt, caring responsibilities, relationship breakdown, and even job loss. What do you have in place to support employees going through the various stages of life that can challenge us? Think about what kind of company you want to be; do you want to help those in difficulty, prevent others from falling into a worse wellbeing position or both? Do you want to react to poor wellbeing or try to prevent it entirely?

- **What the competition is offering.** You'll inevitably be compared with other employers, but it's also good to make sure that the ways you support the wellbeing of your people exceed what they can get elsewhere. With wellbeing being a top priority for new candidates, you must be able to show how progressive you are when compared to others. Who are you benchmarking yourself against, and what do you need to do to get ahead of them? If a candidate held your EVP up next to your competitors, which one looks like it will support a person more?

- **How will the support you offer manifest itself from day one?** From their first week working with you, how will an employee see the promise of the EVP come to life? Will they benefit immediately from a flexible working request? Will they get access to their benefits in the first month? What tools will be available to them while they go through their first month – a mentally taxing time. How an employee experiences your wellbeing support in their first days and weeks will play a massive part in how they engage with it in the future.

This new EVP is a fundamental shift from what we designed historic people strategies for (the employer) to who we now need to design them for (the employee). While I've been banging that drum for years, we now have some hard evidence to back it up. A recent global survey by Edelman asked almost 20,000 people across 14 countries who was the most crucial stakeholder in an organisation. Just under 50 percent of them said the employee now is, and just 12 percent said shareholders are[112]. This marks a *significant* change in attitudes towards how we value employees. Employees are seen to be more critical to our organisational success than our customers, investors and shareholders are, so delivering an EVP that supports employees' lives is paramount.

While many organisations are likely halfway between the shift towards more people-centred workplaces, the fast-paced nature of change in society means there is no time for us to waste; the most successful organisations in 2022 and beyond will understand employees as their primary stakeholders. They will see people as an investment, and that their valuable adaptability, innovation, and decision-making will depend on them being happy and healthy at work.

The most progressive organisations will soon put wellbeing at the top of their EVP. Creating more conscious, supportive, and compassionate workplaces isn't a leftist, liberal idea reserved for the Apple and Ben and Jerry's of this world. It's now the way the most successful organisations design employee experiences. But when we design experiences at work, we must consider how those experiences support a broader mission for creating safer spaces, more fairness and prioritises employee wellbeing. Whether looking at onboarding, choosing your benefits, how you communicate, what tech you use, or how managers are trained, employees are laser-focused on several ways they now expect employers to support their wellbeing. We must make those feature prominently in our EVP.

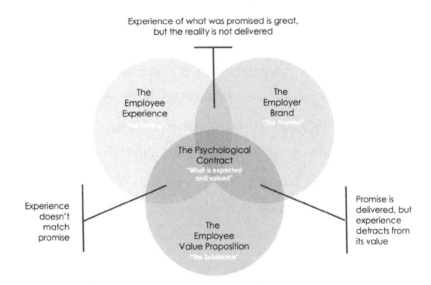

Fig. 7. The cross-section between the employer brand, EVP, and EX (Nadin, 2022)

Your EVP will be where a new employee sees 'the wellbeing promise' and 'the wellbeing feeling' come to life. So, as well as ensuring our employer brand is designed with wellbeing in mind, we must also ensure that 'the promise' matches the reality.

There is rarely a week that goes by when an employer isn't in the news for the way an employee has been poorly treated. This might be because a manager texted an employee who called in sick and demanded they return to work; a tribunal found an employer dismissed an employee unfairly because of their mental health; or constructive dismissal over rising workloads. It's very common that the actions of a few senior leaders don't align with the wellbeing promise of the organisation.

Now I don't believe these examples above make those in question bad employers. But these real-life and recent examples illustrate my point perfectly. In all of these examples, the employer had a very public and visible commitment to employee wellbeing and mental health. They've won awards for their approach to looking after their people and have signed mental health charters. However, it seems that despite these efforts to support employee wellbeing, the actions of one single manager didn't reflect them. This will happen in every organisation – not every leader or manager will buy into your wellbeing strategy. This is why it is so vital that we consider wellbeing through the lens of the promise, the actions and how the experience makes employees feel. Aligning what we say and do as employers is critical to successful wellbeing at work. Your employer brand, your EVP, and the everyday experience an employee gets with you must be saturated by wellbeing. It's not enough to say you care; you have to show it. Managers have to understand and live your strategy fully. When the promise and reality don't meet, distrust creeps in - and that can negatively impact employee wellbeing.

Trust - the foundation of wellbeing at work.

One of the biggest lessons businesses learned from the pandemic was that employees can be trusted. As we begin to recover from Covid-19 and prepare for new ways of working, employers must sustain this trust and build a wellbeing experience founded on it. There can't be good wellbeing at work if we don't have trust. Without trust, an employee can't tell you their truth, and when wellbeing goes unspoken about, problems arise. Therefore, understanding trust at work and trying to instil a culture of trust is a foundation every organisation needs before they roll out or design a wellbeing strategy.

According to a study conducted in 2019, just one out of every three managers said they trusted their workforce[113]. When the pandemic first broke out, many companies shuddered at the prospect of having to trust their employees and allow them to work 'behind closed doors.' Employers spied on employees and bought hidden software to track them, according to newspaper reports[114]. But as the pandemic raged on, the way we worked started to change forever. More than half of employees felt their colleagues were more productive than usual[115] and 90 percent of companies say they believe their culture improved during Covid-19[116]. The pandemic forced employers to do something the most successful organisations had already grasped – they *had* to trust their people. And trusting employees produced some amazing wellbeing results.

When we compare those organisations with low trust in their employees to those with high trust, we see a huge difference. Those organisations who trust their employees show 74 percent less employee stress, 13 percent fewer sick days, 76 percent higher employee engagement and 40 percent less burnout[117].

The UN's World Happiness Report in 2013 looked at how the global financial crisis impacted individual happiness[118]. People's wellbeing was less severely affected by the economic crisis in nations with high levels of trust. Almost ten years late, the 2020 World Happiness Report once again emphasised the importance of trust at work[119]. It found a third difference in overall wellbeing between those who live and work in a high trust environment and those who live and work in a low trust one. At work and in society, there are solid links between trust and wellbeing[120]. Trust can even impact employees' levels of mental health distress[121]. Trust at work makes us feel better.

When we trust our people to work in a way that works best for them, we are giving them autonomy and control. As we'll discover later in this book, these are two big parts of employee wellbeing. I believe this makes things like flexible working far less about policy and more about wellbeing and how much we trust people to make the right decisions. If we aren't letting and empowering our people to make choices of when and how they work, we are saying we don't have trust in them and that harms employee wellbeing significantly.

Guest Expert View: Jason Brennan

Psychotherapist, Author, Leadership Coach & Director of Wellbeing and Leadership, Benefex

Jason Brennan is an experienced Psychotherapist with a BA in Psychoanalysis, a Certificate in Humanities, a CBT practitioner, and a certified Transactional Analyst. He also is a founder and director of The Irish Transactional Analysis Assoc (TIATA) and an honorary lifetime member of the UCD Psychological Society.

Jason has experience in all sectors and as a mental skills coach has supported several high-profile sports teams. He has co-written the bestselling book "WIN: Proven Strategies for Success in Sports, Life and Mental Health".

_____

Some years ago, Patrick Lencioni wrote an influential book titled, The 5 Dysfunctions of a Team, in which he places "the absence of trust" as the foundational platform upon which his pyramid of dysfunctions sit. Trust (or what he describes as the team's inability to be vulnerable) sits at the heart of what a functional team needs.

Without the ability for employees to show vulnerability, there is no closeness, honesty, or healthy conflict. The net result of this leads to the top of the dysfunction pyramid, where avoidance of accountability and inattention to results sit. Effectively, Lencioni is highlighting the lack of productivity, commitment, and overall lack of wellbeing in a team where trust is absent.

It is no surprise then that employees leave environments where there is a trust dysfunction and where toxicity develops. But what of the toll this takes on the individual employee? How long does an employee endure this sense of un-wellness before they act and move on? What of the often-unseen harm created by an unhealthy work environment, the impact on the employee's mental health, and physical and emotional wellbeing? How it interferes with their home life and the havoc it can create in personal relationships, or through the financial insecurity it can often lead to?

Let's also look at the other side of the equation; what is it like to work in a team with high levels of trust? Research shows that when an employee has a good connection with their colleagues and their workplace, where they have a real sense of contribution and where they are growing and developing in their role, they are more engaged, more productive and have a greater sense of wellbeing in relation to how they are spending their time and energy at work.

Trust then is not only a cornerstone for team function, productivity, and engagement; it is also a key factor in health, wellbeing, and long-term mental health. So why is this? The ability to allow oneself to be vulnerable in sharing thoughts, feelings or opinions relies to a large degree on the ability to trust the other person's reaction. Looking for others to be open-minded, caring, understanding, and acknowledging, as opposed to reactive, defensive, discounting, dismissing or hurtful. In effect, a person needs to have a sense of feeling 'psychologically safe' to express themselves, which only grows through a sense of trust built over time and through regular safe interactions with colleagues and within a team environment.

The role of the leader is key here; it is the leader of any group that sets the tone, drives a culture, allows healthy behaviour to foster and grow through reaffirming and recognising it, and who intervenes when unhealthy behaviour is exhibited. It is why employee wellbeing is so necessary for a manager of people to prioritise if they wish to create a highly functional and productive team environment.

Managers need to give team members permission to speak up and genuinely show an interest in how their staff are doing - professionally and personally. They need to create a mechanism to do this regularly, thereby giving a sense of fundamental importance to employee welfare in as much as they would any other aspect of employment such as targets, KPIs etc.

The good news is that this is a fundamental human experience we can all relate to. The need for us to share our thoughts and feelings and for these to be respected, acknowledged, and heard is what makes us such intelligent communicators and so successful in the animal kingdom. Trust then is not an ethereal or magically in-accessible concept but a real-life relational experience that plays out every day in every workplace. The successful managers are the ones that consciously put time and energy into creating a safe, open, acknowledging, and enquiring environment.

The recent global pandemic has gone a long way to helping all workplaces understand the importance of nurturing and supporting the health and wellbeing of their employees, and it can be the beginning of the new inherently trusting and insightful way of working better together. Employees and managers collaborate to create a healthy, trusting, wellbeing-focused workplace.

Gathering support for your strategy.

Support from senior management is essential to building a successful wellbeing strategy. Management buy-in is critical for funding purposes, obtaining support throughout the organisation, and approving policies and processes related to a wellbeing strategy.

Your wellbeing strategy will impact many areas of your organisation, including the customer experience, so, if possible, you should try to build a cross-department group of senior employees willing to support your strategy. This team will also help you to link your strategy with broader business goals like recruitment, retention, increased customer loyalty etc. This helps to position a wellbeing strategy as a fundamental part of overall business plans, rather than just a HR or reward and benefits issue.

When obtaining buy-in from senior management, employers should consider the following:

- **What are your organisation's short- and long-term priorities?** Link to as many of these as possible. Show that investment in wellbeing will help your organisation to achieve its priorities. For example, one employer I work with were able to link their CEOs priority of reducing absence rates and their wider Environmental Social and Governance (ESG) goals directly to their wellbeing strategy.

- **What do you hope to achieve through investment in wellbeing?** What other benefits do you expect to see? (i.e., higher engagement, more customer advocacy, better innovation etc.). What existing organisational challenges might our strategy impact? (i.e., low engagement scores).

You should also give some thought to the role of the C-Suite in your wellbeing strategy and who does what. The buy-in from this team will be critical to the success of your wellbeing strategy. When leaders (especially CEOs) share their own wellbeing experiences, it permits employees to open up about theirs. It rejects the idea that some workers think their leaders are 'superhuman' and don't struggle like the rest of us. Data backs up that when leaders buy into wellbeing, they set a positive example for the rest of the organisation[122]. Wellbeing that the boss sponsors works best.

Chief Executive Officer - Figurehead

The CEO is ultimately responsible for making it clear to the business why wellbeing is a priority. This is often achieved by showing how a commitment to employee wellbeing enables core business objectives. But the CEO must also lead by example. Empowering employees to take their wellbeing seriously requires them to see their leaders do the same.

Robbert Rietbroek, ex-CEO of PepsiCo Australia and New Zealand, famously told his leaders to "leave loudly" to ensure all staff were comfortable using their flexible working policies. Use your CEO as a figurehead for your strategy.

Chief People Officer - Culture enablers

Wellbeing needs to be personalised to the individual and in line with changing needs and lifestyles. The CPO owns the company values, its culture, and the employer brand, so they'll want to see a strategy aligned with those. They can bring you the metrics on wellbeing, engagement, diversity, and inclusion to predict future trends and success. The people strategy that your wellbeing plan should align to.

Chief Information Officer - IT gatekeepers

There will inevitably be technology to integrate with your wellbeing strategy (especially if you create a digital 'home' for wellbeing or use a benefits platform). Figuring out how all of this works together so the employee has a seamless journey where all elements are connected in one place is essential.

Chief Financial Officer - Number centric

There is unequivocal evidence for the financial impact of workplace wellbeing. Quantify the impact on recruitment, retention, absenteeism, and productivity in your business case, so the financial payback is clear.

Chief Marketing Officer – Champions of your strategy

The cross-over between consumer and employer brands is now so strong that customers and potential employees are looking for a sense of purpose and meaning on either side of the brand. Involving the marketing team in your strategy will ensure that the world knows about all the great things you are doing and how seriously you take employee wellbeing as part of a broader corporate mission and purpose. It will help ensure your employer brand has wellbeing at its heart.

Every Employee

Employees should play a critical role in ensuring they are supporting each other, directing, and signposting struggling colleagues towards help. Employees should also be fully aware of the support you provide and consider this as part of their overall package - the same things may not be on offer elsewhere. Providers like Benefex can assist with the communication and rollout of new wellbeing initiatives, so lean on their expertise.

These stakeholders will play a significant and vital role in wellbeing. In 2022, HR thought leader Josh Bersin analysed 80+ capability areas and correlated those with the growth rate of thousands of companies globally. He found that among the top characteristics of high-growth companies, consulting with C-Level executives was the number 2 HR capability that led to success[123].

Guest Expert View: Yulia O'Mahony

Global Head of Health & Resilience, Philip Morris International

Yulia leads the development and implementation of a global wellbeing framework and strategy at PMI, a role she took up in 2021. Previously, she was Head of Wellbeing & D&I at

John Lewis Partnership, where she also led strategy development, piloted, and rolled out several innovative solutions, working with tech start-ups as well as charities, and worked as part of the JLP team to help improve taxation for mental health-related benefits in the UK (Working Well coalition).

Yulia has a wealth of experience in strategy and operations, having worked for leading consulting firms as well as holding senior commercial roles in JLP. She holds an MBA from Harvard Business School, PG Certificate (distinction) in Psychology and Neuroscience of Mental Health from King's College London, and an MA in computer science from Moscow State Academy of Management.

The notion of what wellbeing strategy entails have evolved over the recent years, and there is a lot more conversation now about a holistic approach to the employee experience: wellbeing being an outcome of lots of different things done right, rather than a standalone 'wellbeing initiative'.

This makes it more exciting but also challenging – as we are talking about culture change, and many stakeholders need to be involved, from employees to HR teams to managers to senior leadership teams. But significant culture shifts start with small but consistent steps and a growing momentum; so implementing a successful wellbeing strategy is akin to starting a movement.

The best starting point is an inspiring vision for people to get behind, as well as articulating a clear role they can play in making it a reality. Senior leadership buy-in and role modelling gets the ball rolling, but broad co-creation and active participation are key. One of the best ways to involve people is to create a bottom-up volunteer movement – wellbeing champions networks.

Most companies credit such networks as essential factors in shifting the conversation on mental health and wellbeing. It is important to ensure these volunteers get appropriate training, ongoing support, recognition, and celebration of their efforts – which needs to come from the senior leadership team. This would send a clear signal that it is essential for the company.

The other important step is ensuring congruence across benefits proposition, policies, and management and leadership training pathways. Everything needs to point in the same direction – especially at the critical points in the employee life cycle, such as induction, promotion, moving teams, life events, etc. For example, the policy for taking vacation, expectation to disconnect – all these will signal the intent to support wellbeing. But this also needs to be supported by the integration of the importance of self-care into training programmes – e.g. all line manager training needs to offer modules on self-care and looking after employee wellbeing explicitly – then it will be viewed as 'this is how we do things here' – obviously, supported by the role modelling of senior teams.

And finally, very important stakeholders are comms teams – there is a lot to be said for the ongoing drumbeat of consistent communications and campaigns – not just one big splash a year, but ongoing attention to wellbeing, with the clarity, simplicity, and consistency of messaging.

Chapter 3

Assessing the wellbeing market

As employee wellbeing grew as a trend, the workplace often responded by buying digital health solutions. As part of assessing the market, reviewing those buying decisions you may have made pre- and post-pandemic is critical. Look at what wellbeing tools you currently have, or have considered purchasing, to check their effectiveness. Hundreds of employers I work with raced to support their people during the first stage of the pandemic in 2020, which meant buying tools to support a disparate and desperate workforce through the crisis. But two years later, I'm frequently witnessing apps with little to no engagement from staff and tools that may have helped at the start of the pandemic but are no longer effective. Eighty-three percent of UK employers say they used a wellbeing app to help their employees during the crisis[124], but downloading our way to better wellbeing at work is challenging as it seems tech development is outpacing the science.

"Given the current state of the research, clinicians may wish to consider cautiously incorporating apps as an adjunct to treatment or recommending apps to clients."
- Joyce H. L. Lui, David K. Marcus, and Christopher T. Barry, Washington State University

In the UK, many consumers have turned to digital health to take the pressure off the healthcare system and seek help while trying to avoid in-person contact during the pandemic. In 2022, just under half of Brits say they have used a health app – an increase of nine percent since 2021[125]. Of those who have used such apps, 84 percent say they found them to be 'very' or 'somewhat' helpful. But interestingly, very few found or used these apps because of their employer. Most digital health app users found the app themselves, had it recommended to them by a friend or family member, or was encouraged to download it by a healthcare professional such as a GP, nurse, pharmacist, or hospital doctor. While digital health apps play a large part in supporting stretched healthcare services and dominating the workplace wellbeing market, their popularity brings some new problems for employers.

More than 900,000 digital health apps were released as the pandemic took hold in 2020. The total figure now sits at more than 350,000, according to IQVIA[126]. Apps designed to help manage specific diseases or health conditions account for

47 percent of all digital health apps. Those apps focusing on mental health, diabetes and cardiovascular disease make up almost half of all condition-specific apps – around 87,500! That widening choice and growing concern over evidence of effectiveness is throwing a spanner in the works for employers.

As well as an increase in the number of apps available to help us manage our mental health, there has also been a significant increase in usage[127] and searches for apps during the pandemic. Even doctors reported a 6,500 percent increase in searching for apps they could recommend to their patients to deal with the increase in patient numbers and wait times. But worryingly, despite the considerable rise in and adoption of mental health apps globally, it's suggested that most of them – including some of those endorsed by the NHS in the UK – are clinically unproven and potentially ineffective.

In 2017, research published in Professional Psychology[128], Research and Practice warned that "Given the current state of the research, clinicians may wish to consider cautiously incorporating apps as an adjunct to treatment or recommending apps to clients" such was the unknown at the time, not only about the effectiveness of many apps but in some circumstances the idea that some apps may prove to be iatrogenic. Concerns that have prevailed[129] over the years[130], including one study[131] suggesting many mental health apps can lead to an over-reliance and anxiety around self-diagnosis.

Evidence of efficacy is lacking.

Following the concerns raised in 2017, by 2019, another large study published in Nature Digital Medicine[132] found that many mental health apps were overplaying their efficacy to users. The researchers studied almost 1,500 mental health apps and found that while 64 percent claimed they had evidence of their effectiveness, only 14 percent provided any evidence. Similarly, another 2019 Australian study[133] conducted a significant review of app marketplaces like the Apple App Store and Google Play Store to find apps that offer treatment for depression/anxiety. Overall, the researchers found that just 3.4 percent of apps has research to justify their claims of effectiveness.

While the pandemic has driven millions more to use mental health apps since 2019, according to one 2021 landmark study[134], many mental health apps suffer from a "lack of an underlying evidence base, a lack of scientific credibility and subsequent limited clinical effectiveness." As of later 2021, of the 20,000 mental health apps available for download in the US, just five have been formally vetted and approved by the FDA[135].

As a result, there is growing evidence 136 that despite an initially high number of downloads, only a tiny portion of those users actually use these kinds of apps for a long time. Even by January 2022, new studies[136] continue to question the popularity of digital wellbeing, with one saying it has failed to find any "convincing evidence" that many wellbeing apps significantly helped people with common wellbeing issues.

The high availability of but low evidence has become a cause for concern for those who support the digital app space. ORCHA, the Organisation for the Review of Care and Health Apps, told MedTech[137] in 2021 that their biggest worry was that despite the progress in digital mental health support, most apps would fail their assessment process. ORCHA found that only a third of apps would score above their baseline of acceptability, which sits at 65 percent.

ORCHA's research into mental health apps, in particular is quite worrying. While they dominate the workplace wellbeing market, there are a total of around 22,000 mental health apps available. In his blog, UK television presenter and reporter Rory Cellan Jones interviewed ORCHA's founder Liz Ashall-Payne. Ashall-Payne told Cellan Jones that just five percent of apps dealing with severe mental health issues were of good quality and that we all needed to become better informed about health apps and understand which can be helpful rather than harmful[138].

Another thing employers should consider when rolling out wellbeing apps to their people is that some studies have cast doubt on how they handle data. A 2018 study[139] found that fewer than half of the more than 100 apps for depression studied had any privacy policy. More alarmingly, a 2021 study[140] even found that some common mental health apps were sharing data with Meta and other companies for targeted advertising. The same has been found among other wellbeing apps like period trackers. ORCHA found that 84 percent of period tracker apps were sharing data with third parties[141]. Following the Supreme Court decision to overturn Roe v Wade in 2022, The Guardian reports that many American women are now deleting period tracking apps from their devices amid fears that the data collected by the apps will be used against them[142]. With trust underpinning wellbeing so strongly, this should be a concern for employers and data privacy has to feature in how an organisation assesses the wellbeing market.

Wellbeing apps have an inevitable future.

This all being said, it's clear that the new dispersed global workforce and the ever-changing diversity of needs among the workforce mean there is a place for wellbeing tech in the modern organisation. The pandemic highlighted the considerable opportunity for mental health apps to support the

State and healthcare professionals with rising patient numbers and make care pathways more accessible to millions of employees.

In addition, the privacy of downloading an app to your device and seeking help and support can aid those who still feel a stigma around asking for help. Surprisingly, while many younger employees are happy to disclose a mental health condition, fewer are willing to ask for help[143]. They were almost three times less likely to seek treatment for a mental disorder than those over 40's are. So digital healthcare can bridge some of these gaps.

Digital mental health is a way of extending the resources available to people, reaching far more at once than ever before, beginning early intervention methods and taking a much longer and preventative way of managing our mental health. The pandemic tore our historic 'brick and mortar' view of mental health support. When writing this book, the strain on NHS England means that 8 million people are without help[144] – in addition to the official waiting list. So, these apps are clearly going to be the way forward if we are to take hold of the mental health epidemic, especially as there is some promising new evidence we should be aware of. Recent studies[145] have found that online therapy can work just as well remotely through technology as in person, ratifying many employer decisions to offer access to virtual support.

But we (as employers) must be clear on the function of these apps and who exactly they are designed for. There is a big difference between an employee who has a diagnosed mental health condition like depression and one who is going through a difficult time in their life. So, in reality, we are looking at these types of wellbeing and mental health apps in one of two categories: those that connect an employee to a qualified individual and those that don't.

A new problem for employers.

It's fair to say that the lack of evidence of effectiveness for many mental health apps could be down to a lack of data gathering and the fact that so many of these apps are at the early stage of their development and usage. However, it highlights employers' importance in conducting in-depth market reviews before rolling out apps to their people.

The other challenge for employers is the sheer volume of solutions – even those just focused on the workplace. While choice is inherently a good thing, it also means that assessing the effectiveness and choosing a supplier to work with has become a monumental task. In 2019, Benefex CEO Matt Macri-Waller and I spoke at a wellbeing conference on the worrying growth of workplace wellbeing options and the growing confusion for buyers[146]. It's fair to say, bolstered by the pandemic, that choice has become even more complex and confusing.

In 2021, almost $5 billion flowed through mental health apps around the world[147]. By early 2022, that figure was already $1.5bn more. We are seeing around 500 new mental health start-ups appear in the market each year – that is a lot for employers to get to grips with, understand and kick the tyres off. For many organisations, it's an impossible task now to review and assess the wellbeing app marketplace.

You should also be aware of and be cautious of working with wellbeing providers who sign exclusive partnerships with brokers and benefit providers. Arrangements likes these tend to be designed to benefit the providers over the employer in my view. They limit options and competitiveness for you. You shouldn't be commercially coerced into choosing a wellbeing provider that might not be the right choice for you.

Since early 2018, Benefex has been conducting our in-depth wellbeing research and has spent time with hundreds of employers to discuss workplace wellbeing. It's clear that a wellbeing strategy that spans organisational structure changes, policy updates, employee benefits and third-party tools is the most successful. This has led to a unique opportunity for benefit platform providers to support employers in finding the best wellbeing and mental health apps.

As a trusted advisor, providers like Benefex can review entire wellbeing markets, assess providers, check for evidence of efficacy, run trials and pilots, and constantly review their success. By removing this workload from the shoulders of HR, reward and benefit teams, we are freeing up time not just for strategy development but also helping to implement the most effective interventions. Employers should seek out these types of partnerships with those who can become a trusted advisor that can help them navigate their growing and complex wellbeing tech market. Brokers and tech providers can assist you in proving the efficacy of common apps and help you to find a shortlist of tried and tested services that can make a real difference to your employee's wellbeing.

Guest Expert View: Lorena Puica

CEO Syd™

Lorena Puica is a global AI leader in advanced healthcare with five degrees in mathematics, economics, and finance, is a published author, and has a decade in investment management working with portfolios of over £200billion while also being an extreme athlete with two Guinness world record events.

Following three years of personal health challenges, Lorena founded syd as a Science-Backed, AI-powered Preventive Precision Health platform – leveraging 1 million research papers to deliver a set of tools that give people the power to understand their own biology & behaviour via a digital twin as a guide to since backed recommendations and a real-time population analytics platform for enterprises.

The corporate demand for employee wellbeing solutions has grown 15 percent per year over the last three years. I've made two observations:

A. Vendors and health providers have rushed to the market to meet demand by selling legacy systems with the new language of 'wellbeing' on the packaging.

B. Corporations are still waiting for objectively measurable wellbeing data with verifiable impacts delivered to improve productivity and employee satisfaction.

The downside of this exponential growth in a nascent market is also growing confusion due to the lack of measurability of effectiveness. This is where there I think there is a growing need for:

1. Scientifically robust solutions with independently validated effectiveness and measurable outcomes both for the employee and employer.

2. High privacy and data security protocols to ensure the trustworthiness and integrity of solutions to the benefit of every individual.

3. Measurability of interactions focusing on fun/enjoyable personalisation for increased engagement.

Enterprises can quickly reveal if any proposed provider system can deliver improved wellbeing impacts to their employees and company by checking:

1. The system provides a dashboard of continuous and persistent live wellbeing improvement data with independently validated medical, health and wellbeing science measures.

2. Employees immediately see exactly how much better off they are over a period of time.

3. Employees know exactly which wellbeing aspects of their lives are improving, as well as which parts need to be improved.

4. The provider has automated tracking and reporting of all employee wellness measures across their enterprise, with

clarity on proving exactly where the value of their benefits, communications and investments are driving greater employee wellbeing and productivity and where more significant investments will drive better results in any domain. 5. Company and its employees have clear and continuous engagement with the wellbeing system

Potential questions you can ask to validate the quality of any wellbeing technology solutions you are reviewing:

- What is the scientific foundation of the product? What independent studies have you done to validate outcomes for your product?
- How have you measured success for your past customers? What success metrics can you share?
- What privacy protocols do you have in place - above & beyond the GDPR requirement? How do you ensure people feel safe & trust your product?
- How can you measure the value your product creates for us? How can we see these measurements in real-time?
- How do you address risks in your product?
- What life quality improvements can you prove you can deliver?
- What ROI (Return on Investment) does your product deliver?

- What impact does it have on health equity in the organisation?

- What measures of UX do you use (NPS / utilisation/return rates / dropouts etc.)

- Do you adopt interoperability standards with Fitbit/ apple health/ etc.?

- Do you meet any clinical safety standards or approaches?

- What is the level of personalisation (i.e. personal goal setting)

The need for wellbeing is here to stay, and it will grow. The more clarity and measurability you can bring to the selection process - the more employers can sincerely deliver a higher quality of life for everyone - consistently and impactfully.

A return on the wellbeing experience.

As you prepare to design a wellbeing strategy, inevitably, the cost and resources needed to build it will come under scrutiny. But the evidence supporting an investment in workplace wellbeing is now vast and compelling. Compiling this evidence as you prepare to build your strategy means you are forearmed with the data you need to build a solid business case for investment in wellbeing. While many organisations told Benefex the return on investment for wellbeing is "obvious", and a commitment to wellbeing is simply "the right thing to do", having a business case that clearly shows a return is frequently enabling organisations I work with to roll out more effective strategies[148].

Those organisations with high levels of employee wellbeing have outperformed the stock market by around two to three percent per year over a 25-year period[1]. Those UK FTSE 100 companies that demonstrate best practices in employee health and wellbeing show a higher-than-average shareholder return (61 percent instead of 51 percent)[149]. Organisations promoting health and wellbeing are considered three-and-a-half times more likely to be creative and innovative[150]. The evidence is compelling, but often unknown to those who make the funding decisions, so compile the evidence so that it is clear to your stakeholders that your plans make financial sense to the wider organisation. I've summarised some of the best evidence I think we have throughout the rest of this chapter.

We have some excellent employer case studies demonstrating this return on investment in wellbeing. The London School of Economics analysed data from the Royal Mail, where an investment of £45 million generated a £225 million return on investment over three years[151]. British NHS Trusts that score highly on the health and wellbeing index (measured annually through the NHS Staff Survey) have better performance across various measures, including financial, spending on agency staff, patient satisfaction and fewer acute infections[152].

The Harvard Medical School tells employers that emotional wellbeing should be seen as an investment in the organisation[22]. For every £1 spent by employers on mental health interventions, they get £5 back in reduced absence, presenteeism and staff turnover[23]. If employers want to do the best for their people and ensure they are happy and healthy, then an investment in emotional wellbeing is worth making. Yet, in 2021, just 26 percent of UK employers increased their wellbeing budgets in the face of the pandemic[153], despite this growing evidence of a positive return on investment (ROI).

In 2019, Deloitte reported that the total cost of poor mental health for UK employers was around £42-45 billion. However, by 2021 that figure had ballooned to £52–56 billion[154]. By 2022, 16 percent of workdays are lost to sickness due to poor mental health – almost double what that figure was in 2009. But with these increases came an increase in the return on investment (ROI) that can be achieved by supporting employee wellbeing at work. Individual ROI is now set at £3.50 for every £1 invested. For the organisation, the return is now £7.30 for every £1 invested. With the cost to employers of poor mental health sitting at around £2,300 per employee per year for the average worker, establishing the return on investment for your wellbeing strategy is going to be *very* important to getting the investment and attention you need.

However, despite this considerable ROI, Aon's Global benefits survey: A European Perspective, found that only 41 percent of European multinational employers have a documented global health and wellbeing strategy in place[4]. So, in the face of the enormous financial benefits of getting workplace wellbeing right, employers are still struggling to articulate and create a strategy that works for their organisation. This is why gathering this evidence base is so important. We must make wellbeing at work hard to argue with. But I believe another part of the problem is our failure to demonstrate a return on the wellbeing experience outside of monetary terms.

Historically, wellbeing ROI was designed around how an initial cost outlay would be returned to the employer – usually through objective measures such as absence rates or turnover. But as the wellbeing market and employee attitudes have evolved, these old metrics are no longer the only way to measure the return.

For example, a strong statistical relationship exists between employee wellbeing at customer satisfaction[155] and employee wellbeing correlates with productivity[156]. So when building out an ROI for your wellbeing strategy, be sure to include the ways in which you expect the organisation to improve, even where a monetary figure isn't applicable or available.

Making a real commitment to employee wellbeing.

In my experience, one of the most fundamental aspects of a successful workplace wellbeing strategy is the belief in and reasons why an organisation is committing to wellbeing; I don't think wellbeing at work can be faked. I don't think purely benchmarking a strategy and offering more than your competitors will get you to the culture of wellbeing that so many employers aspire to. Wellbeing must *become* your organisation. As we've already read in this book, the most progressive set of wellbeing initiatives and awards achieve very little without the belief and commitment of your organisation. Some of the most successful wellbeing strategies I've judged have been able to achieve these with small budgets from a passionate team that genuinely believed in what they were doing.

It is estimated that around 80 percent of large US employers now offer a workplace wellbeing program[157], but according to the CIPD, only half of employers have a standalone wellbeing strategy in place[158]. Despite the massive change in societal attitudes to wellbeing over the past four years, this figure is only 10 percent higher than it was in 2018. Alarmingly, almost a quarter of employers say they still aren't doing anything at all to support employee wellbeing, despite it being on the agenda for 75 percent of CEOs. This leads us to talk about why workplace wellbeing initiatives often fail.

One of the largest ever studies into workplace wellbeing looked at 33,000 employees over 18 months at the US retailer 'BJ's Wholesale Club'[159]. Some employees were randomly assigned to a workplace wellbeing programme; the rest were not. While those employees who were enrolled into the wellness program reported they exercised more and watched their weight more, the researchers found no significant differences in outcomes like lower blood pressure or other health measures. They didn't even see any differences in healthcare costs.

A similar study was conducted by the University of Chicago Harris School of Public Policy Associate Professor Damon Jones, along with University of Illinois faculty members David Molitor and Julian Reif, who designed and implemented the Illinois Workplace Wellness Study[160]. The randomised study covered 12,500 people and divided them into a control and treatment groups. The researchers found virtually no difference in health spending between the control and treatment groups. There was no difference in sick leave, gym visits were almost identical, and smokers were among the least likely to participate in wellbeing initiatives.

I think these two extensive workplace wellbeing studies show that we are focussing on the wrong areas. Rather than dictate what we believe employees should be doing, we should follow the evidence to ensure that all work elements support wellbeing rather than focus on traditional initiatives like weight and exercise. The most significant risk factors for poor wellbeing at work include burnout, workload, conflict, lack of control, lack of support, pressure, and stress. If we continue to focus on initiatives that seek to reduce things like healthcare costs, we will never succeed. Wellbeing at work has moved way past activity challenges, motivational posters, and free fruit—instead, its permeated everything we do as employers.

HR and company policy's impact on wellbeing.

As more of us realise the importance of designing the employee experience with the needs of the employee at the centre, we are starting to understand the potential contribution HR and company policies can have on employee wellbeing. To explore this further, for an article I wrote in HR Zone in late 2019, I had some secret conversations with HR, reward, and wellbeing leaders from across the globe[161].

It became clear that far too many organisations over-engineered their HR policies and procedures. Too many rules and too much specificity in policy can actively undermine employee wellbeing. To rein in a few bad apples, these policies tend to be too paternal and attempt to regulate employee behaviour. In many of these situations, the individual drafting the policy can recall the person it is intended for. In my experience, this mindset has kept us from expanding things like our remote working experiments. We were held back by our concern that certain employees may exploit a new manner of working.

Another typical observation is that some HR and company policies are unnecessarily lengthy and intricate because we are attempting to cover every scenario. The way forward appears to be shorter policies designed for a human being. There are several HR handbooks online with wordy, pointless dress code regulations. However, the $70 billion US company General Motors demonstrated how quickly we could change that. Their ten-page dress code guide was condensed into two words: "Dress appropriately." This is a fantastic example of how policy can be designed in a way that supports employee wellbeing by trusting employees.

Keeping it simple was the advice I received in large part from the HR leaders I spoke to. You must weigh your desire to have a policy in place against any potential drawbacks if it starts to affect your employees' wellbeing negatively. How we design and roll out standard HR policies and practices has impacted employee wellbeing[162]. In the UK, research by the NHS found that human resource management policies can negatively impact employees' general health and wellbeing[163].

Consider how your wellbeing strategy can be used as a guide for those creating company policy. How can we ensure how we define and design our strategy can be used as a framework for how we word and roll out new policies? For example, if you require your employees to pay for company travel and claim those expenses back, how quickly are we ensuring we pay them, so they don't cause financial stress? How do we encourage managers to use empathy and discretion when enforcing company policy in a way that positively supports employee wellbeing?

Guest Expert View: Anne-Marie Russell

Wellness Consultant

Anne-Marie's background is in HR, predominantly in employee relations. In 2017, Anne-Marie was given a transformative opportunity to lead wellbeing at ACCA. At the time, Anne-Marie wasn't an expert in wellbeing but did have a solid HR background and was starting her journey in training to become a counsellor. But Anne-Marie was passionate and committed to making a difference. Anne-Marie currently leads wellbeing at a large global media company.

A successful wellbeing strategy should have a long-term vision, be aligned to overall business objectives, and be flexible as it evolves. It is not a once and done and is definitely not a tick box exercise. Here are five top tips I would want every employer to know when designing and implementing a wellbeing strategy:

1. Take an evidence-based approach.

Wellbeing is not rolling out initiatives you think your people want or need. Take people on the journey with you, ask what key issues are impacting their wellbeing. Review your data, assess where your pain points are. Look at your current benefits, are people aware what they have access to?

2. Senior Management buy in.

Share with your stakeholders the findings from your data insights. Be clear on your long-term vision and planned wellbeing strategy. If getting buy in is difficult, don't give up, be persistent and doors will open. Be consistent and provide regular updates on the impact of the programme, always backing it up with evidence. Don't be afraid to admit when something hasn't worked; show what you have learnt from it and what you will do differently.

3. It is not a one size fits all approach. Do not build your strategy around one area of wellbeing. Take a holistic view focusing on physical, mental, financial, and social wellbeing; they are clearly linked. Be prepared to tailor your approach based on your demographics. Your strategy is not your EAP; it is not a mental health first aid network; it is a combination of various offerings to empower your people in reaching their full potential.

4. As the saying goes, "Rome wasn't built in a day". I had all my evidence; I knew where the pain points were and was bursting with excitement to get going. I wanted to tackle everything but realised the danger in this. I started with some quick wins and where I could make the most significant impact longer term. Decide on your plan, break it down into key focus areas and consider timescales. Be inclusive and communicate your plan to your people and let them know you have listened. One key piece of advice - don't over promise as you may underdeliver!

5. Internal and external networks.

Don't work in a silo; cross collaborate with other departments and have a joined-up approach. Set up a wellbeing champion network; they are your eyes and ears. Their role is vital in communicating the key messages, encouraging colleagues to engage with wellbeing initiatives and gathering feedback on what's working well and what's not. They can also be trained in mental health first aid, to listen and signpost colleagues to professional help. They are not therapists or problem solvers.

External networking is essential. Engage with other wellbeing experts to help build your knowledge. Use them as a sounding board and take their advice. This was invaluable to me; I learnt from the very best! Finally, remember that your people should always be at the heart of everything you do.

Chapter 4

The Role of Diversity and Inclusion in Workplace Wellbeing

Although a record number of employers are taking steps to support their staff with wellbeing, few are considering how their approach needs to change based on the various challenges of the people they employ. The global Coronavirus pandemic brought the intersection of wellbeing and diversity firmly into the limelight. A recent survey of large US employers found that women of colour and LGBTQ+ employees have the highest share of unmet basic needs[164]. As we learned during the exploration of how we define employee wellbeing, diversity plays an essential role in our health and happiness.

From data collated by the Office for National Statistics (ONS), all minority ethnic groups in the UK were at higher risk of death throughout the COVID-19 pandemic than white groups. Data from the second wave of the pandemic in the UK (1 September 2020 to the end of January 2021) showed a particular intensity in this pattern[165]. Health equity at work means that all employees should have a fair and just opportunity to be as healthy as possible. However, it's clear that many still aren't doing this for their most vulnerable and marginalised groups.

The crisis hit Black households harder than white ones, even considering pre-pandemic socio-economic disparities. Black unemployment[166] was higher than white during the pandemic, and Black households[167] were more likely to have taken on debt during the pandemic. Black Americans were up to three times more likely to die of Covid-19[168]. So, it's probably not surprising to know that poor mental health was far more prevalent among Black adults than white adults during the pandemic. Yet race-related wellbeing support tends to be non-existent in the workplace.

"For patients being treated in another language, it's amazing that the odds of serious harm, including death, are more than doubled"
- Dr Peter Tanuseputro, Physician and Scientist, Ottawa Hospital School of Medicine

The importance of creating an inclusive and safe environment for the wellbeing of diverse groups cannot be underestimated. A landmark new study published in the Canadian Medical Association Journal has doctors and healthcare professionals "staggered" by the results[169]. The study assessed nearly 190,000 patients who spoke French or English. The researchers found that when a French-speaking doctor treated French speakers, they had a 24 percent lower chance of dying in hospital compared to those whom a non-French speaking doctor treated. The odds were more than doubled among non-French or English speakers, rising to a 54 percent lower chance of death if a person was treated in their native language. This study highlights how important it is for us as employers to ensure we are tailoring our wellbeing initiatives to the diversity of our people, making sure they are heard and understood and that the support we put in place is appropriate for them and their diversity.

For a long time, socio and economic factors have meant that women have been at greater risk of poor mental health than men[170]. At the time of writing this book, one in five women has a common mental health problem such as depression, anxiety or self-harm. But it's only recently that gender-specific wellbeing initiatives have become common in the workplace. Marginalised groups are suffering varied, and complex wellbeing needs just because of the colour of their skin, their gender, or their sexuality, and employers need to acknowledge and accommodate this.

LGBTQ+ employees and wellbeing.

According to the ONS, one in 25 people under 24 in the UK identifies as lesbian, gay, or bisexual. However, LGBT+ people are less satisfied with their lives than the general UK population, and experiences of mental health issues are around a third higher in LGBT+ employees[171]. According to research by Stonewall, more than half of LGBT+ people have experienced depression in the last year, and almost half of trans people thought about taking their life in 2017[172]. LGBT+ youth are four times more likely to self-harm than their heterosexual peers[173].

As a result of the discrimination they face, LGBT+ employees are less likely to seek support for mental health issues for fear of more discrimination. In one study by Stonewall[174], an LGBT+ person being treated following a suicide attempt was told by a nurse that their mental health issues were because Satan was in his soul. With an increasing number of employees seeking health and wellbeing support through this workplace, these are fundamental considerations employers need to make when designing workplace wellbeing strategies or initiatives.

While there has been very little research into the pandemic's effects on the wellbeing of the LGBTQ+ community in particular, the data we do have is surprising. A larger share of LGBTQ+ adults reported that they or someone in their household experienced a job loss through the pandemic - 12 percent higher than straight people[175]. In addition, LGBTQ+ people were almost twice as likely to report that the pandemic hurt their mental health than non-LGBTQ+ people. The data shows that the pandemic disproportionately negatively impacted LGBTQ+ employees (like almost every marginalised group). Yet, for many employers I've worked with, the support offered to LGBTQ+ employees is the *same* as that is provided to straight, cis employees.

Racism and emotional wellbeing.

The largest representative survey conducted on the UK's almost four million minority ethnic workers in 2022, found that more than 120,000 employees from Black and ethnic minority backgrounds have quit their jobs because of racism[176]. More than a quarter say they have faced racist jokes at work. TUC General Secretary, Frances O'Grady said the report should be a "wake-up call" for employers, calling for more changes in the law to protect workers and to prevent the harm caused by racism in the workplace.

In 2021, one in three UK adults experienced[177] or witnessed racism at work. Around a third of employees subjected to racism at work have said they've taken a period of sick leave as a result[178]. Unsurprisingly, this is hurting the lives of racially diverse employees. Research has also found a 73 percent increase in suicide attempts among Black US teens this year[179].

Almost half of Black and Latinx employees have left a job, at least partly for mental health reasons[180]. According to Mind, Black men are far more likely than others to be diagnosed with a severe mental health condition and are far more likely to be sectioned under the Mental Health Act. Structural racism among ethnic minority groups can also exacerbate inequities in housing, employment, and the criminal justice system, all of which can severely impact health. Racism and prejudice can have a harmful impact on the physical and emotional health of persons from ethnic minority groups, according to the latest research from the King's Fund[181].

While specific gender wellbeing support is growing in popularity in the workplace, ethnic-specific wellbeing support is almost non-existent. Yet, in its many forms and many ways, racism shortens lives and hurts the health of ethnically diverse people[182]. With our most marginalised employees being at a higher risk of certain diseases and with the mental health impact of everyday racism, it's imperative that we consider our wellbeing strategies through the lens of these diverse employees.

In early 2022 the Chair of the British Medical Association's council told the BBC that the NHS is "riddled with racism"[183]. In the US, structural racism exists within some health care policies[184]. Many studies have shown that systematic racism often means that people of colour and others belonging to marginalised groups do not receive the wellbeing support they need. Racism blocks access to leading a healthy lifestyle for many employees of colour[185]. Seven in ten African Americans believe they are treated unfairly because of their race or ethnicity when they seek medical help[186]. As a result, more than half of African Americans don't trust the health care system.

For employers, our wellbeing strategies have to consider how we can provide access to wellbeing professionals that are informed, perhaps have lived experience, or can deal with the specific wellbeing requirements of diverse groups. For example, is an employee with a sexual health issue able to speak to someone of the same sexuality as them? Can a Black employee who is experiencing racism access a Black counsellor if they wish to?

Diversity and physical wellbeing.

While some of the common causes of heart disease, such as high blood pressure or cholesterol, are universal, the burden of these risks also falls disproportionally on people of certain races and ethnicities[187]. So, when we think about how we support health behaviour change in the workplace, is that advice changing based on our location or the diversity of the people we seek to help?

Large-scale surveys have long demonstrated that diverse groups are more likely to report worse rates of illness overall, and that certain diseases begin earlier among diverse people than in White British people. Ethnicity even has a greater impact on the prevalence of certain diseases than other socioeconomic factors, according to quite a few studies:

- Some ethnic groups have a worse health situation than others. According to the UK Parliament, Pakistani, Bangladeshi, and Black-Caribbean people have among some of the worst UK health, while Indian, East African Asian, and Black African people have the same health as White British people. In contrast, Chinese people tend to more have superior health to white people[188].
- Compared with the white population, disability-free life expectancy is estimated to be lower among several ethnic minority groups[189].
- Mortality from cancer, dementia and Alzheimer's disease is highest among White groups[190].

- Women are twice as likely as men to worry about their post-pandemic lives. They are disproportionately carrying the burden of worrying about their parents, children, education, and work-life balance, according to the National Centre for Social Research (NatCen)[191].

Employers must recognise that not all employees are created equal and the wellbeing challenges they face can differ significantly. Simply understanding the disadvantages your diverse employees face can help you build a wellbeing strategy that accommodates the varying needs of your employees.

There are many groups in our societies whose wellbeing is adversely affected when compared to the majority. The reasons for these inequalities are often complex and long-standing. But whatever groups exist within your organisation, there are a few key considerations you should give to your wellbeing and mental health strategy to ensure you are supporting marginalised groups:

1. **Better access to support that specifically considers employees needs and preferences.** Employers must consider services designed to meet the needs of Black communities better as much of the state-provided

support does not offer culturally appropriate support to those from ethnically diverse groups. In addition, gender-specific wellbeing initiatives should be considered.

2. **Expand benefit offerings to meet basic needs.** How can benefit schemes make up for some of the ways society is holding back certain groups by supporting access to better housing, finances, and transport? Health inequality hinders a diverse employee's ability to find, receive and afford care. Around a third of Black, Hispanic, Latino and LGBTQ+ employees say they have considered switching jobs for better health benefits[192].

3. **Consider the impact of health insurance.** It's been suggested in some research that health insurance may reduce racial and ethnic disparities[193]. Women without health insurance are more likely to receive a breast cancer diagnosis[194].

4. **Make benefits inclusive and accessible.** Removing barriers to representation within benefit schemes by using gender and sexuality-neutral language. Ensure same-sex parents are visible in policy documentation

and offer support to the specific challenges of diverse employees, such as transitioning. Diverse employees are more likely to find resources that support benefit choices more helpful than other employees[195].

5. **Representation.** This has always remained an essential part of diversity at work, but it also has a role to play in wellbeing. When employees feel safe and included, they report higher wellbeing. Simple initiatives that show diverse employees they are recognised can have an impact. Just sharing gender pronouns on employee email signatures has been found to attract more diverse employees[196].

Employers should consider how they can support the mental health impact of racism or homophobia and ensure representation exists in all the ways you support so an employee can speak to someone who can identify and empathise with them. As it stands, Black adults are the least likely ethnic group to access counselling or therapy in the UK[197].

Using lived experiences.

One of the most successful ways to support people's wellbeing has been to use 'permission' and 'social proofing' to allow employees to openly discuss their mental health. For many, seeing a celebrity or CEO open up about their challenges permits them to do it, too, without feeling shame or weakness for doing so.

With many marginalised groups and cultures still experiencing a stigma around mental health, using those who have lived experience of poor mental health which belong to these groups can help others[198]. Research has found that it can promote hope and allows people to think more constructively about their own mental health[199]. An inclusive and supportive workplace culture can help to create an environment where workplace wellbeing not only caters for the unique challenges faced by different groups but also supports them in a way they might be getting elsewhere.

One in four women experience depression compared to one in 10 men[200]. Black men are more likely to have experienced a psychotic disorder in the last year than white men[201]. While these stats may not reflect the true extent of poor mental health among women and Black people, they do highlight the inequality that exists not just in the causes of poor mental health, but the support that is offered too. You need to tell these stories at work.

Creating policies that include people.

If an organisation is committed to providing a positive work experience for its people and ensuring they develop a culture of wellbeing, policies that protect the marginalised from poor wellbeing must be put in place. As we learned in chapter one, our individual wellbeing is closely linked to the experiences we've had in life. Many diverse employees pay what is called an 'emotional tax' whenever they are made to feel different or excluded. Effective workplace wellbeing initiatives accommodate the different needs of employees and recognise that pillars like emotional wellbeing are a diversity issue. So impacted is our wellbeing by our diversity, the two go hand in hand.

Sexual harassment policies

Sexual harassment at work is generally unlawful under various acts across the world. Violating someone's dignity and creating an intimidating, hostile or degrading, humiliating or offensive environment can greatly impact the individual's wellbeing. More than a third of women say they have experienced sexual harassment in the workplace[202]. So a sexual harassment policy is crucial to discouraging inappropriate behaviour but also protecting employees' wellbeing.

Two essential conditions must be met for a sexual harassment policy to be effective. The organisation must back it and have faith in it. The most crucial component of a company's sexual harassment policy is often not the policy itself but rather the organisation's genuine desire to eradicate sexual harassment. If a written policy is not followed, it is meaningless.

Secondly, adequate training on both sexual harassment prevention and the policy itself must be provided to all employees. Every employee needs to understand the importance of not being dismissive of claims made. This is all very important to employee wellbeing because sexual harassment has been found to negatively impact a person's health, money, and relationships. One US study tracing women over 20 years found that sexual harassment was linked to financial insecurity[203]. Women and men who experience sexual harassment at work have significantly higher levels of depressed mood than non-harassed employees[204]. Many victims of sexual harassment exhibit symptoms of Post-Traumatic Stress Disease (PTSD) and suffer from long-term physical and emotional impacts[205].

The National Union of Teachers (NASUWT) say that an effective and acceptable sexual harassment policy should include[206]:

- A policy statement
- A definition of sexual harassment
- Scope of the policy
- Procedure and guidance
- A complaints procedure
- Confidentially provision

Trans inclusive policies

Research consistently finds transgender employees sustain worse health outcomes than cisgender employees[207]. Almost a third of transgender people live in poverty in the US, compared with less than 8 percent of the population at large[208]. Transgender employees tend to make less money than cisgender employees do, and more than 15 percent of transgender employees say they have been verbally harassed, physically attacked, or sexually assaulted at work because of their transgender status[209].

In the workplace, trans employees' wellbeing is harmed in several ways; a third of trans employees have been bullied, insulted, or intentionally called the wrong pronouns; almost a quarter have been socially excluded at work, and almost 20 percent have been actively excluded from work projects[210]. So, it is essential for us to develop and support trans-sensitive policies to support our culture of wellbeing at work.

According to a report by Gender and the Economy and Pride at Work Canada, fully inclusive trans policies must include[211]:

- Executive leadership support
- Employee training on gender identity and gender expression
- Inclusive recruiting practices
- Onboarding training on gender identity
- Employee resource groups
- Targeted mentorship and allyship
- Diversity and inclusion managers with a trans inclusion mandate
- Networking with community organisations to develop insight and expertise

Employers should also consider health coverage for trans employees and ensure inclusive benefit language. Companies may significantly improve the lives of transgender people and contribute to a societal shift toward transgender inclusion by prioritising the wellbeing of transgender employees in the workplace. New research finds benefits to employees and employers when they educate and implement trans allyship measures. Research from Bath University shows that a substantial diversity and inclusion climate underpinned by robust policies can help generate support and advocacy for trans employees, even among those who historically held prejudicial views[212].

Policies that prioritise employee wellbeing

With such close links between wellbeing and diversity, it is imperative that employers create environments that are welcoming and supportive of different backgrounds and tailor their mental health support to the specific needs of those groups less likely to be able to access adequate support outside of the workplace. While we have covered just a few scenarios here, there are plenty of other policies that ensure the wellbeing of your diverse and marginalised employee groups are taken care of. For example:

- **Codes of conduct:** There is a moral element to workplace wellbeing; for many organisations, that will be the guiding principles that influence employee conduct. How committed the company is to the wellbeing of its people will come through in a code of conduct policy. How employees are expected to treat one another, the discouragement of bias, intimidation, and discrimination etc.

- **Flexible working policies:** The very nature of allowing employees to have some control over when and where they work not only enhances wellbeing, but it actively includes people. Those with caring responsibilities, for example who, can much easily fit their lives outside of work into their working day. Where many caregivers still tend to be women, flexible working policies actively encourage working mothers to the workplace and remove the stigma of working reduced hours or part-time working.

- **Bullying and harassment:** The adverse mental health impact of bullying and harassment has long been known and researched[213]. However, new research is even finding that bullying and harassment at work has physical wellbeing implications too. Those employees who have been bullied at work are more likely to develop cardiovascular disease[214].

- **Reasonable adjustment policy:** Reasonable adjustments are changes made to remove or reduce a disadvantage related to an employee doing their job. This could mean changes to the workplace, changes to equipment used to do a job or even just providing information in an accessible format. For example, in a mental health context, this might include allowing staff who have a mental health condition to take more regular breaks or working more closely with them to manage their workload.

- **Whistleblowing policy:** Protecting the wellbeing of those who raise concerns within our organisation is very important – especially as the concerns they raise may well be to do with how the organisation treats its people. Whistle-blowers can often feel victimised and pressured at work.

The policies we create in the workplace no longer just guide or restrict employees; they send a clear message about how much you value their autonomy, how much you trust them and how much you care about them. Some of the most common company policies send a very clear "we care about you" message.

Chapter 5

The role of the physical workplace

The Coronavirus pandemic has been a good excuse for us to think about what an office is, why we want them and how we can build better workplaces designed around wellbeing. I believe the physical workplace will remain a place for wellbeing, even in those organisations where remote and home working are starting to dominate. So, the office must coexist *and* compete with the home. This all matters to wellbeing because if we are lonely, if we don't feel connected if we don't have friends or positive relationships at work, our workplaces are doomed. And while technology is helping us maintain positive relationships, it's not helping us create them in the same way as face-to-face does. So, we must balance the new desire to work from home with the need to have a workplace. These two lives are not mutually exclusive, and they need each other to survive.

Remote work is good for our health… mostly.

Because of the pandemic, millions realised the wellbeing benefits of home and remote working. Removing an often long and frustrating commute was replaced by more time for rest and relaxation. A pre-pandemic survey of more than 3,000 employees found that remote work had a "huge" or "positive" impact on the quality of life of 97 percent of employees[215]. But the wellbeing benefits of remote and home working go even further; as many as 83 percent of remote workers say the way they work positively impacts their levels of stress[216], and many say they even found themselves practising healthier habits because they were able to work from home[217].

But remote work is also important to inclusion at work, and we know that the more disadvantaged an employee is, the lower their wellbeing is likely to be. Poor mental health is higher in rural areas where long-term unemployment has tended to be higher[218]. But remote work is now enabling many living in these often-deprived areas to find better quality work and gives them more choice over roles and employers. Home working is also a much stronger desire for women than it is for men[219], typically because many women at work carry the burden of childcare and eldercare responsibilities that are made easier with remote work. For women, remote work can ease the burden and pressure of their home lives. Surprisingly, remote work also appears to be more inclusive to LGBTQ+ employees too[220]. Bigger cities tend to be more inclusive of diverse groups, so living in a big city but working for a company in a smaller one opens up new opportunities for employees. CNBC report that for some LGBTQ+ employees, remote work has been a 'game changer'[221].

But like with many things in this book, the advance of remote and home working has just been the continuation of a trend rather than the emergence of a new one. In 2019, hundreds of US employers reported that a third of their workforce were already working from home some of the time, and another report found that 66 percent of US employers allowed employees to work from home if they wanted to. But as of late 2022, UK workers report going into the office less than one and a half days a week[222] – and that could be a problem for wellbeing.

In the book 'Back to Human: How Great Leaders Create Connection in the Age of Isolation, Dan Schawbel found that remote employees spend half their day using technology to communicate rather than relying on face-to-face or even telephone conversations[223]. As a result, slightly more than half said they very often or always feel lonely. This is a big issue for employee wellbeing because not only have feelings of loneliness and isolation been on the rise in the modern workforce (even before the pandemic started), but loneliness can have a detrimental impact on our wellbeing.

A 2019 report from Igloo Software found that 70 percent of remote employees say they feel left out of the workplace while working from home. They report that they often miss out on information, are excluded from meetings, and struggle to access important documents[224]. So while there are clear wellbeing benefits to more home and remote working, these new ways bring new wellbeing issues. There is also a largely hidden impact of more remote work on physical wellbeing too. Nearly half of employees working from spare bedrooms or sofas report developing musculoskeletal problems[225]. This poses a problem for employers: how do we balance what employees want to do and what we think they should do? While many may be able to see the immediate benefits in their bank balances of a lack of commuting, some of the ways their wellbeing is being harmed will take much longer to manifest.

There are obvious pros and cons to remote working, but the evidence is clear – whether we work in the office, at home, or both, that choice will impact our wellbeing. During the pandemic, Microsoft found that more than half of those workers forced to work from home were happier for it[226]. But it seems the negative effects of working remotely are strongly influenced by the levels of support an employer puts in place[227]. When employers provide additional physical and mental support, and when they foster more connectedness among their colleagues, they can lessen the negative impact on employee wellbeing. When the employer steps up to support home and remote workers, the benefits of this type of work are improved and the negative effects reduced, showing how influential the organisation can be in making this new way of working successful for their people.

Redesigning the office with wellbeing in mind.

While employers continue to balance the pros and cons of more remote, home and hybrid working, a common conversation appears to be how the physical office needs to change. If so, much of office workers' historic tasks can now be done elsewhere; how does the office need to change? Rather than compete with home working, can the physical workplace offer something employees can't get at home? Will it become a place where we foster connectedness, community, and social interaction?

While many consider the future of their workplaces, it might be helpful to remind ourselves that even how we design the physical workplace can impact employee wellbeing. White, grey, or beige walls have been found to cause feelings of sadness[228], whereas introducing colour and vegetation to urban environments has been found to improve the wellbeing of people living in city centres[229]. More plants in the workplace can lead to a decrease in tension and anxiety, depression, and fatigue among workers[230].

An increase in indoor air pollution has been found to cause errors in the decisions made by players in chess tournaments. Warmer temperatures have been linked to lower exam scores, and high noise environments can impact memory and tiredness[231]. A review of almost 3,000 research papers exploring the relationship between workplace design and employee wellbeing reveals some interesting results[232], while open-plan offices and background noise appear to harm wellbeing, in-person interactions help it. There is a complex set of factors at play when we think about the place someone does their work and how that changes their wellbeing. But this isn't unique to the physical workplace – remote workers face new wellbeing challenges too.

Remote work by design

A much-discussed area of enabling more home and remote working is how we encourage our people to step out of their homes during the working day. For remote and hybrid workers, we are far less in control of their working environment and while on one hand that is good for wellbeing, on another, it really isn't.

For example, in one slightly bizarre but fascinating study from 2019, researchers looked at the habits of people using Twitter regularly. They found an interesting way to make tweets more positive – go to a park[233]. The researchers found that when people tweeted from a park, they were far less likely to use negative words like "no", "not", or "don't". Users who sent tweets from a park saw their positivity increase by as much as tweets do on Christmas day. But how do we encourage employees to spend time outdoors now that they aren't walking down the street to get to the office or going out at lunchtime? It is these new problems that plague those seeking to improve employee wellbeing as we arguably have less influence over our people than we did before the pandemic and unless we change the narrative around what the workplace is for, we won't get people back to the office more than a day and a half a week anytime soon.

The modern office isn't working.

One of the reasons I think remote and home working has become so popular for office-based employees is that many of them can create better working spaces at home that compete heavily with what the traditional office offers. Many psychologists are interested in the physical workplace, specifically what they call 'cues of belonging'. These are signals embedded within our workspaces that tell us if we are welcome there or not – if we fit in or if we don't. Sapna Cheryan has researched this a great deal, and in one study, along with her colleagues, she commandeered a space at Stanford University where they created a stereotypical classroom and a non-stereotypical classroom.

The latter was filled with science fiction books, Star Trek and Star Wars posters etc. After just a few minutes in the non-stereotypical room, male students expressed a high interest in pursuing computer science, but female students were less interested. But the female students' interest increased significantly (and exceeded that of the men) after spending time in the stereotypical classroom[234]. This and subsequent research conducted by Cheryan has found that the place we work can heavily influence our thoughts and, I predict, our wellbeing.

How we feel in the places we work, and our sense of ownership over them has long played a part in performance. Many studies have shown that sports teams tend to win bigger games when they play on their home grounds. The spaces we work in not only have to make us feel like we belong, but they also need to provide us with cues of identity, our interests, our sense of humour, our achievements, and our hobbies. We have growing evidence that people are more confident, capable, and productive in spaces they consider their own. In fact, the difference in productivity can be as much as 30 percent between working in a bare space like a plain office compared with working from home, where a person's sense of belonging is heightened[235]. So, while our home working allows us to establish these 'cues of belonging', the traditional office doesn't.

Whatever your view on the future of the office, it's clear the old ways of working needed to change. When researching my first book, I dedicated a whole chapter to the failure of the open plan office. Bürolandschaft was a German movement in the 1950s to open-up workplaces and install open-plan offices. Bürolandschaft was designed to encourage egalitarian management and create an environment that would produce more communication and collaborative working. But as the world embraced this way of designing offices, it wasn't long until evidence emerged that it achieved the opposite of what it intended to do. The proximity to our colleagues gave us too much communication and spontaneous meetings/conversations that were eating away at our productivity. We have to find a new balance.

According to a global LinkedIn survey, around 70 percent of employees say they want the office to help them collaborate and socialise. Half of them say they don't want to return to the office and just do meetings they could attend at home[236]. So, we must look at the office through a wellbeing lens – the office (like so much of what we discuss in this book) must make work a positive force in our lives. Employees must feel better off having come to our workplaces than they would have at home, and I think that's where the social element of work becomes critical. How do we create such fulfilling communities at work that our people and their wellbeing is better *because* they choose to work with us? We'll pick this up again in Chapter 10.

The workplace can have a significant positive effect on our mood and wellbeing when designed in the right way. My first book focussed heavily on the work environment and its impact on wellbeing, so I won't go into too much detail here. But it makes us think – if the work environment is now more out of the employer's control than it was in 2019, how can we ensure employees work in a way and in an environment that promotes positive wellbeing?

How we design offices, the furniture we buy and even what lighting we choose have all been found to impact employee wellbeing[237], so we must feature these things in how we think about our wellbeing strategy. How do we design workplaces that encourage social interaction, that discourage a sedentary day or that alleviate stress caused by commuting or the costs associated with travel? How do we encourage our people to build healthy habits into their daily lives when working from home, and how can we influence or control the workspaces our people use outside of the office? These are all considerations for anyone tackling wellbeing at work to be aware of and to make allowances for. But it seems that the most important question is how we do we create cultures where we support our workers' wellbeing and empower them to work in a way that is best for them – regardless of where the physical location actually is?

Chapter 6
Making Wellbeing Work

Now that we have considered how we might define what wellbeing at work means to our organisation and us and have understood some of the best practice that exists, it's time to learn about the evidence that the workplace positively impacts employee wellbeing. Using some of the definitions from the start of this book, we will follow the latest thinking in the ways, every employer can ensure they become a positive force in the lives of their people and develop an authentic culture of wellbeing.

Raising the employee voice.

The evidence suggests (quite strongly) that when an employee participates in workplace decision-making, this positively impacts employee wellbeing. Giving employees a say in how work is planned and carried out positively affects employee wellbeing according to at least seven studies by Health Scotland[238].

From an early age, courting and listening to the opinions of people has been shown to positively impact overall wellbeing. When students' views are sought and used to inform the creation and development of their curriculum or place of education, it highlights the importance of adolescent social functioning in their overall wellbeing[239]. But even as adults, this voice behaviour positively impacts our psychological wellbeing[240].

The views and opinions of our people have long been useful to us as employers. They help to prevent errors and drive innovation at work[241]. But employee voice plays an important part in our wellbeing at work. Having a voice at work benefits occupational wellbeing[242] as well as individual psychological wellbeing[243]. Thankfully, many of you already court employee voice through surveys. Gartner report that around 75 percent of global employers use a formal survey to ask employees questions[244].

It's now very rare that I meet an employer that doesn't run an employee survey. Gathering employee feedback has evolved into an incredibly important part of our experience at work. Whether it's annually, monthly, or daily, everyone reading this book has probably completed an employee survey at some point in their career. However, the way these surveys are run and acted upon can have the opposite to the intended impact and push wellbeing in the wrong direction.

I once worked for a UK FTSE 100 organisation that sent their employee surveys out a few days after they issued all employee annual bonuses. For the one month of the year that our employer helped us to clear our debts, buy new cars or book holidays, we were asked how we felt at work. Even as a young manager, this felt quite contrived. Did we really care what employees thought? Or were we just trying to get high scores? After all, a low score meant we had to do something about it, which meant more work for the management team, so we didn't tend to like low scores as they meant we'd have to answer some difficult questions from our seniors.

As a management group we used to spend hours at a time discussing our lowest scores. One question was 'am I proud to work here?' We debated about how we could make people prouder to work at the company. Could we do more charity work? Were people embarrassed to say they worked here? Was there a stigma attached to our brand? Did people think their jobs were boring? The reality is, none of us really understood the question ourselves or even why we were asking it. Which is quite surprisingly a fairly common experience; asking the questions we think we should ask, rather than the ones we really want to.

I see many employers asking employee survey questions that if responded to negatively, they wouldn't or couldn't action. Which begs the question, why ask it in the first place? Would you say to a friend 'do you need a lift tomorrow?' if you had no way of offering one? This is where

I think courting employee voice has a negative impact on employee wellbeing; when we ask for their views and ignore what they tell us. Between 20 and 25 percent of employees say they feel actively disengaged at work when they take part in a survey and hear no follow up or see no actions being taken[245].

Social desirability bias.

Although most employee surveys are anonymous, if you don't look after a huge team, as a manager it can be quite easy to narrow down responses to one or two individuals. This causes us a problem as social desirability bias can kick in. This is the idea that an employee has a desire to present themselves in a positive light. Many employees don't want to be a 'problem' or give the impression they are struggling or aren't happy, so if they feel like they might not be anonymous, they don't tell the truth.

In research by the University of Colorado, even when surveys are guaranteed to be anonymous, social desirability bias is still prevalent[246]. So, it's important we create a culture of honesty and transparency that encourages employees to give us the honest answers to our questions. There is no point sending out a survey if your employees don't trust you. Employee surveys are not designed to measure engagement, they are designed to tell you what needs to improve. Without getting honest answers, nothing changes.

In mid 2022, Fortune reported that younger employees were using TikTok to share their views on anonymous employee surveys[247]. One employee completed his company's 'anonymous' survey and the following day was called into a meeting to discuss his response. Another was given a writing warning for refusing to attend a meeting to discuss his answers to the survey as he was told it would be anonymous. With videos like these racking up millions of views, it seems many don't trust that their views really will be confidential. As a result, among the hundreds of thousands of responses to these types of TikTok videos, many employees say they simply refuse to complete company surveys as they believe their views will not be private or worse, not listened to. This is detrimental to wellbeing.

You might be familiar with a UK TV programme called 'Four in a bed'. The premise is that groups of bed and breakfast (B&B) owners spend the night in each other's businesses and then rate them. The bed and breakfast with the most points is crowned the winner. They will rate each other's establishments on things like quality of sleep, how good the breakfast was, how clean the place was, what the hosts were like and how good were the facilities.

There's one last question they are asked (and the most important one in my opinion) – 'would you stay here again?' It's this question that I think holds the secret to a good employee survey. While the results could let the owners know what areas could do with improving, ultimately if the answer to the last question is yes, everything is pretty good.

On the balance of all the elements involved in a good night's stay, someone who says they will return is happy with the bed breakfast and happy to recommend it to others. In an employee survey, if we ask the question 'do you think your pay is fair?' it's likely that an employee will say no (multiple studies show that half of us believe we are underpaid[248]). Plus, whether we think we are underpaid and whether we are, are very different things. One is a fact; the other is a feeling.

Research shows that if you ask a group of people whether their IQ is higher or lower than the average, 80 percent will say their own IQ is higher. In psychology this is called illusory superiority – a cognitive bias where people overestimate their own qualities and abilities when compared to others. This can be troublesome when we ask questions like 'do you think you are recognised often?' or 'do you think your peers work as hard as you?'

A more important question I think we should be asking is 'what more could we be doing for you?'. I think this takes the whole wellbeing experience as one collection of good and bad things and asks you to focus on the areas important to you. They might not be very happy with their pay, but they are extremely happy with their autonomy and flexible working arrangements. So, on the balance of how good their experience is at work, it's likely to be good overall. If it were 'Four in a Bed', they'd probably say they'd stay again.

We tend to focus on the lowest scoring areas in employee surveys, as they are perceived as being the place where action is needed. Re-framing some of those in the context of the whole experience, I think, can be quite useful. Now when an employee says they aren't happy with their pay, you can explain that you benchmark etc and why you can't pay them more − but then you can ask them what else you could be doing for them. You might be surprised at the responses you receive, especially if this is more broadly focussed on wellbeing.

I once managed someone whose response to this question was "I don't like the public recognition you gave me. I'd rather it in private" and "can I get a chair with a bigger back? This one hurts" Suddenly, I was having a wider conversation about their whole experience at work, and hopefully made some small changes that would add up to a big difference to their wellbeing. However, if the right conditions haven't been created, it's difficult for us to get the truth from our people. So, it's here that creating a culture and a foundation of trust really starts to help wellbeing come alive. Our people must believe that:

a) We really care about what they think

b) We are going to act on what they tell us (if we can)

c) We genuinely care about their wellbeing

An employee engagement survey or a specific wellbeing survey is traditionally designed to establish the levels of engagement or wellbeing within an organisation. However, I believe they have now evolved to include being a way of finding out what we are doing well, what needs improvement and the levels of subjective wellbeing within our organisation. Asking our people what they think of us, how we are doing, whether they like the levels of support we offer is critical to how we run wellbeing within our organisation. But also, subjective measures of wellbeing like employee surveys, may still be one of the best ways we have of measuring wellbeing at work.

Guest Expert View: Nick Court

CEO, The People Experience Hub

Having worked in HR for companies like Tesco, Carlsberg and Associated British Foods, Nick went on to set up The People Experience Hub to help organisations understand the experience their people have at work and how to transform this to make a real difference. He has a background specialising in HR, People Analytics, HR Technology Reward and Engagement. Nick is passionate about doing good in the world and The People Experience Hub are an award-winning B-Corp.

I think about wellbeing as an Outcome. This allows me to look at how wellbeing comes about and is when it is positively or negatively impacted by work.

I often see that employers are focussing on only mitigating this outcome rather than exploring how they can influence any cause. This is not surprising when a supplier-led wellbeing agenda is focused on selling a solution that mitigates the issue (mental health apps, wellbeing products, wellbeing webinars etc.). Often, these are deployed to all employees irrespective of their wellbeing needs.

This does not mean I am anti these solutions, far from it; they are a vital part of how an organisation supports its people's wellbeing and shows that they care. But it cannot be the only solution, and this is where a great employee feedback solution can help.

One of my mantras is "Go where the problem is and fix it". Understanding what is going on in different parts of your organisation is key to this. Employee voice through surveys lets you add a dataset to your other organisational data (labour turnover, sickness and absence rates, productivity etc.) to give a fuller picture of your people.

This thinking lets you see that the wellbeing issue to tackle first in the Finance team is X, and the wellbeing issue to tackle first in manufacturing is Y (you can dive deeper into demographics, but you get the gist!). You are then able to put initiatives in place and target specific issues. Of course, this means more effort to communicate and procure solutions, but it has to be worth the effort, right?

You also need to know what is happening at work that could be causing some wellbeing issues. The framework we use explores three areas: The Perceived Environment (you own this – a controllable element), The Felt Experience (you cannot own this – a variable element) and The Observable Outcomes. This framework allows us to create pathways to the outcome, showing an organisation clearly what environmental factors could be contributing to a poor or positive outcomes (wellbeing).

A survey isn't just a bunch of questions to stick in a chart or a table; this is research and should give you insights to act upon and think about. Too often, a survey is used to ask how people are doing without thinking about the actions to be taken.

Environmental Factor – More work than I can cope with

Experiential Factor – Reduced enjoyment at work/frustration

Outcome – Poor mental health

In the above scenario, the answer is not to implement an app without also thinking about how to solve the workload issue. The workload issue is probably a more complex thing to solve for most organisations, but if your employee voice suggests this is a primary issue, then you should probably have this as part of your wellbeing strategy. This is what a good survey, and a good survey company will help you with.

Embracing subjective measures of wellbeing.

Employee surveys are an example of subjective wellbeing. According to Diener, Lucas and Oshi, 2002 and ratified by Positivepsychology.org.uk, subjective wellbeing is defined as 'a person's cognitive and affective evaluations of his or her life'. What do we think about our life, our work, our relationships etc. What are our moods and feelings and how do we assess our daily experiences? I, (and many others) agree that in 2022, subjective wellbeing is emerging as a more successful way of measuring wellbeing at work and is taking the place of other common objective metrics like tech engagement and absence rates.

Most modern digital wellbeing interventions in the workplace measure their success by taking a snapshot of a point in time. This is often looking at traditional engagement metrics like logins. But I don't think this technology-led way of measuring engagement works with wellbeing. A login or indeed time spent using a digital health platform doesn't tell us much about how we supported an individual or how their wellbeing changed because of the support we may have provided.

In addition to tech engagement, I don't think the traditional objective measures of wellbeing at work should have much influence either. Objective measures have become problematic; they tend to examine observable factors that affect someone's wellbeing. At a high level these would be do they have a job? Do they have a roof over their head etc? When it comes to wellbeing, what do the traditional objective measures really mean anymore? Absence rates are underreported and commonly inaccurate. Does someone's level of income really determine their financial wellbeing? Is the absence of a diagnosed mental or physical health condition telling us that nothing is wrong in that person's life? That their wellbeing is intact?

For psychologists, wellbeing is about how people experience their lives, not the objective facts of their lives. This is important because we take as a starting point this idea that people have preferences over fundamental aspects of their own wellbeing. This theory is grounded in the economic principle of 'Revealed Preference', which states that a person's informed choice is the best criterion for judging what increases their wellbeing. Subjective wellbeing measures an employee's perceptions, not their utility – and I think that is important. Think back to the 'Four in a bed' question – "would you stay here again?" – the individual perception is far more important than actually what was in place during their overnight stay.

Subjective measures of wellbeing are being championed by many experts as the best way to measure wellbeing (including an extensive report published by the OECD in 2013 and championed by the National Research Council in the US in 2014[249]). Subjective measures are also increasingly being used by economists[250], and advances in the measurement of subjective wellbeing are now profoundly influencing the social sciences and policy analysis. Subjective measures of wellbeing have now become key outcome measures in program evaluation research, often yielding deeper insights than traditional measures according to some studies. Subjective measures capture employees perceived wellbeing; objective measures have only ever told us half the story.

Subjective wellbeing comes from the hedonic tradition we mentioned at the start of this book and includes life satisfaction. In my view, subjective measures are the best way to measure those areas of wellbeing. Employee surveys help us to look for quality of life indicators – many of which we discuss in this book. Do I feel included and represented at work? Do I have a voice? Is autonomy facilitated here? Do I have the opportunity to build social connections at work? etc. So as well as courting these subjective measures as a way of supporting individual employee wellbeing, surveys can also help us (the employer) to effectively measure the ways we support employee wellbeing at work. We'll come back to this in chapter 13.

Guest Expert View: Marcus Herbert

Health & Wellbeing Strategist

With over 15 years' experience and two degrees in the wellbeing industry, Marcus has worked with individuals, elite athletes, and executives on enhancing their own personal wellbeing and reducing their risk of lifestyle

diseases through effective behaviour change strategies.
Transferring this experience into the corporate setting
Marcus has worked with organisations from micro to global
on their approach to organisational wellbeing and how to
develop an effective and meaningful wellbeing strategy.
More recently Marcus has developed training courses to
support Directors, Line Managers and Employees on the
most effective ways to embrace health and wellbeing at work.

When it comes to wellbeing at work one of the most important things to consider, is what your workforce needs (and wants) are from your wellbeing programme. The most common mistake I see is employees being provided with a long list of wellbeing initiatives that the employer thinks will be well received and yet most employees are not even aware they exist. This is frustrating because the employer has the best intention of supporting their workers by providing initiatives, they *think* will make a positive impact and yet the wellbeing spend isn't being utilised and therefore isn't meaningful or impactful.

The best way for me to put this importance across is to compare complex organisational wellbeing programmes with simply putting together an action plan for an individual client that wants to improve their health and wellbeing. In my time working as a health and wellbeing Physiologist, I saw over 2,000 clients and each time I would complete a series of physical tests to assess their risk of lifestyle related diseases i.e., diabetes, hypertension, or obesity. Following the series of tests I would analyse their results, which would be compared to normative values so I could outline if there were any areas that may benefit from improvement. We would discuss the different lifestyle changes they might be able to make to help lower cholesterol or lose some weight or increase their fitness. But we would only ever agree to lifestyle changes they would be willing and able to make. It had to be led by them. If I were to prescribe what they should be doing, regardless of whether they would want to or not, they simply wouldn't listen and wouldn't change their behaviour. Ultimately omitting their opinion from the lifestyle change strategy would result in failure.

When it comes to workplace wellbeing programmes, I have found the most success when the employee voice has been captured (through multiple formats such as surveys, focus groups and feedback from team meetings) and then matched to wellbeing initiatives that the employees will make use of because they match their needs (and wants). Admittedly, even when this approach is taken, employees will always want more than what is provided but wellbeing is about much more than initiatives. It should consider the entire experience of being an employee from the induction to the regular training and support, to the working environment and the organisational culture and leadership style. By capturing the employee voice in the first instance, organisations will be able to decipher where their focus needs to be for enhancing wellbeing across the organisation and better equipped to see meaningful outputs from the changes they make.

Facilitating more autonomy at work.

In 1991, one of the most famous workplace wellbeing studies took place in the UK. What became known as 'The Whitehall Study' began in 1967 and ran until 1988[251]. The study investigated the degree to which seniority within the civil service impacted morbidity across 17,500 employees. What the researchers found was that health and wellbeing was lower in those employees with 'lower status' jobs. Even after normalising factors such as propensity to smoke, higher blood pressure and lower height to weight ratio, the study found that those with lower status jobs were still at a greater risk for a heart attack. The reasons behind the differences would change the way many managers managed for decades to come.

In the Whitehall study, it was concluded that 'decision autonomy' was responsible for the differences in health risk. The researchers found that the more autonomy an employee had within the civil service, the less likely they were to develop serous health conditions. When an employee can make decisions over when and how to perform a task at work, their heart rate, blood pressure and stress hormones reduce. While there is no universally agreed reasons for the results in the Whitehall study, to me at least, it gives us some evidence of the effectiveness of managing people by allowing them to manage themselves.

But even in the present day, evidence continues to mount that autonomy at work has positive effects on employee wellbeing. Researchers at the University of Birmingham examined changes in wellbeing relative to levels of autonomy across two years and 20,000 employees[252]. They found that those working in management reported the highest levels of autonomy at work with 90 percent saying they had 'some' or 'a lot' of autonomy. For other employees, much less autonomy was reported with only around half of the lowest skilled workers have any autonomy. The study found convincing evidence that flexibility over timing and location of work, manner of work, pace of work, task order and job task were all impacting employee wellbeing. The results of this study and others have been even more pronounced when women are given more autonomy at work[253].

What is surprising about the latest research is that even in environments where traditionally very little autonomy existed like contact centres, giving employees more empowerment helped them to resolve more complaints and improve their own wellbeing[254]. But the researchers in the Birmingham study also highlighted that many managers remained unwilling to offer their employees more autonomy at work, because their role was one of 'control of effort extraction', which tells us a lot about the role of the manager in employee wellbeing – which we will come onto shortly.

Guest Expert View: Rob Baker

Founder of Tailored Thinking & author of Personalization at Work

Rob is a specialist in bringing positive psychology to life within organisations. He is the founder and Chief Positive Deviant of Tailored Thinking, a pioneering evidence-based positive psychology, wellbeing, and HR consultancy who were named HR Consultancy of the Year 2020 by the CIPD.

Rob is a TEDX speaker and author of Personalization at Work and world-leading when it comes to enabling and encouraging job crafting and personalised people experiences. His work, ideas, and research on personalised approaches to wellbeing and how people can bring their whole and best selves to their jobs have been presented at academic and professional conferences around the globe.

Autonomy is an often overlooked, but foundational aspect of wellbeing. It can be thought of – and is often cited as – a foundational human need. The ability to shape our own path and destiny in how we navigate our environment is baked into us from birth. This will be immediately evident to any parent who has seen their toddler fiercely assert their right to "let me do it" and the often (tear and rage filled) consequences of taking choice and freedom away from them.

The sad reality is that many of us are starved of autonomy in our workplace. Whilst this doesn't (often) lead to tantrums and tears it can erode people's levels of engagement and energy at work. Leaders can directly promote and seed autonomy into the workplace by directly encouraging and people to shape how they do their jobs. A practical way to do this is through personalised job design and specifically a concept called job crafting.

Job crafting encourages people to make small, positive, and iterative changes and improvements to their job, so it is more aligned to an individual's strengths, passions, and needs. Through job crafting people autonomously make changes to how they act, interact, and think about their work and – where possible and appropriate - personalise when, where and how they do their jobs.

There is a wealth of evidence that demonstrates the compelling connection between job crafting and positive outcomes such as performance, health and wellbeing and growth.

Allowing people to personalise their roles, brings reality to the rhetoric that organisations want people to bring their whole and best selves to work. Rather than treating employees' diverse strengths, passions, and experiences as a threat to be controlled, genuinely people-focussed organisations can use this as a source of competitive advantage.

Not only does evidence suggest clear business benefits of creating this more inclusive and human approach to working, but it is also fundamentally and morally the right thing to do.

Personalised job design enables people to craft autonomy, control and connection into their work which should be a foundational component of any holistic organisational wellbeing agenda.

Managers need to empower their people more.

The pandemic was a huge experiment in trust and autonomy. As millions of workers worked 'out of sight' for the first time ever, leadership had to get comfortable quickly with letting their people be more autonomous. But the impact here wasn't just that employees were feeling more engaged and happier at work, it was significantly impacting their health. Thirty years on from the Whitehall study, the pandemic fuelled new evidence as to why managers needed to empower their people more.

Amid the pandemic, the Indiana University Kelley School of Business found that mental health (and even mortality) had a strong correlation with the amount of autonomy an employee has at work[255]. Using data from more than 3,000 Wisconsin residents over a 20-year period, the researchers found that job control buffered the positive relationship between job demands and poor mental health. They concluded that when a person had more control over their work, their physical health was better too, and their chances of dying were lessened - that's significant! A recent longitudinal study found that work control is linked to rates of mortality. It's why they called their study "This job is (literally) killing me".

While the evidence to support autonomy's role in employee wellbeing is compelling, like with anything, too much tips the balance too. A 2020 study looking at autonomy and job control in the workplace found that excessive job autonomy can start to have a negative effect on employees[256].

This link between work control and health has been discovered in many studies. When employees have more influence and task control in an organisation, they show lower levels of illness symptoms for 11 out of 12 major health indicators. More job control has been found to correlate with lower absence rates and less depression, according to a study of 8,500 Swedish workers. Similarly, a study of employees from 72 different businesses in the US found statistically significant negative associations between work control and self-reported anxiety and despair[257]. If we truly want to create workplaces cultures with wellbeing at their hearts, we must seek to end micromanagement and 'command and control' leadership.

Being more flexible with our people.

In 2022, the most important driver when choosing an employer was work-life balance according to Randstad[258].

Theis remains the highest driver, regardless of if an employee is considered 'white collar' or 'blue collar'. Even looking at those who intend to stay with their employer and those who intend to leave, work life balance is still the most important factor. When McKinsey surveyed employees about the top reasons why they accepted a new job in 2021, 40 percent stated 'workplace flexibility' – higher than compensation and career development[259]. Even for those out of work, flexibility ranked in the top two desires for returning to the workplace.

But asking for more flexibility at work comes with some barriers. One study involving 14,000 people found that we have a "overly pessimistic view" of how likely an employer is to respond to requests such as a change in working hours or days[260]. So, while accommodations are quite commonly agreed to, employee's perceptions are that their employer will say no, even when that isn't the case. But with the benefits of more flexible working patters being so good for both employee and employer, understanding them and ensuring management understand the benefits is key to breaking down this barrier. This is an example of how important it is to get leaders to buy into your wellbeing strategy.

When an employee has more flexible working hours, they benefit from a reduction in stress and improved employee wellbeing[261]. Allowing an employee to change their hours can reduce workplace stress by as much as 20 percent [262]. Almost half of those wo are allowed to work flexibility say it has improved their mental health[263]. Allowing employees to have more choice over when and how they work has very clear positive benefits to employee wellbeing.

Conversely, erratic, and unpredictable working patterns are harming employee wellbeing[264]. If we look at young adults who work on zero-hour contracts, we can see some alarming correlations. Those working under zero-hour contracts have been found to be at a higher risk of poor mental health than those employees with stable jobs. In fact, they were more twice as likely to report suffer from mental ill health[265]. Zero-hour contracts also lead to financial insecurity and increases levels of stress and anxiety[266]. But again, what benefits the employee tends to benefit the employer too. Greater stability in working hours has been linked to an increase in sales and productivity in a retail setting – where zero-hour contracts are commonplace[267]. Unpredictable and inflexible working patterns are driving a type of precarious employment that is taking a huge toll on the wellbeing of employees.

Flexibility in where, and when we work.

Globally, more than half of employees now say they will quit their job if they aren't provided with the flexibility they now want, according to EY[268]. One of the largest global surveys of its kind discovered that flexibility at work was now considered 'normal' and more than half of employees believe that more remote working has improved organisational culture.

In fact, the desire for more flexible working patterns is now stronger than the desire to work more remotely according to one study, with 95 percent wanting to set their own hours at work[269]. Obtaining a better work life balance is so strong the average US worker now says they would need to be offered an additional $10,000 a year to give it up[270]. With the average US salary at around $50,000 a year, that equates to a value of 20 percent of pay being placed on work/life balance. In the UK, the average worker says they would give up seven percent of their pay in return for better flexibility at work[271].

On the back of the pandemic, record numbers of American employees are quitting their jobs. But McKinsey have discovered that parents are more likely to have left their jobs over the last few years than their nonparent counterparts[272]. Because of the competing pressures of home and work life and the re-assessment of their home-work-life balance, many parents have been forced to make some difficult decisions over who they work for. Interestingly, the research also found that parents are more likely to be those who provide the important social support within their teams.

During the pandemic, women tended to support the wellbeing of their colleagues far more than men did[273], and with women mostly carrying the burden of childcare, not being flexible to parents could have some pretty devastating effects on our workplace cultures and subsequently employee wellbeing.

Cisco's 2022 Global Hybrid Work Study asked 28,000 full time employees across 27 markets how hybrid working had impacted their lives[274]. On average, around 80 percent of all employees say hybrid working led to improvements in their wellbeing. The results from this large study show us the detail of just how significant more flexible working has been to employee wellbeing.

- **Financial wellbeing** – Employees report an increase of 14.25 percent in average disposable income because of hybrid working.
- **Physical wellbeing** – 82 percent of Indian employees, 79 percent of Chinese employees and 78 percent of Brazilian employees say they are eating healthier because of hybrid working.
- **Emotional wellbeing** – 82.2 percent of hybrid workers say they are happy in their lives than they were before hybrid working was an option.

Results like these are not to be taken lightly. Cisco's is one of many similar studies, but it was a very large sample size and covered most employees across the world. As the authors of the study put it "leaders must acknowledge that a point of no return has been reached". While at the time of writing this book many still continue to push for a wholesale return to the workplace and the nine-to-five, we cannot ignore the impact this way of working has had on wellbeing. Not without its challenges, hybrid and flexible working has done more for our collective wellbeing than almost anything else and going back to our pre-pandemic ways of will surely harm that.

Time away from work.

An important part of workplace wellbeing is actually how we encourage time away from work. Employee health and wellbeing improves after an employee vacation of 14 days or more[275]. In women, evidence is emerging that paid vacation leave can even protect against depression[276]. But it seems employees need more encouragement to take time off.

In 2017, the average US worker said they had taken only around half of their paid time off over the last 12 months[277]. By a year later, this figure had increased with Americans less likely to take their paid time off by 2018[278]. In the UK, almost a third of workers say they leave around five days unclaimed at the end of the year[279]. More than 57 million days of British annual leave went unclaimed in 2020[280]. I think this is partly because we don't see time away from work as critical to sustaining productivity and work relations, and we don't make it clear that time off is critical to wellbeing. More than 50 million days off wasted are 50 million missed opportunities for our people to decompress from work, destress and recharge. With that UK number alone being so big, that should be of *great* concern to anyone managing wellbeing for a British employer in particular.

In fact, some employers are now so concerned with the volume of employees who aren't taking enough time away from work that they are experimenting with 'mandatory time off'. The most notable employer experimenting in this way is Goldman Sachs, who are combining unlimited vacation with a new policy that will require their senior employees to take at least 15 days off each year – which must be consecutive. Other employees have been given enhanced vacation with a few additional paid days added each year. The bank told CNBC "Our global vacation program (is) designed to further support time off to rest and recharge".

So why don't employees voluntarily take this very important time away from work? When employees are asked why they don't take their full vacation entitlement, one in ten admit there is no-one else to do their work if they don't. Others say they see annual leave as "pointless" as they'll come back to more work or be expected to work through their time off[281]. Yet at the same time, more time off frequently tops the lists of benefits that most employees want. The guilt associated with taking time off is stopping employees from improving their wellbeing. Millions believe that time off will harm their career or lead to missed opportunities at work[282]. In addition, workloads, and fear of losing their job are driving more and more people to not only not take their full vacation entitlement, but to actually go the other way and work more hours.

"There is sufficient evidence for us to be concerned about the potentially negative effects of working long hours on physical health."
- UK Health and Safety Executive

In 2021, the World Health Organization (WHO) report that long working hours led to 745,000 deaths from stroke and ischemic heart disease – a 29 percent increase since 2000[283]. In the first global analysis of the impact long working hours were having on our wellbeing, WHO estimate that the number of deaths from heart disease due to long working hours increased by 42 percent. Working 55 or more hours is now associated with a 35 percent higher risk of stroke. It's obvious that we can't talk about wellbeing at work without addressing long hours and paid time off. But even aside from the impact on physical wellbeing, we have emerging evidence of how time away from work impact our mental health too. A major longitudinal study concluded in 2019 that there is a clear link between paid vacation leave and depression – especially in women. For every ten additional days of paid vacation, the odds of depression in women are 29 percent lower[284].

A fascinating study looking at consultants found that longer working hours didn't actually change much for the organisation. Erin Reid, a professor at Boston University found that she was unable to find any material differences in the work of consultants who worked long hours, when compared to those who worked normal hours[285]. So, if longer working hours don't benefit the organisation and harm the employee, it begs the question why we don't do more to discourage employees working more and taking less vacation?

We have to fix the crack that exists between our people needing time away from work and the reasons why they don't take it. Those reasons appear to be based around perceptions within the workplace. The feeling that time off makes a worker less engaged or less committed. In the context of wellbeing, we have to drive the clear message that taking time off and going home are not only the characteristics of a successful worker, but they are also the actions of one who takes care of themselves. So, as well as ensuring we offer adequate paid time off, how we communicate the value of this is so important.

But it's not just time away from work that appears to improve wellbeing, it's encouraging our people to go on a vacation that also helps. The idea of 'travel therapy' is growing in popularity and research is following. A research collaboration between Edith Cowan University (ECU) Centre for Precision Health and School of Business and Law has found that many aspects of a vacation could have a positive impact on those with mental health issues[286]. The Covid-19 pandemic forced many employees to go without a break away for almost two years and the impact of this made us realise a bit more that travel had value beyond what we originally thought.

Flexibility in employee benefit choices.

While the coronavirus pandemic affected every single employee, it affected each one of them differently. The crisis brought to light how diversity affects employee wellbeing in particular. Employers now face a significant challenge in meeting the diverse needs of a varied workforce.

At Benefex we saw a significant increase in the number of global employers starting to personalise wellbeing experiences for their people through the introduction of wellbeing spending accounts. By offering these wellbeing accounts, employers can encourage their people to personalise their approach to employee wellbeing. This flexibility in benefit funding is enabling employees to make decisions over their workplace wellbeing like they've never been able to before. Giving employees the ability to choose what works for them at any given time, employers are able to offer a uniquely personalised approach to wellbeing without complexity and increased costs. By allowing employees to shape their lifestyles in this way, wellbeing spending accounts can be used to help employees understand the intricacies of their wellbeing and promote healthy habits.

Similarly, offering an online benefits scheme allows employees to do the same. Under traditional benefit offerings, many employees may be getting benefits or coverage that they don't want or need. By giving employees flexibility over the benefits on offer, you and they pay just for what is needed. And most importantly, this choice and flexibility can evolve as an employee's requirements do. So as their wellbeing needs change, so can the support they are offered. For example, introducing online benefits that encourage healthy behaviours and protect against poor wellbeing. We'll talk more about employee benefits later in this book but offering choice over benefits available is a key part of a successful wellbeing strategy.

A flexible future.

I firmly believe that when we give employees choice, we get the best results – and there is a mountain of new evidence to support this. For employers who are struggling to understand these levels of choice and flexibility, take the lead from your people. They've had first-hand experience of remote working for more than a year now and while normal circumstances wouldn't involve a pandemic, they have got an idea of what works best for them; when they are most productive, what challenges they and their team have had, what they want from the physical workplace etc.

The world's first pilot of flexible working on construction sites has had a significant impact on employee wellbeing[287]. Four of the UK's largest construction companies recently ended an 18-month pilot that found that flexible working can be successful in the most unexpected places and roles. The pilot tested a consultative method of setting shifts that took workers personal preferences into account. It also tested enabling workers to accumulate hours to take additional time off and based working hours on output, rather than time. Employee wellbeing increased significantly (in an industry with a historically poor record), overwork decreased and trust in colleagues increased. The impressive results show that even those employers who thought more flexibility would never work in their organisation are probably wrong.

Employees around the world have embraced more flexibility at work as way to balance their home and work lives. McKinsey summed it up perfectly when they said, "flexible work is no longer a temporary pandemic response but an enduring feature of the modern working world". At the time of writing, 58 percent of American workers say they can work from home at least one day a week, with 35 percent saying they have the option to work from home five days a week[288]. When given the option to work more flexibly, 87 percent of employees take it[289]. Regardless of demographic, occupation and location, the frenzied desire to better balance their wellbeing is driving flexibility to become not just one of the most popular ways to support employee wellbeing, but one of the most evidenced too.

If the significant improvement in employee wellbeing doesn't incentivise you to offer more flexible working arrangements, maybe one of the largest studies into it ever can. Standford University found that after nearly a year of home working productivity increased by 13 percent [290]. Other studies have put this increase as high as 77 percent. So rather than continue to push against this evolution, employers should embrace these new features of our post-pandemic world as way of better supporting us and our organisations.

The pandemic thrust more flexibility, choice, and personalisation at work onto employees and their work life balance reached dizzy new heights because of it. But even after the pandemic, events continue to ratify our decision to achieve more work life balance.

The UK rail strikes in June 2022 were some of the biggest we'd seen in 40 years. But while rail workers went on strike, Google searches for 'remote jobs' surged by 260 percent. This marked a new record in searches for remote work online[291]. At the time of writing this book, the Dutch parliament approved legislation to establish home working as a legal right, making the Netherlands one of the first countries to enshrine flexibility in law[292]. Flexibility at work in all its forms is here to stay, and I think employee wellbeing now requires it to thrive.

Guest Expert View: Gary Cookson

Author, HR's Most Influential and Director, EPIC HR Ltd

Gary is a father of four, husband of one, running a successful business in his spare time. He's an expert in workplace performance, with extensive experience leading and directing HR, OD, and L&D functions across all sectors. He's a leading expert in the design and delivery of online / virtual training programmes, as well as an inspiring and entertaining keynote speaker and trainer on a range of leadership and HR issues. He was recognised in HR Most Influential: Movers and Shakers and is an HRD Connect Thought Leader. His book, HR for Hybrid Working, was published June 2022 by Kogan Page.

Wellbeing is higher on almost everyone's agenda now though – the Covid-19 pandemic made many leaders focus on their more human qualities and raised awareness around mental health and wellbeing. The nature of forced remote (and now hybrid) working means that it can be much more difficult for leaders to notice when a person's wellbeing is suffering. The experience of forced remote working also highlighted an important difference between good and not-so-good managers. The impact that managers have on any worker's mental health is stark, but it became particularly important for managers of remote workers to do more than cursory check-ins, and to find out much more about individual mental health and personal circumstances.

One of the prime causes of poor health and wellbeing for remote and hybrid workers is likely to be poor work-life balance. This could be true for other types of flexible workers too. Having one's home and work in the same location can be tricky and finding that separation and managing it in a way that doesn't detrimentally impact wellbeing is difficult.

Humans need connections with other humans, and technology can help with and hinder this when working remotely. Isolation because of technology and burnout related to increased use of technology can lead to significant mental health issues, but the same technology can help disconnect from work and connect socially with others, something remote, hybrid and other flexible workers need more of.

Many surveys have pointed out how many adults have eaten less healthily since the Covid-19 pandemic began, particularly during lockdowns, which of course tie in with increased remote and hybrid working. People's routines changed completely from a daily commute into a face-to-face office and working at home may make it harder to stop for lunch or make it easier to snack through the day, or more difficult to take regular exercise. As a qualified personal trainer, I appreciate the difference that a quality nutrition and hydration routine can have on performance and productivity, and yet I also suffer from making bad decisions when working remotely.

Forced remote working during the Covid-19 pandemic has also affected physical health, specifically on musculoskeletal issues. Workstation and home-office assessments are even more important where the individual remote or hybrid worker is responsible for their own setup.

It may also be necessary to help people look after their eyes due to the increased strain caused by longer screen usage for remote and hybrid workers – again there are relevant health and safety regulations on this but more needs to be done to educate all concerned of the risks for remote and hybrid workers.

Empowering leadership.

Managers play an incredibly important role in wellbeing. Yet during the pandemic, there was a significant difference between how leaders felt they acted and how employees did. In 2022, around 88 percent of executives think they made "excellent" leadership decisions during the pandemic, yet only 53 percent of workers agree[293]. It's obvious in this post-crisis world that leaders must invest a reasonable amount of time and effort in attending to their employee's wellbeing requirements.

When managers are empowered, it positively correlates with their commitment and wellbeing at work[294]. Employees of empowered leaders say they actively take on more responsibility because they know the support is there if they need it. When employees feel supported in this way, it encourages them to speak up and take responsibility for their own wellbeing at work. Empowering leadership has the capacity to raise the all-important trust between managers and their people. When this happens, employees feel more at ease discussing their wellbeing. Research has also demonstrated that empowered leadership can reduce perceived stress levels and have a favourable effect on workers' mental health[295].

Managers can have a direct impact on the wellbeing of their people in several ways; making time for them; being more caring and empathetic, giving them permission to speak up about their wellbeing and signposting them to the best support available.

Making more time for our people.

Developing the habit of spending quality time with their team members has long been a challenge for any manager. When I managed a team of 20, spending just two hours a month with each of them would take up 25 percent of my time – and that doesn't include writing up development plans or training requests etc. But time with your manager is an incredibly important part of wellbeing at work. Employees who have regular meetings with their manager and three times more likely to feel engaged in their job an thrive in their role[296].

Historically many managers have held meetings with their employees on a quarterly basis, but the latest thinking suggests this should be a weekly practice. Employees today now expect their leaders to be an active partner in their personal needs[297]. So, while regular face to face time is important to employee engagement, community and belonging at work, it might not impact other areas of wellbeing without some attention. Only a third of managers say they could recognise the signs that one of their team members were struggling[298]. Six in ten say they aren't getting any training to help them recognise and handle mental health and wellbeing issues among their team members[299]. Eighty percent of employees say they are scared to speak to their manager about their mental health, partly because they have concerns that their manager isn't capable of having that kind of conversation[300] - and three quarters of managers agree they aren't[301]. But for so many employees, their experience at work is driven almost entirely by their relationship with their manager, so ensuring our leaders have the tools and resources to respond to poor wellbeing must play a key role in workplace wellbeing.

Creating more caring leaders.

One 2018 study looking at employees working on the front line in a Chinese manufacturer found that "line managers are a strong determinant of employee wellbeing"[302]. The way we are treated by our managers at work has a very long-lasting impact on our wellbeing. Recent research has looked at coach leadership in professional sports – specifically the NBA. Controlling for tenure, salary, team winning percentage, and absence due to injuries, multilevel modelling showed that exposure to abusive leadership influenced both the trajectory of psychological aggression and task performance over players' careers. Those players with an aggressive coach saw this negatively impact the rest of their careers[303].

"In my professional sporting career (and in business), leaders that care and value their people have always become the most successful in their field. By being curious about your people and curious about high performance, you can create a thriving environment where success is achieved on a consistent basis rather than a rollercoaster of success that leaves a trail of burnt out and unhappy people - that comes from not putting people first"

- Jack Green, Double Olympic Medallist & Head of Performance at Champion Health

Aside from the impact on the employee, aggressive ways of management harm productivity too. Data collected from 30,000 workers in 149 factories across China shows that workers who report their supervisor "often" shouts or yells at them are three times more likely to say they need to redo their work, in comparison to workers of whom their supervisor "sometimes" shouts or yells at them[304]. The data also suggests that those who work remotely are more likely to experience this kind of bullying at work[305].

The top reason given by employees leaving their job in 2022 was "uncaring leaders" according to McKinsey[306]. Following the effects of the pandemic, people have never needed caring and understanding managers more and so the impact of our leaders on individual wellbeing is has never been magnified[307]. When employees report that their leaders are empathetic, they:

- Are more likely to be engaged at work
- Think about leaving less
- Feel more included at work
- And have a better work life balance

The last point is particularly interesting because one study conducted at nursing homes found that when a manager was more accommodating of an employee's responsibilities and life outside of work, those employees had fewer risk factors for cardiovascular disease and even slept better[308]. Those employees who rate their manager as caring and empathetic also report higher wellbeing more generally – they report less somatic complaints[309].

But the way managers support their people can also buffer the effects of poor wellbeing driven by factors outside of work[310]. Better manager support has been found to counteract the negative effects life can have on employees. When we have a good manager at work, it decreases the likelihood that we will have conflict at home[311]. But conversely, when our managers and leaders don't give us the right support at work, it has been shown to increase the chances of an employee reporting pain in their lives[312].

Leaders' strong ability to enhance both negative and positive emotions among their people is having a direct influence on their wellbeing[313]. Employee wellbeing can be improved through the actions of our leadership teams, but also within the team environment that the manager cultivates. In 2021, one study concluded that "the negative relationship between manager care and employee-rated manager role overload is exacerbated in a team environment where employees fail to care for each other"[314]. The researchers concluded that managers shouldn't be expected to "go it alone" to support employee wellbeing.

The way managers create and support psychological safety within a team now accounts for a significant amount in the variation levels of employee common mental health problems symptoms and wellbeing. Managers even appear to be able to influence these symptoms through their individual behaviours[315]. When a manager is concerned with employee wellbeing, overall employee wellbeing is high[316]. When managers believe it's their responsibility and show genuine care towards their team, their employees report above average levels of overall wellbeing.

Giving our people permission to speak up.

As the stigma around talking about things like poor mental health and money at work is fading, employees are becoming more confident in discussing their wellbeing at work. In 2021, Benefex surveyed global HR leaders and found that nine in ten reported greater numbers of employees discussing personal issues at work[317]. But there appears to be a disconnect between what HR teams and the wider employee group think.

While discussing poor wellbeing at work is improving, two thirds of workers in 2022 still say they would not share their mental health problems with their employer[318], meaning we have returned to the pre-pandemic levels of employees hiding poor wellbeing at work[319]. UK workers report taking as many as nearly four days off a year due to poor mental health, but more than half who do are calling in with a physical illness instead of telling their employer the truth[320]. Poor mental health is now the most common reason for an employee to lie about taking a sick day[321]. Despite our efforts to remove the stigma of talking about mental health at work, that figure that has barely changed in more than ten years[322].

The data tells us that we still have a problem with employees being able to talk about their wellbeing at work. Through the pandemic, a million Brits who experienced poor mental health for the first time ever say they didn't speak to anyone about it[323]. Employees say they are increasingly putting pressure on themselves to "put on a brave face" at work, especially those who are now working remotely[324]. But when managers encourage employees to be open about their wellbeing at work, it improves employee's health. Empathy therefore plays a critical role in creating the environments to empower and give permission to our team to be open about their wellbeing challenges. During the pandemic, this was heightened, and the evidence emerged that during times of crisis, this empathy should be a first priority[325].

One 2018 study looked at the ways managers react to and support employees with depression. They found that the more a manager avoided talking about depression at work, the more likely an employee with depression would take time off[326]. Yet we know that when an employee is encouraged to talk about their wellbeing at work, it makes a difference to their recovery. When a person just believes they can do something to improve their mental health, they tend to have higher wellbeing[327]. Which leads us onto another way managers can help the wellbeing of their people – making sure they are aware of the support available to them.

Signposting employees to support.

Managers should play a critical role in supporting employees and signposting struggling colleagues towards help. All employees should be fully aware of the resources available to them and their value as part of the wider reward package.

In May 2020, the CIPD urged employers to step up their mental health support for employees in the wake of the Coronavirus pandemic. Research by the CIPD and Simplyhealth found that only a third of managers were sufficiently confident to initiate discussions around mental health and direct employees to the appropriate support[328]. Research by RAND[329] and VitalityHealth[330] indicates that although most employers now offer a range of wellbeing initiatives at work, access to those is an issue for employees. Less than 20 percent of employees say they are aware of where to go to access their wellbeing initiatives.

One of the primary recommendations of a 2019 report by the Federal Reserve[331] and a 2017 report by HM Treasury and the FCA[332] was to give staff a user friendly, web-based portal so that staff can access information, education and signposting that will help with their financial wellbeing. As financial concerns are the biggest wellbeing worry for employees during this crisis, this is a great place to start.

As a direct result of the pandemic experience, a group of researchers tried to discover what the top six key insights from research on leadership were when employees were facing times of crisis[333]. This research backs up the suggestions made in this chapter. They found that leaders needed to:

- Remain optimistic in their communications
- Adapt by empowering their team members
- Provide additional resources to staff
- Be present and available to their people
- Be empathetic

Their analysis of the research (published in the British Medical Journal in 2021) concluded that focussing on these six areas would not only improve the wellbeing of leaders, but also help their people to navigate more effectively through times of crisis, easing the burden on the workforce. Similar studies have concluded that during times of crisis, leadership has a material impact on public health[334].

Leaders significantly underestimate how much their employees are struggling with their wellbeing[335]. Across all the main pillars of wellbeing, leaders underestimate how much their people are struggling by as much as a third[336]. Which leads us onto one of the most symbiotic areas of employee wellbeing, financial wellbeing. More than other area of wellbeing, financial wellbeing is the most significantly underestimated in the workplace. While 81 percent of managers say their people's financial wellbeing is "good" or "excellent", just 40 percent of employees agree[337]. This huge disconnect between how leaders think their people manage one of the most stressful areas of their lives is causing huge problems.

Guest Expert View: Steven Hargreaves

Leadership & Culture Specialist, Author & Founder of The Compassionate Leadership Company

The Compassionate Leadership Company is a coaching, culture, and leadership development company which

specialises in helping organisations and their leaders to inspire, build and sustain a more compassionate workplace where everyone can stay well, thrive, and achieve. As its founder, Steven has 20 years' experience as a senior leader, having worked across a range of sectors, leading, and transforming large scale, multi-site operations and people services across commercial, regulated care and charitable services. Steven is also cited as one of the Top 40 Global Organisational Culture Champions 2022.

The contemporary workplace is one where relationships, connectivity, wellbeing, and purpose now takes centre stage. Therefore, it is time for us to seize the moment. For leaders to lead with renewed energy, enhanced compassion, and purpose. For a more connected, personal, and relational approach to leadership to emerge and become business as normal for everyone. What people need and want from leadership has changed. It has been changing for a while, and leaders and organisations need to maintain pace with those changes. Leadership needs to pivot, but not panic. This is not about ripping everything up that we have known about management and leadership. Much of that remains valid and an important foundation, but it is now about changing the emphasis of leadership and building a new leadership profile.

We need to consider what this evolving role and purpose of contemporary leadership is. We then need to show how this adds value to a more modern, more relational world of work.

If leadership doesn't bring and create value, then what is it for and why do we need it anyway? Organisations may respond to the need to support employee wellbeing with well-meaning initiatives and through the provision of an Employee Assistance Programme. They are important and we should value them – however my worry is that if organisations and its leadership look at wellbeing in isolation to what is causing employee suffering and what is getting in the way of their people thriving, achieving, and staying well to begin with, they may be more focused on treating the symptoms rather than the causes.

If organisations, can through a more holistic, compassionate, and relationship-based approach, address the causes, rather than purely focus on the symptoms then the employee experience stands every chance of being that best it can be. When organisations and its leadership acknowledge and accept that the workplace can cause suffering which impacts on employee wellbeing, performance, and productivity, they can begin to put compassion first, put relationships first and work to reduce and prevent that suffering and the potential for it to arise.

Organisations need to place greater emphasis on appointing, developing, and supporting leaders who, whilst having the requisite management skills, also, and to a much greater extent, have the required relational skills. These are leaders who demonstrate the values, purpose, and qualities necessary to put relationships first – because they know by doing so, they are doing the best for their people and the business.

The value of modern leadership is how through its actions, behaviours, and decisions it creates and sustains the conditions for the organisations people to do their best and be their best. It is not enough for the modern leader to merely be good at their own job, they must help everyone else be really good at theirs and to enable them to thrive and stay well as they deliver what is required.

Chapter 7

Supporting Financial Wellbeing

Since 2007, The American Psychological Association has been surveying the US public to find out what the biggest factors that drive stress are. The results have consistently shown, that regardless of someone's income or the economic climate, money and finances remain the number one stressor for Americans[338] - and this is having a significant impact on their overall health. The same survey in 2022 revealed that Americans' money stress levels are at their highest since 2015, with rising inflation causing the most stress[339]. Living through wide scale traumatic events that eroded financial resilience for millions is why financial wellbeing has become such a crucial part of workplace wellbeing.

The PwC 2021 Employee Financial Wellbeing Survey also found that money was the number one cause of stress to workers – above their jobs, health and relationships combined![340]. In 2022, 42 percent of Americans said money is having a negative impact on their mental health. Most say they are stressed, anxious and overwhelmed by their financial situation. For half of Americans, just looking at their bank account triggers these negative emotions[341]. Experiencing financial stress can lead to physical pain[342] and a loss of IQ[343], so in my view, it plays a pivotal role in workplace wellbeing. Yet rarely gets the same attention as mental health in the workplace.

At the time of writing this book, a massive 41 percent of employees are living pay check to pay check – more than before the pandemic[344]. Just 30 percent of employees agree that they are getting by financially[345]. Yet research by Zellis reveals that only 12 percent of employees believe their employer is effectively supporting their financial wellbeing[346]. But most worryingly of all through a financial crisis like the one experienced in 2022, three quarters of employees have never *once* talked about financial wellbeing with their manager, making it a well-hidden wellbeing issue[347].

Among some of the most common causes of poor financial wellbeing are low pay, high house prices, high cost of living, high rental costs and lack of financial education[348], but low pay is fairly consistently a reason for poor financial wellbeing across the globe.

Paying a living wage.

In the UK, the National Living Wage does not guarantee employees the minimally acceptable quality of living that society generally tends to feel we all should be able to achieve, according to research by the Centre for Research in Social Policy at Loughborough University[349]. To meet this standard, a single individual would need to make £20,400 a year. At present, the National Living Wage pays less than that. The Real Living Wage is a rate set by the National Living Wage Foundation in the UK. Now paid by more than 10,000 UK employers, the real living wage is a more accurate measure of how much some of the lowest paid in our society should receive. The living wage is aimed to ensure that a minimum salary provides for all a worker's needs, as well as some discretionary income for emergencies.

Many studies have shown that when an employee has insufficient income, it is associated with worse outcomes across almost every area of wellbeing, including life expectancy[350]. The Living Wage Foundation's Life on Low Pay report made the connection between low pay and poor mental wellbeing very clear[351]. According to the study, 46 percent of full-time employees who were paid less than the real Living Wage believed their income had a negative impact on their anxiety levels. Another victim of low pay was healthy connections, which are essential to lowering the risk of mental illness. According to 34 percent of respondents, poor relationships with family and friends are a result of low pay. I find that shocking – money is affecting that all important community wellbeing.

The risk of having mental illness is also disproportionately high for low-paid workers. When a living wage is given to employees, US studies have found that employees subjective wellbeing improves, and depressive symptoms decrease[352]. Some studies across the US have also linked a living wage with decrease in premature death across all causes for 24- to 44-year-olds. Examining the various increases in the national minimum wage (NMW) in the UK from 2016 to 2018, researchers have concluded that increases in the NMW have a significant impact on employee mental and physical wellbeing[353].

The impact of paying a fair wage can be significant on employers too. Large global employers like PayPal say they attribute some of their success as an employer by ensuring they pay a living wage[354]. Policy Scotland found that when an organisation pays a living wage, recruitment costs reduce, employee engagement increases, absence rates reduce, and organisational capacity gets better[355]. In my mind, adequate, accurate and timely pay is therefore a wellbeing issue – but again, how often is pay mentioned as part of a wellbeing strategy?

Pay sick pay.

Sick pay played an almost hidden role in employee wellbeing until the pandemic unearthed its influence. Whilst this was seen across the world, it became a great source of fierce debate among public health officials in the United Kingdom. Despite the UK having some of the most advanced and progressive private sector employee benefit schemes in the world, the UK has the lowest levels of statutory sick pay of all the OECD countries. In the same week that I discovered this fact, I was told by a legal and HR advisor that companies they work with don't want to offer sick pay because "staff will abuse it". The exact same day, a friend of mine was forcing themselves to go to work during the pandemic because they couldn't afford not to, and sick pay wasn't offered.

According to the ONS, nearly seven million UK workers don't qualify for Statutory Sick Pay (SSP) of just £96 a week (which the TUC sees as being "woefully inadequate"). The way it is structured also means someone on SSP will normally receive no payment for the first three days. While this pay is low by international standards, it was also clear that the lack of access to sick pay undermined our attempts to control Covid-19. There is evidence that levels of compliance with the UK's instructions to self-isolate were hampered by the lack of decent sick pay.

In 2021, the CIPD found out that a massive 70 percent of employees were using their own vacation leave when they were ill. This mirrors other recent research suggesting the number of employees working while ill could be as much as a third[356]. We have created workplaces that are giving ill employees no other option but to come to work and we did that at a time when by doing so, lives were being put at risk.

During the midst of the pandemic, I wrote an article for HR Zone magazine about sick pay in the UK and as part of the research for this, I spoke to a friend anonymously about their experiences with not having paid sick leave. They told me.

"I can't afford to get ill… I can't take the risk to go out and do the things I want to in case I catch the virus… I have to decide for every train journey, every activity if it is worth possibly losing a week of income which will literally endanger the roof over my head. It's too big a risk to take. This will be a very long winter"

Employees are having to make some tough decisions when their financial situation is influencing how they take care of their wellbeing. Research shows that both full and part time workers without paid sick leave are more likely than workers with it to attend work while ill[357]. Those without paid sick leave are also three times more likely to forego medical care for themselves when compared to those with paid sick leave. This poses a huge problem for employers who don't offer paid sick leave. You are effectively forcing employees into a situation where they are too ill to work, but too poor not to. Lack of paid sick leave encourages ill employees to come to work and this has much wider wellbeing concerns for the rest of the workforce.

We have evidence that when employees come to work while ill, not only is the quality of their output lowers, but the individual's psychological wellbeing declines too[358]. The Royal Society of Arts (RSA) said that the UK's lack of adequate sick pay threatened and impeded our ability to contain the Covid-19 pandemic; those that couldn't afford to stay at home while ill with the virus, came to work and assisted the fast spreading of it within the workplace. I have no doubt that a lack of paid sick leave contributed to unnecessary pandemic deaths.

But even before the pandemic, in 2018 the Brookings Institute was warning employers of the dangers of a lack of sick pay. Two years before the Coronavirus outbreak, America suffered its worse flu year since the 2009 swine flu pandemic. The Brookings Institute reported that flu rates decrease significantly when workers get access to paid sick leave through state or city-level employer mandates[359]. However, as of 2018 only nine US states had passed paid sick leave laws. I can't help but think the wellbeing of employees all over the world would have weathered the pandemic better if we had listened to the advice that was being given just a few years before the Covid-19 crisis started.

Employees are poorly protected.

During the pandemic we saw an employee benefits renaissance. Overnight, millions turned to their benefits packages for support and as a result, the demand for certain financial and wellbeing products skyrocketed. But discerning employees began to see through useless and gimmicky wellbeing benefits and instead began to demand those with real, tangible benefits to their lives[360]. Namely, those that protected them against poor financial wellbeing in the future.

The pandemic reminded us of our finite lives and the fragile state of our income and savings, so demand for life insurance and income protection grew significantly[361]. As a result, more than half of employees now say their benefits package should be designed to help them with their wellbeing[362]. And with very good reason:

- Critical illness insurance has been found to reduce the financial burden of patients with high medical costs[363]
- Access to more affordable preventative dental care decreases the disparities in oral health[364]
- 1 in 4 Income Protection people who make claims at one of the biggest insurers in the UK also accessed

support services that resulted in 82 percent of them seeking therapy. This insurance product not only insures against ill health, but is effective at getting people the support they need too[365]

Around 15 years ago, when I did my first set of Chartered Insurance Institute (CII) qualifications it was common to advise people to settle their financial affairs in a certain order, the first objective being to protect your income. The advice is still as relevant now as it was then, but in retail terms, income protection is still a little known and very misunderstood benefit. Seen as complex and expensive, I frequently come across employees who have either never heard of it or don't understand what it is. When bought in the right way, however, income protection will be one of the most important financial wellbeing products an employee will use.

Despite the long list of positives to offer employees protection against ill health, only around a quarter of employers offer staff with cancer access to benefits like income protection and critical illness insurance[366]. Alarmingly, around 20 percent of employers in this study say they wouldn't know how to support an employee with a cancer diagnosis. Even employees themselves aren't aware of the financial support offered to them, with almost half of those who are living with cancer saying they were unfamiliar with the resources available before their diagnosis[367].

More than one in four income protection claims are now trigged by mental health issues[368]. In 2021, British insurer Royal London paid out more than £632 million in protection claims with the most common reasons for a pay-out being musculoskeletal, cancer and mental health[369]. Aviva paid our more than £1 billion in UK claims with the two largest reasons being musculoskeletal and mental health[370]. In 2022, mental health now accounts for the *top* reason why income protection claims are made[371]. So why isn't income protection more widely invested in by employers?

Poor financial wellbeing at work is costing UK employers £1.56 billion every year through increased absenteeism and presenteeism[372]. Over the last 12 months, it is estimated that half a million British workers have taken time off due to their financial wellbeing – that's over 4.1 million lost days of work. Insurance benefits like income protection can help to ease the financial stress cause by external pressures like a pandemic.

The Covid-19 led millions more UK employees to take out financial wellbeing products like income protection. More than half of new income protection customers in 2021 said the crisis influenced their decision to take out a policy – up from 37.4 percent from the start of the pandemic[373]. Just knowing someone who has experienced a negative health event in the past influences our intention to buy an income protection policy[374]. Yet in 2022, less than one in five employees protect their income[375].

But we have a problem and that is that most employees don't understand the protection benefits many employers pay for, subside, or make available to their people. MetLife UK found that one in five employees had never heard of income protection[376]. A quarter didn't know what critical illness was and 20 percent who were aware of such products didn't understand them. Industry jargon is acting as a barrier to this understanding with only half of adults saying the language used to describe insurance products is easy to understand[377]. Employers must do more to improve employees' understanding of these protection products to boost their take up and build important financial resilience in the future.

This book was published during one of the worst cost of living crises the world has ever seen. New research shows that more than a third of adults across the UK felt their health deteriorated as a result of this crisis[378]. Worrying about money is causing poor sleep and growing anxiety which is putting people at a greater risk of developing serious medical conditions. Employees are unprotected against the financial impact of another pandemic, long term ill health or common diseases. And now a quarter are turning to unhealthy habits like smoking or drinking more in order to cope with stress of an uncertain financial future.

It's fairly well documented that during times of economic hardship, people tend to gamble more[379]. Consumer confidence appears to be directly linked with "luck-based" gambling like scratch cards, lotteries, and bingo and lottery consumption increases during recessions[380]. For employers, this should be a big concern. When financial stress pushes employees to develop more unhealthy habits, it begins to make the job of supporting wellbeing so much harder. Gambling related harm affects more than 300,000 people in the UK and around 1 percent of the entire US population[381]. While the financial impact on employees who gamble is probably obvious, the wider health implications are less so. Those with gambling problems have lower self-reported health, higher rates of stress-related physical ailments and lower quality of life scores[382].

It's important for us to fully understand the relationship money has on our overall wellbeing. Whether that is being forced to work while sick, gambling our salary away or being poorly protected against life's knocks, financial wellbeing is so inextricably linked to our health that unless we are finding ways to help our people deal better with their finances, we will fail at supporting their wellbeing.

Chapter 8

A Commitment to Physical Wellbeing

The benefits of good physical health are well known. When we are more active, we sleep better, our bodies are stronger, and our weight is managed well. Physical activity can improve our cardiovascular health[383] and even reduce the risk of cancer[384]. When we look after our bodies, we protect ourselves from illness and disease and become more resilient to some of the thing's life will throw at us. The health benefits from regular exercise that should be emphasised and reinforced by every employer include the following[385]:

1. Improved sleep
2. Better endurance
3. Stress relief
4. Improvement in mood
5. Increased energy and stamina
6. Reduced tiredness that can increase mental alertness
7. Weight reduction
8. Reduced cholesterol and improved cardiovascular fitness

Mood and stress relief are interesting additions to the traditional list of the benefits of regular physical activity. Exercise spikes the stress response in our bodies which makes us experience lower levels of stress hormones.[386]. We know also know that more exercise has a positive impact on more serious mental health too[387]. A very large study involving 1.2 million people across all 50 states of the USA, found that those who exercise regularly take, on average, one and a half fewer days off work due to poor mental health than those who do not exercise[388]. What's more, all exercise types were associated with a lower mental health burden than not exercising at all. Team sports showed the biggest positive impacts, followed by cycling and gym activities. With cycle to work and gym memberships being common among the top global benefits offered by employers, this gives us a new dimension for us to consider these benefits with.

Physical activity and mental health.

The latest research continues to enforce the idea that physical activity doesn't just maintain good mental health, it protects mental health too. When we move more, our bodies produce a mixture of hormones which make us feel good. While it takes a certain level of activity to release endorphins, even moderate levels of exercise can boost our mood. Physical activity has also been found to be effective in treating clinical anxiety[389].

In an analysis of more than 1,150 global studies, 89 percent found a statistically significant, positive relationship between physical exercise and mental health[390]. The strongest associations across almost every study were for depression. Depressive symptoms are reduced when physical activity is increased. But even for those with post-traumatic stress, schizophrenia, anxiety, alcohol abuse and bipolar disorder, exercise was leading to better outcomes. In some studies, the effects of exercise on treating depression were on par with antidepressant drugs[391]. But Smithsonian Magazine raises a very interesting point:

"There's a flip side to this coin that's especially relevant during the Covid-19 pandemic: If exercise stabilizes mental health, then anything that prevents people from working out is likely to destabilize it"
– Bob Holmes

Data collected from over 3,000 US adults, pre and post pandemic showed that those who were usually active, but during the pandemic were less active, were more prone to report depression and stress[392]. The nature of lockdowns, working from home and the closure of gyms and team sports events meant many employees couldn't be as physically active as they used to be. When active people were forced to be less active, their mental health declined.

Surprisingly, the evidence is also mounting to show that this kind of physical activity doesn't need to take place in person in a gym or exercise class. Home workouts became popular during the pandemic and many employers put them in place. In one study, the antidepressant effects of exercise applied equally to participants doing exercise classes in person, in a group as it did for those working out at home following instructions[393]. Some studies have even found that just mild 'placebo' exercise (where a person is barely moving/stretching) can positively impact mental health[394]. So even minimal physical activity has its place in improving employee wellbeing.

For those employees who are already suffering with poor mental health, physical wellbeing can also play a very important part in their treatment. What is being referred to as the 'therapeutic promise' of physical activity is now informing mental health treatment. Exercise improves mental health outcomes among those already dealing with depression or anxiety[395]. While the reasons why exercise is so beneficial to mental health is still up for debate, it does seem like physical activity triggers the release of a protein known as brain-derived neurotrophic factor (BDNF) – one of the key molecules that helps us to grow new brain cells. Experts believe this new cell growth may be taking place in the hippocampus, which tends to be smaller in people who have depression or anxiety.

Better sleep.

While one of the most important functions of our bodies, sleep is frequently the thing that is often disturbed by life's events. A major 2022 study showed that improving the quality of our sleep leads to better mental health[396]. While we always tended to assume that poor mental health affects the quality of our sleep, we now know that the opposite is true too. Researchers at the University of Sheffield found that improvements in sleep gives people significant mental health benefits – regardless of the state of their wider physical wellbeing. Improving the quality of employee's sleep may not only reduce the risk of developing poor mental health but improves outcomes for those already struggling.

But as sleep happens entirely out of the workplace for most employees, why is it important for employers to enhance where they can? Mostly because it fuels so much of who they are and what they achieve at work. Sleep has been found to be crucial in our ability to remember things – and specifically the important things[397]. Studies have shown that a good night's sleep enhances our ability to work smarter[398]. But our overall physical health is closely linked to quality of sleep too. A good night's sleep is associated with higher vascular fitness, normalised heart rate and lower blood pressure[399]. Conversely, inadequate sleep is associated with more regular chances of falling into mental distress[400]. So, we must ensure that the workplace isn't contributing to a poor night's sleep as that can lead to worse health outcomes.

An unfortunate truth is that our work stress and schedules do impact our sleep[401]. Work overload, role conflict, repetitive tasks, lack of autonomy are all work factors that have been shown to negatively impact sleep[402]. Those working longer hours have significantly more depressive and anxiety symptoms[403]. Given that we know how much poor sleep impacts overall physical and emotional wellbeing, it's imperative that employers consider the ways they negative impact sleep through the workplace. So rather than try to react to the causes of poor sleep by encouraging better sleep habits, we should first be ensuring those organisational factors that drive sleep deprivation are looked at first.

For many workers on zero-hour contracts, lack of sleep and poor-quality sleep are frequently wellbeing issues[404]. Shift workers are more likely to develop psychological problems and experience higher financial stress, which all contribute to and cause poor quality sleep[405]. Those employees on zero-hour contracts are twice as likely to work night shifts according to the TUC[406]. The TUC says that night shifts in themselves are a "health risk" and reports that two-thirds of those employees on a zero-hour contract want to be on a permeant, secure contract[407].

Activity monitoring.

In my early days at Benefex, our CEO I ran a trial with our people that saw volunteers attach a small digital pedometer to their footwear. The small dome would send data to a website that would allow employees to track various physical activity from swimming to cycling, running, and walking. These were pre-Apple watch days and the very early iterations of a wearable activity monitor. Fast forward to 2019 and nearly 86 million Americans are using a wearable device on any given day – an increase from just 25 million in 2014[408]. While back during the early days of the Benefex trial I was sceptical, it's clear that for millions of people, activity monitors are supporting their wellbeing at work.

In 2016, a review of 14 different studies into the effectiveness of activity monitors looked at the results from more than 1,157 participants. The researchers concluded that people with activity monitors were more likely to spend time doing moderate to vigorous physical activity and walked more than those who didn't wear one[409]. A similar study found that using a fitness tracker increases everyday physical activity by an equivalent of 1,235 steps a day[410].

Wearables are still very much in their infancy, but some of the latest thinking is not only fascinating, but incredibly useful for employers to understand. One large study reviewed 179 other studies involving almost 200 different types of wearable device and more than ten million participants[411]. They concluded that wearables can be used to predict Covid-19, track fertility, track the effects of drugs and even measure the effectiveness of psychological interventions. The researchers conclude that wearables "may potentially transform the understanding of population health dynamics and the ability to forecast health trends" in the future.

Physical activity of any intensity is beneficial to employee wellbeing but being able to measure it might be the secret sauce. One of the largest studies in the UK examined the physical activity of almost 100,000 people and it found that being able to use a wearable device to ensure your level of intensity is increased can positively impact health. The study found that increasing the intensity of whatever physical activity you are doing and gradually building that up will improve future heath[412]. And in many ways, the dataset that comes out of a wearable is improving health literacy. By tracking what exercises help them to achieve their goals and by educating employees on effort so far, we may begin to crack the very difficult behaviour change required to get employees to sleep better and move more.

Employee benefits that matter.

One longitudinal study into health insurance in the US found that the mortality rates of uninsured versus insured adults was higher. Health insurance can affect health status[413]. In the UK, the IFS recommends that the UK Government does more to encourage people to take out private medical insurance[414].

These recommendations come with good reason – health coverage appears to make people healthier. A landmark study from 2011 involving researchers from MIT, Harvard and the State of Oregon studied the impact of randomly assigning Medicaid insurance to poor people in Oregon through a lottery[415]. They found that Medicaid's impact on overall health, happiness and general wellbeing was "enormous". After just one year with the insurance in place, those random participants were happier, healthier and under less financial strain than those who weren't included in the lottery. It appears that the insured seek treatment earlier, lowering their chances of falling more seriously ill. The researchers found that having Medicaid in place made people more likely to be admitted to hospital. The newly insured used more of almost every kind of health care service. There were big jumps in the numbers seeking out preventative care like mammograms and more regular doctor visits. People were more proactively looking after their health because of insurance. Just having health insurance in place increased the chances of someone saying that they were in "good", "very good" or "excellent" health. The study also found that the number of sick days dropped by 15 percent among those who won the lottery.

Throughout the pandemic, health-related benefits became more important than I think they have in the 20-plus years I have been working in the industry. The pandemic forced many US employers to enrich their employee benefit schemes with health and wellbeing at their core. When asked how important health benefits have become now, compared to five years ago, every single benefit was ranked as "more important"[416]. Almost half of US employers now say benefits like critical illness, long term disability, hospital indemnity and dental insurance are more important than they were before the pandemic. The impact is so strong, that employers are even reporting that the cost of offering these benefits is now less important than it was in 2018 – by quite a large difference – around 14 percent.

These types of employer sponsored health and wellbeing benefits do make a material difference to individual wellbeing according to new research[417]. Digital health screening, virtual doctor appointments, self-help tools, health insurance etc., are all proving to move the dial on employee wellbeing. For example:

- Making dental insurance available to employees has been shown to positively impact oral health[418].
- Health screening benefits have been shown to reduce inpatient and outpatient health costs for two years after treatment[419].
- Employee Assistance Programmes (EAPs) result in a 50 percent drop in absence rates[420].

Just as in other parts of the world, across the US the lack of state support is driving employees to turn to their employer to support their physical wellbeing. For almost half of employees in America, health insurance is a deciding factor in whether to choose a job or not and more than half say the quality of what insurance is offered is a key factor in whether they decided to stay at a job or not[421]. The more the employer shoulders the burden of healthcare, the more pronounced these feelings are[422].

The effect of the pandemic on health insurance has been huge. In 2022, some private medical insurance providers are reporting an increase in sales of a massive 92 percent since 2018[423]. Employees are demanding this employee benefit more than they ever have as state funded care becomes stretched, waiting times are growing and many question the quality of care provided by the Government. The demand and willingness to pay for private medical insurance is growing rapidly. A report by the UK Institute for Public Policy Research (IPPR) finds that the UK has seen the sharpest rise in paying for private healthcare that any other G7 nation since the 1970s[424]. During the pandemic, more than a third of Brits said they struggled to access the care they needed and that this is fuelling a rise in private healthcare solutions. The evidence is mounting that employees are demanding more of these core health and wellbeing benefits than ever before, but also that their impact on employee wellbeing is significant. However, we also have growing evidence that these types of benefits (expensive as they are) can have a profoundly positive impact on the organisation too.

A 2021 report by the Social Market Foundation in the UK examined the role insurance products like income protection and private medical has on things like reducing workplace absences, facilitating a swift return to work, and reducing presenteeism[425]. The report found that private medical insurance was described as "indispensable" or "helpful" by 82 percent of respondents who had a policy in place at the time of absence or illness. Two thirds said the same about their critical illness policy. Overwhelmingly, for those with these products, the highest rated benefit was the peace of mind the insurances gave employees.

Though much maligned, health insurance continues to play a large part in wellbeing at work for American employees in particular. Picking up where the state is failing, employers are increasingly wanting to support their people in getting access to quick and high-quality care. But even outside of the US, employers are also continuing to bow down to pressure from employees to offer health insurance. Health insurance in the UK now ranks as one of the most desired workplace employee benefits, second only to higher pay[426]. For British employees, I can only see the demand for private health insurance grow as the NHS continues to struggle to look after the health of the nation, and as employers who can, try to find ways to unburden the NHS.

Improving health literacy.

A growing body of research indicates that limited health literacy can lead to adverse health outcomes due to patients' inability to follow instructions on medications, labels, and health messages, especially in preventive care. Research reveals that many members of the public cannot recognise specific disorders or different types of psychological distress[427]. Attitudes and lack of health literacy hinder people's ability to ask for help and recognise problems.

- Research estimates indicate that between one-third and one-half of all adults' struggle with health literacy[428]
- Only about 13 percent of English speakers in the US have proficient levels of health literacy. That means that about 87 percent of people (or nine out of ten people) need help with health-related information[429].
- Health literacy improves health behaviours in those with Diabetes[430].
- A literature review found that the ability to obtain and understand basic health information partly determines the mortality rate of people with heart failure[431].
- Health literacy and the general ability to understand health information impacts health behaviours – specifically in relation to be being physically active, having a poor diet, and being obese[432].

At Benefex we have doubled down on content as part of our strategy to improve employee wellbeing across the world. The compelling data on not only how we digest content in the modern age, but the impact of employees being more informed is fascinating. The pandemic meant that many consumers had no choice but to take charge of their own wellbeing and become more informed – their life literally depending on knowing how the virus might affect them and how to avoid catching it. As a result, we have seen a big shift in people showing more agency and engagement with their wellbeing. According to Deloitte's Health Care Consumer Response to COVID-19 Survey, Americans are now far more likely to engage in health behaviour change content taking more ownership of their wellbeing[433].

Throughout the Covid-19 pandemic there was a significant uptick in people seeking out content online that can better help them to understand themselves and their wellbeing. Limited time spent with healthcare professionals and barriers to accessing state healthcare have become the main reasons why people now say they seek out health information themselves[434]. According to a 2020 study by Vice, young people in particular are seeking out the wellbeing facts more than they ever have[435]. In the last three months of 2021, one in two EU citizens reported they had sought out health and wellbeing information online[436]. The mental health charity Rethink report that people are seeking advice online from them in record numbers. In the 12 months running up to the first UK lockdown, Rethink reported that more than 7.5 million pages were read by people looking for guidance and education[437]. However, in an era of clickbait content and fake news, finding the real or best content from a trusted source has become very difficult. For those who seek out health and wellbeing information online, the credibility and trustworthiness of the information is their primary concern.

Global content consumption doubled in 2020 and shows no signs of slowing down[438]. But finding the best content from the best sources is becoming a challenge. This presents a huge opportunity for employers to improve financial and health literacy of their people, while also providing the information that will be critical to each of them in improving their wellbeing at work. Especially as your people have a direct route to the most trusted institution in their lives – you, the employer[439].

Chapter 9
Prioritising Emotional Wellbeing

The pandemic not only marked a fundamental shift in our collective attitudes to wellbeing at work, but it also actually made many of us change the way we think of work and wellbeing. A 2022 global study of 33,000 employees across 32 countries found that more than half say they are now more likely to prioritise their wellbeing over their work than before the pandemic[440]. This change represents a significant pivot in attitudes towards those employers that prioritise mental health or emotional wellbeing in the workplace. Yet unfortunately, less than half of employees feel that mental health is being prioritised at their company[441].

The causes of poor mental health.

We've covered it already in this book, but I think it's essential to elaborate on. When we talk about mental health in the workplace, I think it's important to be clear on the causes of poor mental health. While work and the workplace can clearly be a stressor and driver of poor mental health at work, most of those that are struggling are doing so for reasons far out of the control or influence of the employer. So even the most progressive employer who is doing all they can to support the mental health of their people will still see high numbers of reported mental health at work.

Among the four major causes of depression, family history, illness, medication, and personality feature at the top of the list. In addition, life events like bad relationships, job loss, divorce or relationship breakdown, isolation, grief etc all play a part too. While the entire causes of depression are still unknown and there isn't a single cause for it, I believe from the research I've conducted, that things like family history and socio-economic reasons account for around half of poor mental health conditions. Which leaves around half that can be modified or improved through lifestyle or behaviour changes the workplace can facilitate or encourage.

The unknown impact of family history.

In 2022, landmark research in India suggests that our life experiences can have consequences that reverberate to our children and even their children[442]. The hypotheses here is that emotional trauma experienced by a child will not only follow them into adulthood but could be passed down to their children too.

It sounds wild, but we do have evidence that an individual's experience might alter the cells and behaviour of any children they have. In some animals, exposure to stress, cold or high fat diets has been shown to change the metabolic make up of later generations[443]. I think this is important to note here as it adds credence to exactly what wellbeing support an employer can offer that is ultimately going to be effective. If diagnosed conditions can be passed down from one generation to the next and now also trauma, it does change the way we support mental health at work. For some employees we are trying to ensure we don't harm their emotional wellbeing, but for others we are supporting an existing condition or experience - and that's a very big difference.

Preventing burnout.

Burnout was cited as one of the top three reasons why young workers are leaving their jobs during 'The Great Resignation'. According to research, almost half of young employees (those under 40) said they felt burned out due to their work and would like to leave their jobs as a result[444]. While the research found that burnout was prevalent across all ages at work in 2022, younger employees were the ones who were far more likely to take drastic steps to make it stop, like leaving their employer entirely.

But resilience should be about how we recharge, not endure through work's stressors and pressures. When we look at the reasons why employee's burnout, they are commonly those that we are trying to avoid through the advice in this book. When employees have clear objectives, positive relationships with their team and management, when they have a voice and are recognised more, they become less likely to burnout[445]. Conversely, when employees work in a team or organisation where trust and psychology safety are high, they recover quicker from burnout.

An employee's vulnerability to burnout can be changed and this is incredibly important to workplace wellbeing as aside from burnout, we are now able to link it to depression and anxiety too[446]. Burnout is a symptom of an organisation not supporting many of the areas we look at in this book. By following the advice and the evidence we present here, an organisation should be able to create a culture where burnout is limited and one where we are better able to support those who are already experiencing it.

Support for everyone, not just those in crisis.

Part of the problem here (especially when it comes to emotional wellbeing or mental health) is that many employees often fall into the trap of believing that this kind of support isn't for them. Throughout the pandemic, the term 'languishing' was used to describe the way many employees experience poor mental health and helps to explain why they may avoid using some of the wellbeing tools we make available to them. Languishing refers to the absence of serious negative mental health, but also the absence of positive experiences.

Research conducted by Professor Rothmann found that 59 percent of people were currently sat in a "thriving" or "surviving" category of mental health where languishing is present[447]. While not struggling or in crisis, these employees weren't excelling either. This can lead to some employees not engaging with wellbeing initiatives because they tend to be aimed at people in crisis. Ensuring your communications target all employees as a way of positively and proactively managing their wellbeing, rather than targeted those with a health problem, will ensure the highest engagement possible.

Guest Expert View: Rob Stephenson
CEO of FormScore & Founder, the InsideOut Leader Board

Global mental health campaigner and TEDx speaker, Rob Stephenson, is on a mission to inspire the creation of mentally health workplaces. Rob regularly delivers keynotes for workplaces and their leaderships teams on how to create culture conducive to wellbeing and why this makes great business sense. The InsideOut Leader Board is a charity that showcases senior leaders who are open about their mental health challenges. FormScore is a workplace wellness platform that helps employees be more intentional about wellbeing and facilitates connection and peer support whilst offering employers real time insights and wellbeing analytics

---

Mental Health & Wellbeing – an essential component of high performance?

The pandemic has elevated mental health and wellbeing in the workplace with more leaders talking about employee wellness and increased investment in wellbeing solutions. Awareness has improved, yet, as we travel through tough economic conditions, we are starting to see a worrying trend or wellbeing budgets being seen as discretionary spend and, in many cases, being significantly cut. This is short sighted to say the least and is likely to have a significant detrimental effect on employer brand at a time when the attraction and retention of talent is one of the key people challenges.

We know from the recent Deloitte research that presenteeism is the biggest cost of mental ill-health, costing UK employers up to £29bn per annum. Presenteeism is where people are underperforming due to sub-optimal mental wellbeing. For many organisations this is a huge opportunity to invest in the mental wellbeing of employees (their greatest assets). It makes great business sense and the right thing to do.

The benefits of getting workplace wellbeing right are significant and include a more productive workforce who are more likely to stay with the organisation. So what does good look like?

1. Senior leadership engagement with c-level executives displaying vulnerability and authenticity where mental wellbeing is concerned. The InsideOut Leader Board is one vehicle that helps achieve this by showcasing those leaders who are open about their challenges.

2. Embed wellbeing as a core strategic priority of the organisation, have a strategy and report on the impact of initiatives.

3. Employ a dedicated wellbeing leader who reports into the CEO or Board.

4. Empower line managers to be better non-judgemental listeners and inspire them to create cultures of wellness in their teams.

5. Recruit champions within the organisation and provide them with both training and clinical supervision.

6. Focus on awareness; support and prevention and work hard on inspiring all employees of the benefits of prioritising their wellness.

7. Use "wellness time" to send a strong message of permission and let employees know that there is an expectation that they invest in their wellbeing.

The risks of ignoring employee wellbeing are significant:

Access to capital – we are seeing increased scrutiny from fund managers on how well companies are doing in respect of employee mental health. (CCLA Fund Managers)

Access to talent – 40 percent of employees say that want to see more investment in wellbeing to improve company culture (LinkedIn Global Talent Trends 2022) and 91 percent of graduates look at the wellbeing benefits of a company before applying. (Bright Network)

Forward-thinking CEO's really do understand the need to focus on the wellbeing of their people. For those who chose not to look after your greatest assets, expect to see this reflected in the bottom line.

Chapter 10
Fostering Community

There is a growing body of evidence that shows when most or all the elements of community wellbeing come together in a positive way, the impact on the individual and the organisation is significant. Some studies have found that when Community Wellbeing is high, staff report less conflict between their home and work lives[1]. We also have evidence that community wellbeing directly correlates with life satisfaction and employee mental health[2]. The more opportunities employees have to talk to colleagues who they trust and socialise with can have a significant positive impact on mental health. This also helps to create a workplace that cares for its individual members.

When employees feel more connected to their workplace and their colleagues and feel part of a community. We've known for quite some time that loneliness can exacerbate ill health[3] but also having people around us improves our wellbeing. A community of people at work that we feel care for us and that we can interact with regularly in a positive way has a huge effect on our health. Both the quantity and quality of the social relationships we have affect our mental health, physical health, and mortality risk[448]. A study of 7,000 people in California found that when participants were disconnected from others, they were three times more likely to die during the nine-year study than those with strong social ties[449]. These results ring true even when we account for age, gender, and health status. In fact, people with unhealthy lifestyles but lots of social ties live longer than those with a healthy life but poor social connections. A large body of evidence continues to fuel the idea that we need other people around us to be well. People who have satisfying relationships in their lives have fewer health problems and live longer[450].

In the small Minnesota city of Alberta Lea, 18,000 residents were part of a community wellbeing experiment[4]. Local shops and restaurants were encouraged to use local produce, people were coached on their purpose and sense of belonging and more connectedness was encouraged in the community[5]. Residents were encouraged to exercise together, volunteer and contribute to meetings with local leaders. The impact of this investment in community wellbeing was huge. The average resident increased their life expectancy by three years. Key employers in Alberta Lee saw a reduction in absenteeism by 21 percent and a decrease in health care costs by a massive 40 percent.

Combatting loneliness.

Before Coronavirus forcibly separated us from our colleagues and made community wellbeing an even more important part of the employee experience, loneliness at work was at worryingly high levels. More than half of employees say they feel lonely 'always' or 'often' with almost half saying they don't have a friend at work[6]. The more connected we feel to other people, the better our overall health. Strong social connections are what make up community wellbeing and now, more than ever, it's time that employers started to build more of a commitment to creating supportive, trusting communities.

The small, seemingly insignificant 'small talk' we have with our colleagues is playing a much larger role in wellbeing than we once thought. One new study has found that although these interactions can distract employees, they are also an uplifting part of work[451]. Employees who experienced regular 'small talk' felt more positive emotions, resulting in enhanced wellbeing. Creating these connections, reducing feels of isolation and loneliness are all part of why I think community wellbeing is such an important part of wellbeing, but with increasing levels of home and remote working, bridging these physical gaps is a new challenge.

Technology and social capital.

Interestingly for those employers who have remote workers is that some of the evidence behind community wellbeing appears to stack up even in virtual environments. Research into gaming finds that one of the main motivational factors behind the hobby is the building of social relationships[452]. Throughout the pandemic, gaming was found to help create inclusive communities and lessen the effects of poor mental health[453].

A survey of US adults found that gamers who develop ties with fellow gamers build social capital, which in this instance has been shown to be a positive antecedent in predicting both face to face social capital and civic participation[454]. Gaming is finding its place in helping people to build real life face to face communities[455]. Virtual gaming can be used to promote social connectedness even in older adults too[456].

The number of daily users of workplace communication tools like Microsoft Teams have almost doubled over the last 12 months. By the second quarter of 2021, Teams had 145 million users[457]. But there is growing evidence that this kind of technology is having a positive impact on wellbeing. Teams has been found to increase the frequency of communication in the workplace and is helping hybrid and remote workers feel more engaged[458]. Using technology to bring people who work physically far apart together, is one of the best ways we have to build community at work when not everyone wants or can get together as frequently as we used to. At Benefex, we have been invested a great deal into using technology to build better workplace communities, so strong we feel the impact will be.

Instilling a sense of belonging.

But this sense of community is also about belonging, because only one in six employees say they feel strongly connected at work[459]. Within the communities we build at work, we are talking about person-to-person connection but also how connected our people feel to the organisation. New research by Workplace from Meta[460] found that half of frontline workers say they are planning to move on from their current role because they feel disconnected from their employer. But bringing everyone together in the office or workplace might not be the answer to this problem of disconnection. According to one 2022 study, employees working in the office are feeling less connected to their organisation than remote workers[461].

One of the more compelling ways employers are engaging their people in more belonging at work (especially when the organisations purpose isn't as obvious or strong as a vocation) is through the encouragement of altruism and volunteering. Numerous studies have found that when colleagues participate in volunteering and public causes at work, worker wellbeing improves[462]. Six in ten employees who volunteer through a workplace scheme rate their happiness at 70 percent or more, compared to only 55 percent among those employees who have never volunteered[463].

The London School of Economics has attempted to put a monetary value on the wellbeing benefits of volunteering and found that it comes out to around £1,800 per person. The researchers studied 9,000 people and found that the positive effects of volunteering can last three months after the volunteering task had taken place[464]. Similar research has been found across the UK with those who engaged in volunteering regularly appeared to experience higher levels of mental wellbeing than those who never volunteered[465]. The University of East Anglia found that in a post pandemic world, volunteering is associated with enhanced wellbeing, improved life satisfaction, increased happiness and decreases in symptoms of depression. Even those who are already ill show improved outcomes because of volunteering[466]. Elderly people who volunteer are 44 percent less likely to die![467].

But as well as giving our time, giving our money can aid our wellbeing too. While charitable giving has been a feature of many employee benefit schemes for decades, they aren't often mentioned in the same breath as wellbeing. Yet this prosocial behaviour has been found to have a positive impact on individual wellbeing. Generous behaviour increases happiness[468] and donating money releases feel-good chemicals in our brains[469]. When you give money to a cause you believe in, your brain changes. Our brains act the same way when we donate money as when we receive it, so the positive benefits of receiving match giving[470]. Prosocial behaviour like donating money to charity can even cause our body temperature to rise[471] - it literally gives us a warm glow! Giving is consistently good for our health and happiness and so when an employer can create opportunities to give our money and our time, we can see a positive impact on employee wellbeing[472].

Guest Expert View: Sanjay Lobo, MBE

CEO, onHand

Before onHand, Sanjay served on the exec team at two tech unicorns, Lastminute.com and Vistaprint, leading growth teams across the EU and US. In 2019, he founded onHand with the aim of solving some of society's biggest issues, using technology.

onHand is the all-in-one tool to engage your team in environmental and social good. It lets employees learn and take action on the issues that matter - from youth mentoring, food poverty, and elderly help, to fighting the climate crisis with CO2e tracked eco-pledges.
They've won an armful of awards, including Best Employee Engagement Volunteering Tool 2022.

Simply put, doing good makes you feel good.

You get a dopamine hit when you do something kind - like collecting an elderly neighbour's prescription for them or dropping off your surplus food at the local food bank. You don't really need studies to prove that, but there are loads of them out there that show the clear link between volunteering and good wellbeing. 80 percent of respondents to our own impact report saw an improvement in their wellbeing, thanks to their time spent volunteering using the onHand platform. Even people who suffer from mental illnesses can see "improvement in their outlook and mental health through volunteering. It gives them a sense of direction and meaning".

That's because volunteering helps create 'social capital' which increases people's access to help from others, creating a network of support for people to draw on to help them cope with difficult times. And 'social capital' doesn't just benefit the person doing the volunteering - it supports the entire community, cultivating resilience as people work together and help each other through tough times. It also boosts self-esteem and confidence - in a study exploring environmental volunteering, respondents expressed that they gained a sense of self-worth and felt good about themselves by volunteering for a 'good cause'.

The health benefits are huge. In a hybrid working world, your employees might be less active - spending more time on the sofa and less time on the commute. Local volunteering means getting out of the house and moving around more, whether that be helping someone with shopping, gardening, or a group activity.

All that being said, it's plain to see that a wellbeing programme that incorporates 'giving back' to the local community makes for happier employees. And a happier workforce is a more productive workforce. Bupa's research backs this - over half (51 percent) of people of all ages said they would be more engaged with their organisation overall, more satisfied in their jobs (53 percent), and more productive (47 percent) if the place they worked had strong eco and social commitments.

Employees want purpose, not just a pay cheque.

More and more, employees are turning down cash in favour of impact. In a 2018 LinkedIn study on workplace culture, a staggering 86 percent of millennials said they would take a pay cut to work at a company whose mission and values aligned with their own. In a 2022 Bupa survey, more than half of the respondents (54 percent) said they would take a pay cut to work for a business that reflects their ethics, on average sacrificing more than a quarter (27 percent) of their salary. That's quite a bit!

With employees craving more purpose in their daily lives, it comes as no surprise that reports from Deloitte show 80 percent of employees want to do more for their communities. Clearly, the appetite for community involvement and environmental action is growing, proving that business leaders can benefit hugely from strong social good initiatives.

Sustainability and employee wellbeing.

Employers' approaches to promoting and delivering community wellbeing could be crucial to being more sustainable. Because a healthy environment is so important to our wellbeing; resources that encourage more exercise and healthier diet are also good for the environment; wider economic security impacts a person's financial wellbeing[473]; community wellbeing is altruism[474]; emotional wellbeing is aided by green places and clean air[475]. So how can employers use their wider Environment, Social and Governance (ESG) initiatives to help employee wellbeing? The benefits you offer may be part of the answer.

There appears a core set of climate technologies that I think a benefits scheme could help to support[476]:

- Renewable energy
- Electric vehicles
- Circular economy
- Nature-based solutions
- Carbon removal
- Agriculture and food

We are seeing increasing demand from employees and employers to help staff to make more sustainable choices through the benefits that are on offer. Removing some of the cost barriers to running an electric vehicle, giving employees the ability to move to more sustainable energy choices, offering refurbished technology, reforestation, carbon reduction and locally sourced food. Employers who support their Environmental, Social and Governance (ESG) goals through the benefits they offer may notice a by-product to these efforts: higher employee wellbeing. Countries with higher Sustainable Development Goals, corelate with wellbeing according to the University of Oxford[477]. Sixty-four percent of people say they feel happier when they do something that is good for the environment[478], results that have been mirrored time and time again. A review 78 studies into sustainable behaviour and subjective wellbeing found a consistently positive relationship between different types of sustainable actions and individual wellbeing – and this correlation is stronger when a person is acting consciously (rather than automatically out of habit), like choosing a new employee benefit[479]. What is more, the impact of more sustainable choices on wellbeing is enhanced further among low-income employees[480] - those most likely to display poor wellbeing at work.

"Wellbeing is correlated with the long-term outcomes of environmental policies"
- Dr Jan-Emmanuel De Neve, associate professor of economics at the Saïd Business School and Director of the Wellbeing Research Centre at Oxford

There are strong ties between wellness, sustainability, and economic prosperity, so think about how sustainability features in your community wellbeing strategy. I estimate that around 10 of the UN's 17 Sustainability goals[481] can be positively influenced by the ways an employer supports the wellbeing of their people. Poverty and financial stress affect mental health, learning and development can lessen the effects of mental health conditions[482]. Even high traffic pollution correlates with anxiety levels[483]. This is just some of a growing body of rather compelling evidence that is looking at the impact the environment has on wellbeing.

But we have a new, very interesting angle on the way that more sustainable workplace decisions have on employee wellbeing too – they appear to make staff happier. New research has found that employees who report that their employer is environmentally and socially responsible also report, on average, having better mental health[484]. What's more, encouraging 'pro-environmental behaviour' (PEB) through offering more sustainable benefit choices has been found to strongly link with individual wellbeing[485]. Of almost 40 common green behaviours (many of which can be facilitated by an employee benefits scheme like buying locally sourced food and drink), most of them increase our life satisfaction[486].

Encouraging the option to live more sustainably or make greener choices in the workplace not only benefits the individual, but the organisation too. Employees have been found to be 16 percent more productive when they work in organisations that adopt green initiatives[487]. More sustainable support at work boost employee wellbeing and employee engagement.

 Guest Expert View: Letesia Gibson

Founder, New Ways

Letesia is the founder of New Ways, a behaviour change consultancy that works with leaders to create progressive, anti-racist and equitable organisations that people choose to belong to. Their work helps to create meaningful, lasting systemic change that builds stronger organisations that all kinds of people want to be a part of. They work at the intersection of progressive coaching, organisational development, future of work and creative consultancy to develop leaders and cultures that attract passionate, invested people, have a positive impact on workforce and society and are a beacon of inspirational light for their sector."

The Great Resignation was preceded by the Great Awakening, and at the crux of this was a renewed relationship to meaning and purpose in our lives. The pandemic wasn't the reason for this – pre-pandemic workers were burning out at epidemic rates, we'd normalised living to work, and loneliness and social isolation were rising across all age groups.

But it was a catalyst. I think of it a little like the red pill, blue pill scene in the 90s film the Matrix. People saw with new clarity the way that systemic issues in society impacted on our individual and collective health and wellbeing. The reality of the inter-dependence of public health. Systemic racism, and the way it creates poorer outcomes for Brown and Black people in almost every aspect of life. The profit centric focus on capitalism that saw people as assets, not humans, robbing people of their mental and physical health. The Climate Emergency and the way it creates a two-tier world of those anxious about the existential threat to life, and those in the global south whose lives are already threatened. Throw in Brexit, the refugee disaster, and the cost-of-living crisis, it's no wonder people are asking deep and meaningful questions about what they want for their lives and the work they do in them.

Focusing now on the workplace, there's been a rise in companies seeking to be more purposeful and wanting to have a positive impact in society. But what hasn't been quite so pacy is the recognition of the deep connection between sustainability and health. Sustainability is branded as something happening "over there", focused on "preparing for a better future" rather than being something currently impacting on people *now* - in a variety of different ways. Moreover, the narrow definition of sustainability as only about environmental issues isn't at all helpful for these times. We need to better understand the inter-connected nature of human, social and economic sustainability alongside environmental sustainability, and the way this creates a plethora of impacts that mean life is unsustainable.

Companies that put purpose before profit, with actions that address all our sustainability needs, not only create healthier workplaces with healthier people, but are a magnet for those who share their values. We are in a new era where we need more politically aware businesses that stay credibly connected to the needs of society at large. They need to be ethical businesses, that think about how they show up with integrity and humanity and have the courage to address their own systemic failings that reinforce the inequalities making our people ill. Having commitments to 'save the environment' are not enough. Companies that take sustainability seriously do this as standard. They need to step up and stand up for people by addressing things like presenteeism, toxic cultures, burnout, systemic racism, classism, gender-based inequalities.

The companies that excel will be ensuring they pay people fairly and invest in their people's growth and development. They think about their purpose inside their organisations as much as the impact they have on the outside. Ultimately, it's about care that isn't conditional on profit. We need more companies that genuinely care.

The universe has no purpose, but we do.

This might sound like an atheist view of the world, but through my life I've found that an acceptance of the universe's indifference to us has led me to understand just how important other people are to our lives. There is a great deal each of us can do that can help our fellow humans – I suspect just wanting to read a book that seeks to improve the lives of employees puts you, the reader, in this camp. The way we support and care for each other not only benefits others, but ourselves too. When we think and act in a way that considers how we can help others, it also gives meaning to our own lives. How an employee supports the society or community they live and work in gives them purpose and that in turn has a huge impact on their wellbeing.

Employee expectations for "clear and good environmental and sustainability policies" were sixth in the Aon Benefits and Trends Survey in early 2020[488]. Peakon's 2020 Employee Expectations Report reflects these shifting expectations[489]. One of the four major employee expectation trends found was sustainability. Peakon discovered that employee discussion of environmental issues has increased by 52 percent since 2019. In 2022, most employees want to care for others and the environment – I truly believe that.

Buoyed by the pandemic, employees' attitudes towards the environment and how the workplace supports it are changing. More than half of employees now say they want to contribute more to society and have questioned the purpose of their job[490]. Record numbers of employees want to work for an employer or do a job that is more meaningful and gives them purpose. A massive nine out of ten employees say they are willing to earn less money to do more meaningful work[491]. This journey to more purpose plays a pivotal role in our wellbeing.

Intrinsically relevant values, such as social relationships and contributing to one's community, were shown to be strongly connected with wellbeing, in research of more than 25,000 young adults from 58 countries[492]. Even though the form of these correlations differed by country and culture, the findings all hint to something crucial: money and position aren't enough to make an employee feel happy at work. Employees need meaning and purpose to be well. The work we do and who we do it for matters.

A 2020 study by the University of California, San Diego found that when a person feels they have a purpose in life, they are more likely to feel mentally and physical well[493]. Surveying more than 1,000 adults, researchers found that those "searching for meaning" were less likely than those that had found it to say they were well. But this study (and others like it) highlighted that the "meaning" we get from life can manifest itself in many ways. It's not always about working a vocation or a business with a social purpose, it can be as simple as doing work that we love or our job enabling us to do the things we enjoy in life or spending time with people we care about.

Adults with heart disease have a 27 percent lower chance of suffering a heart attack over a two-year period for every one-point rise on a six-point scale evaluating purpose in life[494]. A one-point difference in purpose can reduce the incidence of stroke by 22 percent in older people[495]. The hugely positive impact purpose has on employee's health and wellbeing is undeniable, yet with the thousands of hours of wellbeing consulting I've run with large global employers, purpose has never *once* featured in the ways employee wellbeing is supported at work.

Our jobs have a big impact on our personal identities, and they account for a lot of our self-esteem. With the collapse of traditional sources of community and social support, the workplace has emerged as the principal forum for meeting social needs. Work has become the main source of personal identity, relevance, and purpose in many people's lives. So how the workplace facilitates that purpose, how it helps employees to identify what is important to them now plays out in our wellbeing strategies.

Research involving just under 8,000 young people in the United States found that when it came to starting their careers, younger workers prefer organisations that prioritise social benefit over those that focused solely on profit[496]. According to a Staples study, most office workers (89 percent) say they seek fulfilment at work[497]. Similarly, 70 percent of employees who consider themselves to be thriving professionally and personally work for a firm that has a strong sense of purpose[498].

Guest Expert View: Perry Timms

Chief Energy Officer, People & Transformational HR Ltd

Perry Timms is the founder and Chief Energy Officer of PTHR – a niche consultancy, with the mission to create better business for a better world. PTHR is in its 10th year of operating, is a Certified BCorporation, a Gold-Standard Four- day Working Week organisation, an accredited Living Wage employer and a Climate-Positive enterprise. Perry is a proud Chartered member of the CIPD and is a five times member of HR Magazine's HR Most Influential list making the top 10 in 2018, 2019 and 2021 and ranked Number 1 Most Influential Thinker for HR in 2022.

He is an international and two-time TEDx speaker and award-winning writer on the future of work, HR, and learning. He is a recently certified Semco Style Institute Expert in Self-Managed systems of work. His 2017 book Transformational HR was named one of the Top 100 Business Strategy books of all time and published as a second edition in July 2021. His second book – The Energized Workplace – was published in August 2020 and was shortlisted for the UK Business Book of the Year 2021.

Perry is Adjunct Professor at Hult International Business School and Ashridge Management School, a visiting fellow at Cranfield School of Management, and Sheffield Hallam University. He is a Top 100 global HR Influencer on numerous lists, a LinkedIn Learning instructor, a member of the European Organisation Design Forum, the Institute for

Organisational Dynamics and the OD Academy and a
Fellow of the RSA.

Wellbeing is rightly a topic of attention and action within the world of work. Whereas once the "hero" mentality prevailed - the stiff-upper-lip, just get on with it, don't panic meme and coming into work despite being riddled with a terrible cold - has thankfully been erased in favour of declarations of struggling wellbeing (be it physical, mental health or both) and the support, comfort, and recognition that we all hit the buffers at times no matter how "resilient" we're told or taught to be.

Resilience - what was once a considered tactic to empower others to find their inner strength - has become a hijacked cliche of how to position someone's wellbeing challenges as something "they can sort out". This now means I recoil from both words - resilience and empowerment - as cliches used by privileged others to ordain self-determination on others as a way of abdicating care, appreciation, and support for others.

I am a big believer in self-managed systems of work: Removing the dominance of hierarchical control and power (and often oppression) to shared, dispersed, and enabling leadership that provides agency and autonomy aligned with accountability and clarity of aspiration and achievement.

Wellbeing is the same for me. Not just "physician heal thyself" but a sense that people - at a low ebb or challenging circumstances around their health - feel they have what they need from both themselves, their colleagues, and the organisation's resources in a way they can enlist, enact, and enable for themselves. Clearly, where someone is lost or feels bereft of choice, there are healthcare professionals and experienced colleagues who can guide them but the idea that someone is helpless in their situation may simply serve to amplify the feelings of despair and damage they face.

It's like the Buurtzorg human-centred care model in their home-based nursing responsibilities. They do not administer medical care to a supposedly helpless patient, but they get to know the individual, their neighbours, friends and family and the patient's own sense of confidence in self-managed care that leads them to lead more positive and sustainable outcomes for their care and treatment.

So, wellbeing at work is not a consumed product or tokenistic service, it's a crucial part of the People Experience of any organisation. Not just "how do we motivate you to succeed" but how we can provide safety, surety, and support when you need it most.

We've gone some way to destigmatise work and our health from what was previously "sick absence management" to wellbeing and care. And at PTHR, we took the decision to go to a four-day operating week at the height of lost work during the 2020 pandemic impacts, so we've seen how much a punctuated, "Wellness Wednesday" becomes a meaningful enabler of self-derived care and attention to living a balanced life.

In summary: it's not about resilience and empowerment. It's about a shared sense of care, self-management of healthy living and working and a human-centred people experience that really counts when it matters most.

Our purpose in our work is not just to perform, it's to flourish.

In PwC's Global Workforce Hopes and Fears Survey 2022, 52,000 employees shared what they think about work[499]. PwC concluded that "meaning matters to employees". Employees want to be themselves at work, they want to find their job fulfilling and they want their team to care about their wellbeing. We have to create environments where we help our people to find and fulfil purpose, to pay back to society and support one another. We also have to take a stand on social and environmental issues as employers and find ways to link the purpose of the individual to our organisation. It's not often purpose is linked to wellbeing, but the pandemic experience brought about a change in attitudes that mean these links have only grown stronger.

The rise of conscious capitalism.

The pandemic changed a lot of our attitudes to various parts of our lives, including the way we view one another. In only a few short years, employees have gone through several generation defining events. Most employees at your company will be under the age of 40, and they are now officially the unluckiest generation in history in terms of economic growth[500]. They suffered the most during the 2008 recession, were most hit by the pandemic, and would be the hardest hit by the 2022 increases in the cost of living.

Unsurprisingly, the most recent research shows that 80 percent of young people in Britain attribute many problems to capitalism, and nearly 70 percent say they would prefer to live in a socialist society[501]. Since 2018, both the UK and the US have seen a sharp increase in that number[502]. According to numerous studies, most young people today are quite unsatisfied with important areas of our society, politics, and economy. New research from the Institute of Economic

Affairs (IEA) shows that 75 percent of young Brits now believe socialism is a "good concept" because of the pandemic[503].

Here, the unequal distribution of capitalism should be noted here, rather than necessarily the rejection of it. While those 40 years of age and older are still far more likely to hold socialist beliefs, there is a clear, developing, and long-term socially conscious trend that is capturing the hearts of young people. This defies the widely held belief that younger people lean left, and older people lean right on issues of politics. It also begins to hint at how the workplace must alter to keep up with the young and the generation that is currently in charge.

Globally, the concept of conscious capitalism is expanding. In fact, the phrases "purpose," "people," and "wellbeing" are included in practically every group report I read these days. More than 62 percent of consumers worldwide want the businesses they buy from to take a statement on social, cultural, environmental, and political problems[504]. Consumers' purchasing decisions are now influenced by an organisation's commitment to their people, the earth, and society.

Organisations are now focusing on the triple bottom line: financial, environmental, and social results. The most prosperous businesses are those that are most socially responsible. Growing corporate transparency and stakeholder influence means investors, board members, regulators and partners are all calling for more data to be shared on people, profit, planet, and purpose too. In 2021 a survey of 600 US investors found that 94 percent wanted to know details of employee wellbeing[505] – a significant shift in behaviour from those funding organisations.

The most advanced organisations now focus on fairness, equality and see wellbeing as critical for sustaining operations. Culture and the employee experience has moved to the front of these organisations. Creating more conscious and compassionate workplaces isn't actually a leftist, liberal idea anymore; it's the way the most successful organisations design employee experiences.

Your employees are the same people who are advocating for large-scale change to make our society more sustainable. Workers have made it clear that they want their businesses' environmental policies to be improved, and when they are, employee wellbeing improves too. Even simple sustainable behaviours like recycling can have a positive impact on mental health[506]. So, it's important that we consider these things in the ways we support employee wellbeing. Do we offer benefits that support more ethical and sustainable decisions? Do we help employees lead the lives we want by making sure we are including people in our workplace? Are we listening to employees when they tell us they are unhappy with decisions we make, or working in a way that matches their own values? Both consumers and employees want to see more conscious organisations, so if employers don't take these expectations seriously, they run the risk of irrelevancy.

Guest Expert View: Craig Turner

Founder, Confido Talent & Jobs for Good

Craig is an experienced recruitment professional and tech for good advocate. His personal mission is to inspire/connect as many people and businesses as possible to have a positive impact on the planet and society. Confido Talent partners with early-stage tech for good start-ups to hire across product and engineering. Jobs For Good is a job platform that allows mission-driven jobseekers to find verified "For Good" companies. He also hosts the Founders For Good podcast, interviewing Founders about their journey building high impact companies.

What we've seen in the last two decades is a shift from functional work, where the expectation of an employer is to pay you a good wage in return for your work. Career advancement was steady and employee loyalty was given lightly.

Now the relationship between employer and employee is much more complex. With the demand for talent far outstripping supply, companies are having to compete at unseen levels to attract and retain their talent.

In the last three to five years, we've witnessed this through salaries increasing substantially, interview processes becoming more streamlined, and candidate focused, plus greater investment in benefits, training, and personal development.

In the last two to three years the focus has shifted to the working environment, with the rise of remote, flexible and hybrid working. How employees are supported has become a much larger focus; how companies create a better work/life balance and support the different needs of their workforce.

Finally, the market has now reached a point where most companies are competing on these levels: good salaries, career progression, flexible working, good benefits packages. Naturally the focus now is on meaning and purpose derived from work. Does the person feel proud of what their company does? Does it align with their values? How responsible or sustainable are the company's practices?

Part of this shift is also due to the new wave of millennials and Gen Zs in business. They are actively looking for companies with a positive mission and responsible approach to running a business. Every study on millennials and Gen Z's and their motivators indicate they prioritise purpose and working for a responsible business over money.

So, the rise of purpose-driven workers is coming from both the newer generations entering the market with their priorities, as well as the current workforce seeing purpose as the biggest differentiator between companies.

I'd also add that founders and business leaders of purpose-driven companies are more likely to invest in their people and double down on their wellbeing. These are individuals heavily motivated to make a positive different to the planet and/or society. Naturally they are going to be more people-focused leaders that have progressive and well-defined people policies.

Look at companies like Beam, onHand, OLIO and allplants. These are organisations that have a clear purpose, strong company values, plus huge investment in their people – they care about running a responsible business. These are the companies winning out in the talent war. The gambling and betting companies, the management consultancies, the big banks, they are struggling to attract and retain talent.

Employers are driving purpose at work.

Employers are driving purpose at work – and that's improving wellbeing. This leads us to a new phenomenon: when we have presidents who are socially irresponsible, business leaders end up pushing corporate social responsibility further than they usually would[507]. Researchers studied the political donations of almost 1,000 CEOs between the mid 1990s and 2005, then overlaid this with data tracking the companies socially responsible initiatives. They found that under liberal presidents, socially responsible activities dropped by around 20 percent. It's suggested that when a president doesn't push the socially responsible agenda, CEOs are more likely to pick up the slack. When the state isn't acting in the way many think it should, businesses step in. There's a theme here...

When an employer can nurture purpose at work, either through the jobs people do or the actions the organisation takes, employee wellbeing improves. One study discovered that up to 40 percent of some workers satisfaction at work could be linked to their sense of purpose[508]. When an employee has a greater sense of purpose in their lives, it sets a foundation for a healthier and happier life. Finding our purpose is even associated with decreased mortality[509] and greater resilience to life's knocks[510].

Helping your people find their purpose can be far easier than we think. Building a positive work environment through connections with other employees can help your people to link their own personal beliefs with that of others. It can also create a support network that be used to uncover strengths and collaboration.

The evidence is clear that regardless of role of company, when an employee can find their purpose at work, its instrumental in our wellbeing. A lack of purpose if frequently a reason given by people as to why their mental health declines[511] and is also linked to lower risk of developing some common health conditions.

Even before the pandemic accelerated some of these views, employees were searching for organisations with more meaning. An early 2019 study found that nearly 40 percent of younger employees have chosen a job because of sustainability, and more than 70 percent say they are more likely to work at a company with a strong environmental agenda[512]. The pull is very strong. The idea that socially responsible employers can even pay lower wages while still attracting motivated people has some empirical evidence[513]. I believe that 2022 will be the year when businesses from all industries begin to integrate more socially responsible activities into their wellbeing strategies, employer brand and

EVPs – as scholars have demonstrated that the effort is worthwhile.

Community wellbeing and employee resilience.

Purpose also plays a part in how resilient we are to life. Purpose has been found to predict health and life longevity, suggesting it plays a part in how resilient we to life's challenges[514]. Employees with a purpose are better at managing stress and have better self-rated health status (SRH)[515]. Purpose can even lessen the chances of developing depression[516].

Many studies over the last few decades have shown various benefits on our individual wellbeing by having an increase level of social support at work:

- Better mental health
- Lowering cardiovascular risks, such as lowering blood pressure
- Improved self-esteem
- Improvement in our ability to handle stress
- Alleviating the effects of emotional distress
- Promoting healthy lifestyles

Research shows that when asked about what aspects of their roles that have the biggest impact on their wellbeing, employees frequently cite lack of social support[517]. But the community that we create at work can also have an impact on one of the most serious and growing areas of employee wellbeing- burnout. During the pandemic, burnout increased significantly. Across the board, American employees reported heightened rates of burnout with 79 percent of employees now reporting having had experienced it[518]. In the UK, The Global Burnout Study 2022 found that employee burnout has increased by over five percent in the last 12 months[519]. In tech, two in five workers show they are at a high risk or burnout this year with 62 percent saying they feel physically and emotionally drained[520].

Earlier in this book we covered limiting the causes of burnout, but for those organisations whose employees who are already struggling with it, burnout doesn't have to be commonplace in the modern workplace. The latest research and thinking shows that when we have increased social capital in our lives, our burnout reduces[521]. One study in Ecuador found that the general health of healthcare professionals correlated with social support[522]. In what is likely one of the largest studies into workplace burnout, social support mediated the negative effects of burnout. Similarly, research by the University of Birmingham in the UK concluded that "social support was found to be influential" on burnout[523].

Increased social support in the workplace has also been found to help nurses cope with stress[524], support counsellors to accomplish more at work[525], help students to burnout less[526] and within Caribbean police forces, co-worker support reduced stress[527]. A drum I'll keep banging in this book is how much our wellbeing is related to positive experiences with other people. Our evolution and mere existence rely on having strong emotional connections to others, and the workplace needs this as much as our home lives do. According to Gallup, just 2 in 10 employees strongly agree that they have a friend at work. Yet Gallup found that if that ratio could move to six in ten, organisations would see 36 percent fewer safety incidents[528]. As well as an improvement in overall wellbeing and a reduction in health and safety incidents, having a friend at work makes work more enjoyable for almost 60 percent of workers[529].

The role for the employer here is to consider the ways they can create a better, tighter community of employees. It can be very hard for adults to open up and be vulnerable with each other but when that happens the benefits for all parties are considerable. When teams work closer together, open up and talk more often about their lives, it transforms cultures from one where individuals struggle alone, to one where they are more likely to ask for help or say, 'I don't know'. Which makes them collaborate more, problem solve together, take risks, and produce better results. They look after one another.

The reason why community at work has such a profound impact on our wellbeing and resilience is mostly to do with having a confidant we can talk to. Being able to talk to someone after a stressful incident and having someone who can listen to our worries is very important. More than half of employees say having a friend at work gives them someone to talk to about their health issues, conflict at work and even their financial issues[530].

Chapter 11
Employee Recognition

Consistently through the literature, employee recognition emerges as one of the most important components of a great experience at work. In fact, in many studies it has emerged as the number one reason why people quit their jobs[531]. Yet recognition plays a significant part in our health and happiness too.

When I look at recognition schemes through the eyes of a psychologist, I frequently conclude that they are wellbeing initiatives. When we get recognised by a colleague for something we've done, it shows us we are valued, and we are seen. As children, we need to feel valued so that we develop our sense of self. As adults, we still thrive on this kind of feedback. This reinforcement of positive self-worth and the validation we get from positive mirroring helps us to feel good about ourselves. But recognition also gives us a deep sense of meaning in our lives. When we have meaning in our lives, we flourish; when we don't have meaning, we flounder. That makes recognition a *large* contributor to positive mental health.

Building closer bonds with other people is a core survival mechanism for us humans. As I outlined in the preface for this book, we only have to look back to the tribe and fire history of human life on earth to see how much we've always needed other people. Gratitude plays a huge part in that. Giving thanks and expressing appreciation have been revered in many cultures around the world for thousands of years. Even in ancient Rome, lawyer, scholar, and statesman Marcus Tullius Cicero famously said that gratitude was not only the greatest of all virtues, but the 'mother' of all of human feelings; it is a core human emotion.

Native Americans have always had a deep tradition of routinely giving thanks. The Ottawas, who live in the northern regions of the Lower Peninsula of Michigan, have regular feast days and ghost suppers going back hundreds of years to show gratitude for the people and the harvest. In these indigenous groups, wealth is defined not my material goods, but the idea that the wealthy are those who give and share with others. Gratitude is espoused daily among these communities because they understand how important it is to the strength of their community.

In 2022, human nature hasn't much changed. Finding ways to work closer together is part of our survival as a race. But it's also shown to be an incredibly important part of building a successful business. Yet the latest research in 2022 reveals that fewer than one in four workers say their recognition needs are being fulfilled and this is now a big predictor of an employee intending to quit[532]. Gallup found that the more recognition someone says they get, the lower their intention is to be looking for a new role.

The pandemic fuelled the need for more recognition at work.

A global theme of the Coronavirus pandemic was appreciation. Millions thanked key and healthcare workers for their help in getting us the goods and services we needed while the world shut down. Social media was full of stories of neighbours helping each other, strangers supporting one another and of organisations thanking their employees.

A YouGov study looking at the appreciation key workers felt from their employers before and during the Covid-19 pandemic shows us the impact recognition can have[533]. Before the pandemic, just 29 percent of logistic and retail workers said they were appreciated, alongside 44 percent of healthcare workers. However, during the pandemic these figures almost doubled. Because of the additional appreciation the pandemic brought upon these workers, between 36 percent and 50 percent say they feel their organisations have changed for the better in the long-term.

I've written a lot about what impact the long-lasting effects the pandemic will have on the mental health of employees, and how lack of investment in supporting employee wellbeing – over the next five years especially – will cause huge problems for organisations. Whatever your reason for implementing or considering a recognition scheme, I urge all employers to double down on their recognition efforts during this time. It's been an incredibly challenging and taxing time for your people, and they need to know they are appreciated and valued now, more than any point in their careers.

The neuroscience of recognition.

When we express gratitude for something or receive thanks, our brain releases dopamine and serotonin – two important neurotransmitters that regulate our emotions – which makes us feel good. By regularly feeling grateful and expressing thanks to others, we can help these neural pathways to strengthen and eventually automate. The more often a neural pathway is activated, the less effort it takes to stimulate the same pathway next time. Eventually, expressing gratitude becomes even stronger and more important to us.

The part of the brain that is responsible for all our emotional experiences is called the limbic system. It's made up of the thalamus, hypothalamus, amygdala, hippocampus, and cingulate gyrus. Studies have shown that it's the hippocampus and the amygdala (the main areas that regulate our memory and emotions), that light up when we feel grateful. So, we can see that giving or receiving small gestures of thanks and kindness activates the hypothalamus and subsequently impacts all our bodily functions that are controlled by the it – including one of the most important areas of our overall wellbeing - sleep.

Several studies looking at gratitude and appreciation have found that, when feeling grateful, people show a marked reduction in levels of cortisol - the stress hormone. Research has shown that grateful people often have better cardiac functioning and are more resilient to stress. This now starts to illustrate how important gratitude at work can be to things like employee performance too.

Fig. 7. The impact of recognition on organisational culture and wellbeing, Benefex (2020)

We can see in this image exactly how neuroscience plays a part in creating the right environment for employees to blossom. Expressing gratitude at work becomes a proactive driver towards building close bonds and fostering psychological safety and togetherness with our colleagues.

Studies have shown that when students express gratitude to parents, teachers, or coaches, they feel closer and more connected to them. Expressing gratitude to the people we work with strengthens our social bonds. By doing so, we increase the sense of community wellbeing, which encourages us to take on bigger challenges in our lives and at work. This becomes hugely important for one of the most vital areas of the employee experience: psychological safety. You're probably familiar with Google's large experiment that looked at what made a successful, high-performing team. Project Aristotle found that psychological safety – more than anything else – was critical to making a teamwork.

When employees practice gratitude and thanks at work, they become more likely to take on new assignments, more willing to go the extra mile and more likely to work as part of a well-functioning team. Research shows us that gratitude at work leads to less exhaustion, higher job satisfaction, fewer absences due to illness and generally more proactive and positive behaviours. So, giving and receiving recognition within in a team, builds those important social bonds and increased connectedness that is so important to team success.

Positive psychology and employee recognition.

In positive psychology research, gratitude is strongly and very consistently associated with greater happiness. Practicing regular gratitude helps people to feel more positive emotions. Psychologists have found that when we express gratitude, it gives us the ability to override negative thoughts and wash away our concerns and stress[534]. A recent Korean study found that appreciation and positive mental health correlate.

We know that our lives need a lot more positive interactions than negative, just to counter the negative ones. When we take time to consider the help other people give us and recognise and appreciate them, the evidence shows that we ourselves benefit[535]. Our joy increases, our life satisfaction improves. Not only do those who regularly appreciate others display more positive behaviours, empathy, and generosity, but they also feel happier themselves.

Numerous studies have found a link between emotional reactivity and an increased risk of heart disease. A physical stress reaction and the production of stress hormones are linked to negative emotions, raising blood pressure and heart rate. According to research optimistic people are less prone to undergo this stress response. Stress can harm the cardiovascular system, but people who tend to see the positive side of bad situations can prevent this from happening as much. Recognition breeds positivity and optimism.

Expressing gratitude and feeling appreciated are both incredibly important parts of mental health. They underpin our social self-perceptions, our self-actualisation and our value as humans *and* the work we do. Gratitude and appreciation reinforce our self-belief and our feelings of competence, which is why it's not surprising to see that recognition enhances productivity and performance too.

Employee Recognition and mental health.

In the midst of the pandemic, a study published in Frontiers in Psychology, found that something called 'The Anxiety-Buffer Hypothesis' was protecting people from developing poor mental health[536]. The hypothesis states that levels of self-esteem can act as a shield against threats to our mental health. This is where employee recognition can have a positive impact on worker mental health, and we have the evidence to prove this. When employees receive adequate recognition at work, their mental health improves[537]. But conversely, underappreciated employees are more like to suffer from poor wellbeing. One 2022 study found that employees who weren't recognised adequately at work were twice as likely to experience poor mental health[538]. The positive, pro-social behaviours that recognition schemes promote are helping employees to build better resilience to poor mental health in the workplace.

A lack of this positive, social interaction is harming employee mental health. A study of 20,000 American employees found that only half have meaningful personal interactions with people on a daily basis[539]. A lack of recognition at work is a predictor of higher levels of loneliness[540], and as we've discovered in this chapter, being recognised is one of our very basic human needs. When our employees experience a lack of recognition at work, they have fewer of those moments that connect them to other people.

The American Psychological Association concludes that feeling valued at work is directly linked to wellbeing[541]. Their research has found that employees who feel valued and appreciated are more likely to report better physical and mental health. When an organisation curates a culture that exudes gratitude and appreciation, it becomes one that is putting the wellbeing of its people at its very core.

Guest Expert View: Kevin Monroe
Global Gratitude Ambassador

Kevin Monroe envisions our world touched and transformed by gratitude — by the power of gratitude, the experience and expression of gratitude. He believes gratitude experienced is better than gratitude explained. And that gratitude is best experienced in community.

To that end, he creates environments, hosts encounters, and curate's experiences allowing people to explore, express, and experience gratitude. His most recent gratitude innovation is the I'M GRATEFUL FOR YOU Movement that is transforming workplaces, communities, and congregations around the world.

Employee recognition and appreciation are in important enough priority that most companies formalize programs to ensure recognition and appreciation happen consistently.

Formal recognition matters! Yet, when recognition and appreciation programs only recognize service anniversaries or performance achievements, they miss a myriad of opportunities to recognize people for their contributions and commitment to the organization.

In recent months, millions of workers across the globe have left jobs, companies, or managers. And many of those exiting employees, cited not feeling recognized, appreciated, or valued as a contributing factor for their decisions to leave.

Disconnects abound

Leaders feel they make significant investments in recognition and reward systems. Obviously, that allows many leaders to conclude "we're doing a good job recognizing our people."

Yet, survey after survey shows many workers feeling overlooked, unappreciated, and undervalued.

Workers wonder:
- Do I matter?
- Am I valued for my contributions?
- Are my gifts, talents, and abilities appreciated here?
- Does anyone see the work I do? The effort I make?

I am intrigued by the disconnect between leaders and workers. Rather than debating why the disconnect exists, let's bridge the gap! Gratitude is one of the most effective ways to bridge those gaps!

BC (a time that seems so long ago — Before Covid!), gratitude seemed optional. For many people, gratitude seemed a "nice-to-have", an add-on or upgrade for those 'perky people' - you know, the ones choosing to adopt a positive outlook or embracing growth mindsets.

However, as we move beyond Covid into the now and next that are emerging, both for the world at-large and, specifically, the world of work, gratitude is an essential skill needed to flourish. This gratitude-fueled flourishing applies to all aspects of life, work, community, and family.

Saying thanks can be transactional

Expressing gratitude is transformational! Let me illustrate. Think back to interactions you've had, either in the giving or receiving of thanks. Many of us are programmed to express thanks as part of good manners or civil interactions. Someone did something for you and your natural response is to say "thanks."

It happens daily in coffee shops, tea houses, and check out counters around the world. A customer places an order. A barista or clerk completes the order and hands the item ordered to the customer. The customer, often without looking up from their phone, mutters something that sounds like thanks or thank you. To which, the worker responds with "no problem" or possibly even says, "you're welcome."

THAT'S TRANSACTIONAL!

Transactions like that happen millions of times each day around the world. What's the impact of transactions like that? Yes, it's proper to extend courtesies and remember your manners. Do transactions like that change anything? I don't think so! Do they happen in workplaces around the world? YIKES! Way more than many of us care to count. Imagine this happening instead:

The barista or clerk completes the transaction and delivers the coffee, tea, biscuit, bagel, or other merchandise.

As they do, you pause everything else you are doing and take a moment to see the other person. You make eye contact with them. Perhaps you see their nametag and call them by name and express gratitude for them — as a person and for the love and care with which they completed your order. At that moment, you share an *encounter*. You connected person-to-person with the humanity of another and valued them for their contribution. YOU EXPRESSED GRATITUDE! Expressing gratitude is transformational!

SIMPLE + SINCERE = SIGNIFICANT

Simple is best! Especially when it comes to expressing gratitude. A simple and sincere expression of gratitude is significant. The impact goes deep and lingers. Expressing gratitude takes several forms. There's no one-size-fits-all.

When you NOTICE someone making either a valiant effort or a valuable contribution, what if you PAUSED in the moment and EXPRESSED gratitude TO THEM and FOR THEM?

NOTICE | PAUSE | EXPRESS is a simple approach to expressing gratitude.

You can take a moment and verbalize your gratitude; you can write a note, send a message, give a shout out on a recognition app, Slack or Teams. Maybe you use one of our

I'M GRATEFUL FOR YOU Cards. These cards contain four words on the front of the card and room on the back for a short note.

It's powerful to express gratitude FOR YOU as a person. To elevate and celebrate a person for their gifts, talents, or abilities. For their commitment, character…and yes, also for their contributions. Perhaps you send a short message - voice or text. I've discovered that meaningful messages often get saved, replayed, and even shared. There is something profoundly powerful about the human voice and hearing gratitude expressed.

A few tips for making the most of expressing gratitude: Be specific. Make it personal.

Express gratitude for who they are not just the work they do or the tasks they perform. Highlight their unique contributions to your team and project. The gifts, talents, and abilities they invest into the work they do. And yes, be sure to use the formal recognition platforms and portals provided by your company…remember to infuse your submissions with gratitude. Gratitude changes everything! Especially employee appreciation and recognition.

Chapter 12

The Role of Communications in Employee Wellbeing

Almost three quarters of employees report effective communications are a driving factor in workplace culture, morale, and mental health[542]. The way managers communicate with their team plays a big role in employee psychological wellbeing[543]. When we communicate our vision and policies clearly at work, they improve feelings of being supported and included[544]. But the challenge here I think, is that too often we are focused on the messages we want to send, and not the *way* we want them to be received.

One of the most successful adverts of all time didn't feature the product it was trying to sell at all. Cadbury's Daily Milk 'Drumming Gorilla' advert was once named the best advert yet didn't feature chocolate or a chocolate bar at all. Lauded by advertising experts for almost 20 years, the advert tells us the importance of communications. In the Cadbury's example, the advert was designed entirely to make sure you didn't forget the brand, so the next time you thought about chocolate, you thought about Cadbury's. I think this same thinking needs to be applied to our wellbeing communications.

While nearly all organisations say they communicated with their employees more about wellbeing in 2020 than they did in 2019, the data tells us that many employees still don't know what is on offer in their organisation. Gartner's 2020 Wellbeing Benchmarking Survey found that while almost every organisation (96 percent) offered emotional wellbeing programs, less than half of employees knew their employer offered them[545]. There is clearly a problem with the way many communicate wellbeing within their organisations.

Cutting through the noise.

Traditionally, email has been used as the main, and often only way organisations communicate employee wellbeing. Yet it has been estimated that the average office worker receives more than 100 emails a day and a lot of those get deleted without even being read[546]. So we must start to think more carefully not about how we *think* we should communicate, but how our people *want* to be communicated with. While some will prefer an email update, others may be more engaged in a collaboration tool like Teams or Slack, so how can we enable an employee to tell us how they want our communication?

Communications will be a driving force behind your wellbeing strategy. However, with so many ways of being communicated to and so many different organisations vying for our attention, finding out the best way to communicate with your employees can be very challenging. A useful exercise I discovered on www.strategiccoach.co.uk was to ask yourself and those around you at work a few simple questions:

1. How do you like to give information out at work?
2. How do you prefer to receive information at work?
3. What is the best time for your employer to communicate to you?
4. When you're stressed or under pressure, what do you need?

Just reflecting on these questions for yourself, you might be surprised at the different ways you answer. For me, it became apparent that while I like the "throw it out and its done" aspect of email for sending out information, I'd actually prefer to receive my wellbeing communications on Teams. Mostly because I tend to use my email inbox as a 'to do' list, so don't want emails clogging it up. You could even formalise this exercise even more and ask a working group of employees to give you their thoughts. The answers to these questions will no doubt reveal how different employees in different roles prefer to be communicated to. For example, drivers may not like having notifications or text messages and shift workers may not want any communications sent to them while they are away from work.

Finally, the last question is an interesting one. We know from everything we've read in this book so far that most employees are under pressure. Knowing the best way to communicate to someone when they are feeling this way is important, especially because our wellbeing communications may be able to help them. So rather than them frustratingly deleting our emails without even looking at them, how do we reach people when they really need help, or when they are pre-occupied? How can our communications provide reassurance to an employee that is feeling under pressure? If I read the Teams message on a bad day, how might just reading it make me feel more supported at work?

We also need to give careful thought to how we construct the communications we issue. A study by Nielsen Norman Group[547] found that people only tend to read around 20 percent of the content on any given page, and that page viewing time doesn't really change regardless of how many words exist. So whatever way we are communicating, are we ensuring we are getting to the point as quickly as possible? Here are some of the best tips I've heard from employers:

- **Make the message easy to consume**

  Employees are dealing with daily information overload, so how can we cut through that noise and not add to it? If people will only read 20 percent of your email, how can we fit the main messages and calls to action within the first few lines? Say only what is necessary.

- **Provide information at the right time**

  How are we allowing employees to customise how we communicate with them? Can they decide if they want wellbeing communications via an app notification, via Teams or over email? Can they turn off notifications and can they personalise what they want to hear about? For example, if an employee is really interested in improving their mental health, can they just hear about that from us? Can a deskless employee opt out of any communications that will require them to login to an onsite system? Content irrelevancy is a huge barrier to getting our people engaged in wellbeing. If you're sending parent and baby wellbeing tips to a childless employee, you'll disengage them.

- **Use varying methods**

  Different employees will appreciate different ways of being communicated with. Allow them to subscribe to newsletters, join a Teams team, follow a Slack channel, turn on notifications, join a WhatsApp group – whatever way they want to be communicated with, try to meet them there.

- **Consider the physical barriers to communication**

  Remote workers, deskless workers, various locations etc all add physical barriers to how we communicate with our people. This has led to digital communication methods becoming the fastest and easiest ways to communicate wellbeing within an organisation.

- **Be a credible voice**

  Among the vast array of ways we are communicated to on a regular basis includes lots of 'fake news' and 'clickbait' content. Think about how you can become a credible voice for your people. How can they trust what communications you issue, so that they are more likely to engage in them?

Changing media consumption.

Something for every employer to be aware of is that the very nature of the pandemic and associated lockdowns meant that we started to consume more media and communications than ever before. Both inside and outside of work, employees absorbed a lot of information in a very short time. An assessment of internet users across the UK and the US revealed some surprising changes in our attitudes to media and communications[548].

Of those under the age of 23, more than half said the pandemic made them consume more online videos more than ever before. The under 37-year-old group also confirmed that they now consumer more online videos than ever before. Overall, 80 percent of people now say they consume more content since the start of the pandemic. Most of us got used to the fact we needed to keep up with changing rules, media updates, the need to improve our health literacy etc., so these habits we formed over the pandemic years are going to be hard to shake. Employees want and need more information from a trusted source. But that became a problem; we don't trust many people to give us the right information.

Just 61 percent say they trusted the information coming from the World Health Organization (WHO) during the pandemic. This figure drops way below 50 percent of people when we look at news channels, local health authorities, news websites, radio, podcasts, and scientific articles[549]. But across the world in 2022, 77 percent of people say their *employer* is the most trusted institution in their lives[550]. Far above Governments and media, more people trust their employer than ever before. This will play a huge part in how we successfully communicate wellbeing at work.

Employer communications that drive wellbeing behaviour change.

As detailed at the start of this book, I believe (to an extent) employers have the ability to positively impact the wellbeing of their people through the encouragement of healthier lifestyles. Evidence shows that modifiable health behaviours contribute to around 40 percent of deaths[551]. Research has found an inverse relationship between the risk of all-cause mortality and the number of healthy lifestyle behaviours a patient follows. That is to say that a large portion of our poor health behaviours can be changed to create better outcomes. We just need to think about how we communicate wellbeing in different way.

Part of the reason why health behaviour change is so difficult for many employees is that the factors needed to adapt behaviour aren't always aligned. Generally speaking, we need the skills to better perform a behaviour, a strong intention to change, and the removal of any environmental constraints. I believe the way we communicate the support we offer our people can help us to help our people to identify those skills and build the intention to change.

When we look at behavioural science, there are a number of obvious and relatively straightforward ways organisations can use this insight to help to support their people (based on those designed by Abraham, Kelly, West and Michie, 2009):

- Improve knowledge about the consequences of employee behaviour (or lack of change)
- Personal relevance – drawing attention to how that change will benefit the individual and their specific needs/desires
- A more positive attitude to wellbeing and the removal of stigmas
- Improving self-efficacy – increasing an employee's belief that they can change their behaviours.

Broadly speaking, the social sciences refer to the above as three high level influences on behaviour – Capability, Opportunity, and Motivation Behaviour model (COM-B). When we understand what these factors are, we can better design wellbeing communication strategies that focus on real behaviour change.

Characterising and designing health behaviour change communications

When we reflect on poor wellbeing habits like overspending or eating a poor diet, what we are usually trying to do is change an employee's emotional connection with something (which is usually entrenched in their upbringing, societal influence, and prior wellbeing experience). When thinking about wellbeing communications, there are broadly nine common behaviour change interventions that we know from extensive research and practice that help people to change their health behaviours: education, persuasion, incentivisation, coercion, training, restriction, environmental restructuring, modelling, and enablement. If we take one area of wellbeing like financial wellbeing (the area that is of most concern to employees in 2022), we can start to understand how we, as employers, can facilitate behaviour change through communications.

1. Changing the usually negative emotions and associations we have with money. How can our communications make money appear more positive? How can we show that employees are at the start of a journey to a better financial future, rather than always focussing on debt and worry?

2. Informing employees of the consequences of inaction/lack of change. While traditionally health behaviour change has tried to threaten or worry people into change (like warning signs and distressing images on cigarette packets, which have often failed to stop people from smoking), how can our communications show people a better future? A future where giving up smoking frees up money for example.

3. Changing the context of money and the impact on the individual – it becomes a tool to achieve our desires in life, rather than something to be afraid of. Saving becomes a life goal, rather than just a pile of money. There is evidence that this approach is effective. Savers have been found to save as much as 73 percent more when they do things like attach images of what they are saving for to their savings accounts[552].

4. Modelling through leadership is how we give our people the permission to talk about their financial wellbeing and admit when there is a problem. Can our communications feature senior leaders talking about taboo issues like money? Can a high earning senior leader talk about a time they struggled with money and give hope to those that are challenged?

Behaviour change and retirement planning.

For context, if we look at one common behaviour change an employer might want to encourage – like increasing retirement provision – we can see how this understanding of behaviour can help.

Although pension scheme membership has been growing in places like the UK, the average level of savings is falling. So, while the retirement savings message appears to be getting through to employees, awareness of how much will be needed, and the options available, are not. This is partly due to the prevailing idea that "because I've been auto-enrolled, my employer is paying in and that's enough". We can also see that a bias towards spending on "the things I want and need today" is overshadowing employee's retirement planning. And lastly, it seems employees are 'put off' by the negativity and perceived complexity of pensions in the UK. So, with all this in mind, we begin to understand some of the barriers to improving this specific wellbeing challenge. So how do employers encourage their people to improve their retirement savings?

Improving employee knowledge of pensions in such a way that people see and understand the incentives has been shown to improve retirement planning. A combination of our own contributions, tax relief, investment growth, pension credits etc. show us the much wider impact of each £1 saved into a pension. Illustrating this payback can begin to incentivise saving and lessen the feeling of 'giving up' money today[553]. Delivering communications that show employees how much they will make and how much they need, significantly increases engagement in pensions, according to research by the Cabinet Office and its Behavioural Insights team[554].

Through the communications, imagery, and language we use, we can also begin to make retirement savings vivid and exciting and change the context of what retirement means to employees. The Retirement Living Standards offer people the education and awareness to see retirement in three simple ways – minimum, moderate, and comfortable, thereby illustrating the kind of lifestyle varying levels of income will offer[555]. This way, employees stop seeing numbers they can't grasp, and instead visualise a lifestyle with specific details around their ability to do certain things like eat out and go on holiday while retired. This frames pensions as more about the kind of life you what to lead as you get older, rather than how much money you have. It changes the context of a pension.

This same thinking can be applied to any wellbeing benefit you offer. When you begin to think about how you position benefits under those three influences on behaviour – Capability, Opportunity, and Motivation Behaviour (COM-B)

– you start to consider what you expect an employee to change as a result of being offered certain employee benefits.

Here are my three tips to enhance your wellbeing communications:

1. Focus on one behaviour change at a time with small, attainable goals

Showing your people they need to fix all these different health behaviours at once is too overwhelming. Behaviour change requires deliberation, action, and maintenance. It's difficult for staff to focus on physical exercise, mental health and clearing debt all at once. So, communicate in a way that focuses on one area of wellbeing at a time throughout the year.

2. Identify the motivation

Our motivations are important predictors of our behaviour. Without a strong personal motivation, employees may never make the right changes. Our motivations are closely linked to our core beliefs as humans, so when we think about providing a safe place for us and our family, that goal to buy a first home becomes much more of a motivator than just 'saving for the future'. The words you use in your communications matters.

3. Knowledge is a key predictor of behaviour change

In almost every theory of health behaviour change I've read, knowledge is either a key predictor of, or a precursor to, change. How can you better educate employees on the wellbeing paybacks of using a tool, choosing a benefit, or downloading an app?

Understanding behavioural science can seem like a hazy route to take when focusing on wellbeing communications. But in understanding the psychological, biological, and social influences on behaviour, you can take practical measures today that will help improve your employees' wellbeing through the way you communicate with them.

Staying connected.

A challenge for almost every employer that was acerbated by the pandemic was our ability to stay connected to our people. While this was far easier when most of your people worked from a few locations, home and remote working has given us a much bigger challenge and that is how do we stay connected to so many people at once?

Historically it has been easier for those employees working from one location to stay well informed. For those who work remotely or at home, it's common for them to miss messages and feel left out. Reaching every employee in a way that works for them is going to be impossible for every organisation to do, but there are a few tips I've learned from employers that might get you as close as possible to that:

1. **Create a dedicated space for wellbeing communications**

   Creating a dedicated place online for wellbeing means that wherever and however an employee works, they can access the latest information from you. At home, at work, on the move, day, or night. But it must be accessible outside of work and multiple devices.

2. **Find a platform that works for you and your people**

   You have a lot of tech options for collaboration these days but committing to one single tool as your 'home' for wellbeing will make it easier for employees to get your messages and find out more information. While the way you advertise getting to this place may change based on employee preference, using consistent technology will help to ensure your messages get through. For example, it's not good practice to email a wellbeing newsletter, then just copy and paste the same information onto a Slack, Yammer, and Teams channels. So created a dedicated space.

Consistency is one of the best ways to ensure we are communicating effectively with our people, wherever they work. Whether that is a similar format, a dedicated brand or look and feel, a specific channel or the timing of your wellbeing communications, consistency will breed *familiarity*. Consistency helps us to build certainty and humans crave that. Being consistent in your wellbeing communications will help to build the trust that we know is so important when trying to get employees to improve their wellbeing at work.

Guest Expert View: Louise Nixon

Psychologist & Digital Wellbeing Manager, Benefex

With a keen interest in the interplay between mental health, physical health and technology, Louise has conducted research with Dublin City University on Fitbits, with Trinity College Dublin on engagement in digital health interventions, and with Maastricht University in the Netherlands on the effects of online interventions on wellbeing. She is extremely passionate about discovering novel ways to enhance and promote the wellbeing of

individuals. Louise regularly attends international wellbeing
events as a keynote speaker and panellist to share her
knowledge and expertise. A strong believer in practicing
what she preaches, Louise enjoys spending her spare time on
hikes with her sisters, cycling, and travelling.

The role of internal communications in employee wellbeing must not be underestimated. Whether through a staff survey, team huddle, or one-on-one check-in, internal communications help employers to better understand the wellbeing of employees at a given point in time. But how exactly do these communications support and promote wellbeing in an organisation?

First, an effective communication strategy in the workplace promotes transparency and builds trust. Employees like to know what is happening within their organisation and so it is vital that employers have active communication channels that reach all their employees. Through sharing information with employees, this transparency ensures that everyone is on the same page and understands the goals and visions of the company, thus creating a trusting environment that enhances employee wellbeing.

Second, adequate communication within an organisation contributes to reducing the stigma associated with mental health issues. By actively communicating and promoting health and wellbeing initiatives among employees, employers are demonstrating that they acknowledge these concerns for their employees and do not see wellbeing as just a 'tick the box' concept. Mental health issues remain a hushed topic within many organisations; it is, therefore, a powerful message for employees to work alongside leaders who are open to discussing these issues and providing support where needed. This recognition of the importance of open communication around sensitive topics such as mental health issues helps to reduce the stigma and boost the mental wellbeing of employees at all levels of the business.

Third, effective communications enhance employees' innovation and creativity. When communication and information flow freely and openly between colleagues, it inspires efforts to collaborate, promotes knowledge-sharing, and provides employees access to one another's skillsets, thereby promoting common goals as well as a more mutually supportive, healthier, and happier working environment. Introducing an internal social media platform allows employees to connect - wherever and whenever they may be working. Encouraging this type of communication enables employees to ask questions and share ideas. Innovation does not always come from the top and such social media platforms give everyone in the organisation their chance to speak up, creating an inclusive culture that improves the wellbeing of all staff.

Finally, communications play a key role in preventing burnout among staff. While research has shown that productivity increases with remote working, this growth in productivity combined with a lack of social interactions can lead to burnout. Internal communications help to prevent burnout by clearly communicating work boundaries, creating space for check-ins, and enhancing the clarity of messaging and delegation so that individuals aren't overwhelmed with tasks. When working remotely, many employees can forget to step away from their workspaces and take a break. This is when good dialogue between managers and employees makes all the difference in reducing burnout and improving wellbeing.

When it comes to the wellbeing of employees, communications are crucial. From the relationships employees have with their colleagues and their sense of value and worth to their levels of involvement and motivation – communication is at the heart of it all.

Chapter 13

The Wellbeing Progress Index

As wellbeing at work was climbing up the corporate agenda in late 2019, by the time the pandemic took hold in early 2020, it became a number one priority. For millions, it was one of the most challenging times of their lives. So, unsurprisingly, this significantly impacted what an employee now expects from the workplace.

Across every country, the pandemic fuelled major shifts in attitudes, attention and budgets allocated to employee wellbeing. Our research at Benefex highlighted just how significant these changes were:

- 71 percent of global HR leaders now say wellbeing is "very important" to their business
- 99 percent of global HR leaders told us wellbeing is their top priority
- The top eight global benefits chosen in 2021 were all wellbeing benefits

But there was one stat that came out of our research in 2021 that I think is the most compelling; 92 percent of employees around the world told us that a commitment to employee wellbeing is the number one priority when choosing a new role. I think this is huge! Employees are now seeking out employers that take care of their wellbeing, and they are looking for that *before* they think about salary. But with these changing attitudes and an explosion of new wellbeing tools and benefits came another new problem – how do we measure success in this new world? One where wellbeing covers so much of what we do, and is no longer just a collection of things we've bought?

Increasingly employers were coming to me in 2022 to ask, "what does good look like?", "am I doing the right things?", "how do I compare to other employers?", "is what I'm doing working?". Measuring wellbeing has long been a challenge for policymakers and wellbeing experts. At present, the evidence on ways to effectively measure wellbeing is lacking. Globally, significant objections still exist over the validity of some of the most common ways to measure individual wellbeing. There is also no universally agreed framework for measuring wellbeing, and modern measures are rare. A study of 42 different measures of wellbeing found "considerable disagreement regarding how to properly understand and measure wellbeing"[556]. A separate study looking at 99 different measures of wellbeing found that most were developed between 1990 and 1999, and the authors were rarely explicit about what theories or evidence influenced their design[557].

Another challenge when measuring wellbeing is that the wellbeing market has evolved to treat the symptoms of poor wellbeing at work rather than their cause. What causes poor wellbeing at work includes exclusion, poor communication and management practices, limited autonomy, lack of control, inflexible working, low levels of employee support, unclear objectives, workload, physical risk, bullying, lack of positive emotions associated with work, recognising, and rewarding the contribution your people make, conflict between home and work commitments, fairness and justice at work, economic insecurity – all the things we have summarised in this book. However, it's very rare that any metric surfaced by a common wellbeing tool measures any of these. Most interventions measure their success by taking a snapshot of an employee's wellbeing at a point in time. This can sometimes work for a mental health app – it can show you that someone's self-reported wellbeing is higher *after* they've used the app for a period. But commonly, wellbeing tech tends to use traditional measures of engagement to mark success, which can be problematic.

For example, if a mental health platform gets 89 percent of employees logging into it every month, does it tell us any real measure of success? We have no idea what they were looking at, what was compelling, what wasn't, and most importantly, how the individual's wellbeing was made better because of the platform. For psychologists, wellbeing is about how people experience their lives, not the objective facts of their lives. Just because an employee has a high salary and a lot of savings, it doesn't mean they aren't suffering financial distress. Just because someone isn't using your mindfulness tool doesn't mean they aren't managing stress well. This leads us back to the economic principle of 'revealed preference'. Remember, this theory states that an individual's informed choice is the best criterion for judging their welfare. Thinking like this means we take a starting point of admitting that each employee will have a preference over fundamental aspects of their own wellbeing. This is a 'subjective measure' – asking employees what they need and how they feel. And I think subjective measures should eclipse the traditional objective measures of wellbeing at work.

Objective v subjective measures of wellbeing.

As we discussed earlier in this book, I think objective measures of wellbeing at work have become somewhat problematic. They tend to examine observable factors that affect someone's wellbeing. What do the traditional objective measures mean when it comes to wellbeing at work? Absence rates are underreported and commonly inaccurate. Does the absence of a diagnosed mental or physical health condition tell us that nothing is wrong with that person's wellbeing?

When we look at what the research says impacts our wellbeing, we start to see a lot of factors – many of which we just can't measure at the moment. But what we can do is follow the evidence that says what an *employer does* that has an impact on wellbeing. Everything you have read so far in this book has been based on almost 600 studies and research projects that illustrate the main things we know help, or hinder, employee wellbeing at work. So, I think that that is more important for us to measure – are organisations doing the right things when it comes to what the evidence says has a positive impact on people's wellbeing at work? We use the Wellbeing Progress Index to measure what goes in (the employer actions and contributions – or lack of them) and use subjective measures to look at what comes out (asking employees). More on what that is and how it works below.

Making sure what you have in place counts.

Can we gauge success by measuring the employer inputs first and then asking their people how they feel about the way the organisation supports them? To me, this seems far easier to do and fits nicely into the subjective ways you already ask your people how they are doing. By measuring what is going in – i.e., what the employer is doing – we can ensure that with the best endeavours, the employer is fulfilling a duty of care and, in many cases exceeding it. With so many things influencing wellbeing, limiting the way we measure wellbeing by input rather than output, I think, is quite interesting. So at Benefex, after years of research and development, we built the Wellbeing Progress Index.

When designing the Wellbeing Progress Index, we asked ourselves a few questions:

- Can we ensure that work is a positive force in people's lives and doesn't contribute to poor wellbeing?
- Can we create a benchmark to give employers an idea of what the best support looks like?
- How can we present an evidence-based view of workplace wellbeing?
- Should we take a combined view of benefits, policy, communications, leadership, diversity etc.?
- Can we track progress over time – as wellbeing is very much a work in progress!
- Can a company like Benefex show its customers where we can help them and show them historically how our support has improved things for them?

This book was written to accompany the Wellbeing Progress Index. The index is one of the first of its kind – one that has so much evidence behind it, it has a book that acts like its operating manual. It is designed to give employers a set of evidence-based questions that will produce an *employer* wellbeing score. This will enable employers to finally benchmark their approach to wellbeing that covers holistically the varied ways wellbeing is enhanced or harmed by the organisation - or by the organisation's lack of action. Employers can see how they compare to their competitors, similar organisations, organisations of the same size, employers in the same region etc. It will also give them a category breakdown, so an employer can find exactly what areas of the organisation, or what pillars of wellbeing they are over, or underperforming in.

Fig. 8. Early mock-up of the Wellbeing Progress Index, Benefex (2022)

The index is driven by academic evidence. It will evolve as that evidence evolves, and for the first time, you will be able to not only benchmark your approach to employee wellbeing, but you'll have a clear roadmap for improvement. Across employee benefits, company policy, leadership, communications, third-party tools, and apps, you'll be able to see exactly what you need to do you get ahead of these new and critical employee wellbeing expectations from an unbiased third party.

Now that you have read the most compelling evidence behind workplace wellbeing, you are in a *prime* position to run your company through the index and determine your score.

But before you do, here are a few final bits of advice when building your wellbeing strategy.

Moving your wellbeing vision to competitive action.

As part of using the Wellbeing Progress Index effectively, here is some advice we learned by helping large organisations build their wellbeing strategies.

- **Make short- and long-term plans** – While many employers made a bigger commitment to employee wellbeing as a response to the way the pandemic affected their people, we must now focus on a longer-term commitment. So, your strategy must serve to help in you in the next five years at least. But we know the next pandemic or cost of living crisis is just around the corner, so making allowances for you to respond quickly to the next stressor is just as important.

  This means a careful balance of things you are putting in place to respond to an immediate threat and the things you are putting in place that will change your culture to be one more centred around wellbeing in the long run.

- **Shake off the old ways of thinking** – Try not to focus on what worked well in the past as a benchmark of what will work well in the future. There were employers with effective wellbeing initiatives in place in January 2020 that failed to support their people by mid-way through the pandemic. Employees expect more and better-quality support at work than they did before the pandemic started, so try to see the crisis as a marker in time. Post-covid-19 requires so much different thinking, it prompted the creation of this book.

- **Prioritise your vulnerabilities** – Wellbeing is a big problem to solve. It's as diverse as your people, and it's a moving target. Giving yourself focus allows you to manage this problem more effectively and over time. The Wellbeing Progress Index is designed to support you in doing this.

   Defining and agreeing on what problem to solve first is a crucial action when designing a wellbeing strategy. As well as using the Wellbeing Progress Index to help you focus, go back to the reason why you want to support wellbeing at work in the first place. Think about what problems you are trying to solve for your people, for yourself and your organisation. Make a clear definition between where you are at and where you want to be and what each step along the way looks like. Creating a culture of wellbeing will take time. Changes in policy, new initiatives implementation, adding new benefits at renewal etc., can all take years to achieve.

- **Align your top team** – Leaders will play a crucial role in the success of your workplace wellbeing strategy, and they remain a common reason why these types of strategies fail. So, prioritise their involvement, get them to buy into your strategy and ensure they fully understand why and how you will roll it out.

Use the Wellbeing Progress Index to tell a story over time to your C-suite. HR is burdened with analytics tools, dashboards and charts and this index isn't supposed to add to that noise. But the index will create a compelling narrative that will help to articulate the wellbeing problem to your leadership team. The output will give you a story to tell that will have:

- **A beginning** – Where we are now. How we compare to our competitors, where we sit on the global stage, what we are doing well, what needs our attention etc.

- **A middle** – What are we doing next? What vulnerabilities are we prioritising? What needs to change now to remain competitive and attractive to our people?

- **An end** – Where do we want to be in three or five years? What is the journey we are taking our leaders on, and how do we get them excited about our continuous improvement and where we hope to end up?

Benefex's in-house experts designed the Wellbeing Progress Index to accompany the evidence behind this book. While far from perfect, it was built after extensive research and work with large global employers to help them get to a place where they could effectively measure and benchmark their approach to workplace wellbeing. It is designed to work alongside many other ways employers might measure wellbeing, whether surveys, activity monitors or mental health apps. Its primary purpose is to give an organisation a view on what they *should* be doing to support their people according to the research, their competitors, and their wider country of operation.

Wellbeing is a journey; no employer will complete it, and the data and evidence we have around workplace wellbeing is evolving at pace. The next crisis will fundamentally change the direction of our strategy, as will new leadership, new ownership, and changes in resources. The Wellbeing Progress Index was designed to measure progress, not success. So, no matter what constraints you may be operating under as an employer, you can follow the evidence and do the most you can to make sure you have the benefits, policies, and processes in place that we know put you in the best position to improve wellbeing in your organisation.

If you would like to know more about the Wellbeing Progress Index, or see it in action, please contact Benefex.

Guest Expert View: Alastair Gill
Founder, Alchemy Labs - A Leadership,
Culture & Growth Agency

Before founding Alchemy Labs, Alastair was giffgaff's Head of People. Reporting to the CEO, Alastair led on all things culture, engagement, peopled development, strategy, inclusion, wellbeing, and people experience. Before giffgaff,

Alastair was a Senior HR Advisor at the London Borough of Hillingdon.

If you haven't got your health, you haven't got anything.

It's what my Dad always says to me. And he's right, but it also applies to business and how we lead, how we operate, and the companies we build. The collective health and wellbeing of the people in your organisation is critical to your success. It's one of your greatest opportunities for improvement, a core source of competitive advantage, and is simply the right thing to do.

For years leaders have said that people are our most important resource but were instead just treated as a resource. Now at a time when lots of things are in a state of flux and the pressure is on organisations to grow, be creative, efficient, and constantly innovate is vast, it's time to *prove* that people are our most important resource and create the conditions for them to truly thrive. And that starts with health and wellbeing.

The link between engagement and performance is now clear (although it has taken some time, and many still want to see the business case), so now is the time to go deeper and focus on the first principle and essential partner of engagement and organisational performance; our health as a collective and individually. The thing is, like with motivation, engagement, and experience previously, it's flipping obvious yet nuanced and complex - but that's the point.

The world of work and the world around us is changing and is more complicated than ever, so the solutions need to be equally evolved and designed to meet that. If the future is human, the key to it is our health.

Creating a culture of wellbeing starts with creating a culture of care, which begins with leaders showing that it's essential. Easy to say but harder to do. One way to do this is to give it your most valuable resource - Time. In a world where BAU, emails, DMs, and packed diaries fill our weeks, it's a leader's role to help pull back from the coalface (like any great coach does) and ensure time is spent on the health of a team and its individuals. Like a time-out. It sounds too easy, but don't let it fool you. Like all good intentions and resolutions, they slip, so make it a habit. Yes, it will be complex. Health is more than physical health, as this book shows - it's personal and human, but that is the role of the leader to explore and understand the factors impacting team health and then support, educate, and design a better environment. Just like exec and sports coaches who to improve performance don't just focus on the job or the task in hand but on the underlying factors impacting the individual from functioning at their best.

Developing and empowering managers and leaders into coaches who see the holistic drivers of performance is one thing, but to be truly effective, it also has to be much wider. I've found that when leaders commit time as a company to learn, discuss, and then ideate around the elements of wellbeing combined with individual conversations, that is where the impact really is and is what will help you drive organisation evolution.

It all starts with learning. So commit the time to learn, share and discuss elements of wellbeing together as a company (I've seen many impactful sessions on everything from sleep, ADHD, nutrition, anxiety, and how to manage personal finances). Audit your existing approaches to wellbeing, find out what others are doing, and then create spaces and time for people to continue the conversations (just like a focus group, but anyone can get involved). Give those groups direct access to the Leadership Team and board to playback their insights and solutions, and ideas to move your wellbeing strategy forwards. The Wellbeing Progress Index will help you do just that.

Create accountability and a process for turning the learning into 'features' of your culture that underpin health and wellbeing.

Chapter 14

Conclusion

This book and the Wellbeing Progress Index are by no means a complete list of everything that impacts employee wellbeing. The reasons behind our wellbeing can be complex and influenced by many factors – some of which we have still yet to understand. Including them all here would be impossible, so we have summarised some of the most interesting evidence that has informed the creation of the Wellbeing Progress Index and the outcome of more than 100 wellbeing workshops with global employers, and the research behind 200+ conference talks over the last few years. No doubt, new evidence would have emerged within the time this book was published, and you are reading it. This moving target of wellbeing is why this book and the index have the word 'progress' in them; no employer will finish wellbeing - there is no end to it. All we will be able to do is progress along a never-ending line, keeping up with changing attitudes, societal influences, and the latest thinking. But here are some final thoughts that will be relevant to anyone tasked with supporting employee wellbeing.

Wellbeing needs to run through the veins of your organisation.

The pandemic profoundly influenced wellbeing in the workplace. Yet while only 56 percent of employees think their company's executive team cares about their wellbeing, 91 percent of the C-suite think their employees do believe they care about it[558]. There is a huge difference between what organisations say and think, and the actions they take to support their people. With more than three-quarters of employees saying their mental health impacted their careers in 2022[559], it is evident that support isn't where it needs to be and, importantly, where employees *want* it to be. When you embark on the wellbeing journey, your aim is to create a culture of wellbeing that permeates everything you do. When you write a new policy, when you choose a new benefit, when you design your communication strategy or even when you update your onboarding process, wellbeing must be front of mind. Successful and effective workplace wellbeing runs through the DNA of an organisation.

Hybrid working is a boost and a ball and chain for wellbeing.

The evidence is clear: the more social support we have, the higher quality it is, the better our resilience to stress, the lower the likelihood of developing an illness, the better equipped we are to deal with poor mental health and the higher likelihood we will live longer[560].

But in a world where millions of employees are now working away from the workplace on their own, this has given us a substantial new wellbeing challenge. Especially as it appears those who work in a hybrid way are far more likely to stay working with you for longer. A 2022 study by Stanford University researcher Nick Bloom found that hybrid work reduces attrition by as much as 35 percent[561] - that could save an organisation employing 1,000 people millions each year. So how do we prioritise employee wellbeing while also doing what is good for the organisation?

Working at home is good for wellbeing. But working on our own isn't. So as the world finds its feet and employees find a way of working that supports their wellbeing, we must remain mindful that the employer still has a paternal role to play. While an employee may want to work from home for economic reasons, work, and the social aspects of it have to factor into that decision and, in many cases, may require the employer to intervene and negotiate a way of working that balances what employees want, and what we think they need. Take this from a senior leader and a remote worker for the last ten years – it's sometimes challenging to know what's good for us.

Guest Expert View: Jamie Broadley

Group Head of Health & Wellbeing, Serco

Jamie helps individuals, teams, and organisations become their best selves by distilling learning from performance sport, healthcare, corporate organisations, and the literature into accessible and actionable approaches and strategies.

Jamie's background academically is in psychology. He holds a master's in health psychology from the University of Leeds and has worked in a variety of NHS psychology settings. Jamie has combined this with a career in professional sport, having played championship rugby and now as a player-coach in the National Leagues.

Jamie believes that these two worlds have given him the privileged position of observing human performance at both ends of the spectrum and has allowed him to develop his thinking and practice to best support organisations, teams, and individuals to achieve their goals while supporting their wellbeing.

Jamie applies this in his role as Group Head of Wellbeing at Serco, having previously been a staff wellbeing lead for five years within the NHS.

———————————

Where there is disruption, there is opportunity, and that is certainly the case in the workplace wellbeing space currently. The pandemic, for all its hardships, has opened our collective eyes to a far deeper and more meaningful version of wellbeing at work, one that we can hopefully all lean into going forward.

Pre-pandemic, conversations about wellbeing at work had the tendency to be sanitised and neatly packaged; we'd talk about nutrition, getting more exercise and time management strategies to reduce stress. Whilst these were important topics, they never felt like they got to the heart of the challenges. As such, engagement with wellbeing content and utilisation of related services was low.

The pandemic and all the difficulties it brought suddenly meant we had to talk about and support far grittier and deeper topics. We had to talk about bereavement and grief, we needed to think about parenting and caring responsibilities, and we wanted to respond to anxiety and stress in far more tangible ways. The blurring of boundaries between work and home meant there was much more on the workplace wellbeing table to be included and considered.

Whilst none of this made the challenges easier, the conversations felt more inclusive and real; we could see ourselves in them, so we leant in. Engagement and utilisation increased. It is this path that I think wellbeing in the workplace must continue on.

To give you a practical example; at Serco, we run monthly wellbeing webinars. Whilst webinars have their limitations, they can be a great amplifier of a message, and they provide rich content which can be repurposed for different audiences (think podcasters chopping out segments of video for their social media channels). Within these, we've sought to give voice to those issues that have remained unspoken previously. Rather than the vanilla topics of old, we have dug into complex and gritty issues such as grief, relationships, parenting, trauma, and finances.

There is an important principle we are seeking to put to work here. If we want a topic to feel comfortable for discussion at work, how can we support a conversation that goes beyond that? How do we make the uncomfortable more comfortable? Menopause, for example, is an increasingly important topic in the workplace; in our attempt to support this, we ran a webinar on sex and the menopause. This quickly made more 'day-to-day' menopause conversations feel far easier.

The key to a successful workplace wellbeing approach, as I see it, is the story that is told about it. With this approach, the story we are seeking to tell is that we see you, with all your human messiness, and we're here for it. Through this, challenges can feel normalised, accessing support has less stigma, and we can design support services with our people, not too them.

I encourage you to explore the conversations that aren't being had but need to be where you work. Give these a platform, make them safe and align your support services alongside them.

The workplace is changing lives.

The evidence is unequivocal – work plays a significant role in our wellbeing. There is a very close relationship between job satisfaction and overall life satisfaction[562]. When we have a purpose and social capital at work, and when we feel like our employer cares about us, our overall life wellbeing improves. That's why getting wellbeing at work right is so important – its consequences on the individual and broader society are significant. In one study of Hungarian teachers, workplace wellbeing and happiness was associated with hope and optimism in life[563]. Work is creating more positive and happy people when wellbeing is done right.

The author and Cornell Professor Lee Dyer once said the new employer-employee relationship was a "collaborative effort to develop high-quality jobs and strong, successful businesses while overcoming the deep social and economic divisions apparent in society today."[564] This sums it up better than I have been able to. HR, reward, and benefit teams are not just adjusting to changing employee expectations over how an organisation supports their wellbeing, but they are having to react to several generation-defining events that are moving the goalposts too. The pandemic wasn't the first of its kind, and it won't be the last, so our wellbeing approaches must keep in mind that our people's needs will change on the spin of a coin.

That being said, as employers and as HR teams, we must stop looking for a course of action and instead become obsessed with getting to the *cause* of action. To make more successful and resilient businesses, we must tackle the growing problem of unhappiness because when employees are happy and healthy at work, they work harder[565]. Sales advisors sell more when they are happy at work[566], and for many of us, work itself makes us happy[567]. But since 2006, the global rise of unhappiness has continued. By 2021, around 33 percent of us said we were unhappy – up from 23 percent from 2007. We are more stressed, sad, and worried than ever. The Gallup Positive Experience Index 2021 found that people report fewer positive experiences today than yesterday[568].

Employees have been struggling through some seriously emotional events over the last decade. Multiple recessions, wars, price rises and a pandemic. This growing uncertainty is impacting our lives, and we are looking for someone to help us. All eyes are looking at the employer. In 2022, more employees are looking for wellbeing support at a new job more than they are looking for higher compensation. According to LinkedIn, among the top three areas, employees think their company should invest in our mental health and wellness[569]. More wellbeing at work is resonating with employees on social media too. Posts that mention 'wellbeing' get more engagement. There has been a 73 percent increase in social posts by employers that mention the word 'wellbeing' and a 35 percent increase in general social posts that mention 'wellbeing'.

In 2022 there was a 13 percent uptick in job titles that reference 'wellbeing' compared to 2019[570], with some organisations dedicating teams and individuals to ensuring we get things like flexible working right. The pandemic gave employees a moment to pause and reflect on what they wanted to do and whom they wanted to do it for. Their conclusion was a general feeling that they could be working for someone better, and I think that (in part) drove the 'The Great Resignation'.

Wellbeing is a huge opportunity for HR. You will be called upon more frequently to advise your organisation on how to engage, support, attract and retain the best talent. People need more wellbeing and financial assistance more than they ever have, and the long-term effect of the pandemic means that desire isn't going away anytime soon. So as part of a competitive compensation package, how you support your people will become critical to how you attract and retain them – and specifically, how you attract and retain the candidates you need.

This presents an opportunity to manage the top thing HR leaders told Benefex is holding them back – budget. There is a lack of understanding at the top of most organisations regarding how to leverage performance using wellbeing. ROI is no longer driven by simple metrics like turnover and absence but will be driven by rising healthcare costs, growing presenteeism, culture change, employee experience challenges, Corporate Social Responsibility (CSR), and Diversity, Equity, and Inclusion (DE&I) strategies. Reward and benefits are on their way to becoming even more important to the employee experience than ever before. There is now a much stronger case for the economics of morale, culture, poor health, development, and inclusion. The opportunity is for HR to become much more strategic regarding wellbeing and the EVP – and, where possible, to lead on both. In my view, employee benefits would still exist if wellbeing wasn't a thing, but wellbeing cannot exist without employee benefits.

Because of the pandemic, there is now the recognition that reward and benefits (especially things like sick pay and living wages) have become wellbeing, Ethical, Social and Governance (ESG) issues in themselves. These new perspectives mean the HR, reward and benefits functions are not cost centres to be reduced, but a vast performance driver. We live in a world where employees are demanding more, and employers are having to offer more compelling compensation packages designed around supporting people's lives. To remain competitive, the EVP must be developed around wellbeing, or 'The Great Resignation' will continue to cause damage to employers who fail to keep their best people.

As a person responsible for wellbeing, your impact on the organisation and the world should not be underestimated. There is a significant opportunity ahead for people like you to play an even more critical role in the new workplace. I have never seen as many passionate and hardworking people working in wellbeing or HR as I have in the last few years. I have seen and have evidence that a commitment to employee wellbeing can have a considerable impact on the health and happiness of the individual and the culture and success of the organisation. But I've also started to see how this commitment can impact broader society. Anyone working within an organisation to promote and improve employee wellbeing is making a better world. I really believe that. Just think of what we've learned in this book; you can help a parent to have a better relationship with their child, you can help someone to live longer, and you can give a person a reason to wake up in the morning and sleep well at night.

The workplace is finally becoming what employees want and need it to be. As the balance of power and influence shifted from employer to employee, we began to see the erosion of centuries worth of workplace practices designed to contain and control people and ultimately harm their wellbeing in many cases. The changes we are seeing will be considered a significantly positive time in our workplace evolution. Almost every employer finally realised that when we put people first, meet their needs and support their lives, they will do amazing things for our organisations.

There is a great quote by Thomas Aquinas that goes:

"If the highest aim of a captain were to preserve his ship, he would keep it in port forever."

If you are to make a material difference to the wellbeing of your people, you must go forth with confidence, compassion, and commitment. This means pushing the envelope, taking risks, and doing what others have yet to do. You will not succeed by following other organisations' old, well-trodden paths. Wellbeing has evolved significantly from motivational posters, mental health first aiders, wellbeing rooms and self-care boxes. To get this right, you have to be experimental, follow the latest evidence and research in wellbeing, and forget most of what those with wellbeing to sell you have taught us about wellbeing at work. I was recently sent a photograph of an email from within an organisation that was seeking to improve employee wellbeing on the back of the extreme stress caused by the pandemic. The email was asking for ideas on the types of poster they could create to let people know they were cared about. This ineffective and glib approach to wellbeing is still too common and is why I felt compelled to write this book. We have to get wellbeing back on track.

As we've discovered in this book, wellbeing will not be solved by those with the deepest pockets or smallest imaginations. In a post-pandemic workplace, wellbeing will only be ameliorated by those who resign themselves to care for their employees honestly. That mindset will guide you to invest your organisation's time and money in the best way.

There is a unique and exciting opportunity for you reading this book to make a material difference to people's lives in this brave new post-pandemic world. I am genuinely excited by some of the things I know you will do, and I'm jealous of the real human impact you will have.

Good luck with your *progress* to becoming a more sustainable and resilient organisation.

"Progress lies not in enhancing what is, but advancing toward what will be"

- Lebanese American writer, poet, artist, and philosopher Khalil Gibran (1883-1931)

Sunrise: A Song of Two Humans

Seeing as you're still reading, I wanted to share something extra with you that seemed significant while I was writing this book. While I was sitting in a hotel room under the shadow of Ben Nevis in the Scottish Highlands, this song came on the radio. I wasn't able to Shazam it, so it took months of research to try and find out what song it was - without any lyrics, this was a big challenge.

The song is by Park Jiha, a Korean composer and instrumentalist who uses a variety of traditional Korean musical instruments to create her compositions.

While you reflect on what you've learned reading this book, take a moment to scan the below barcode into Spotify and listen to 'Sunrise: A Song of Two Humans'.

References

[1] https://psycnet.apa.org/record/2022-15372-001
[2] https://news.harvard.edu/gazette/story/2017/04/over-nearly-80-years-harvard-study-has-been-showing-how-to-live-a-healthy-and-happy-life/
[3] https://www.mckinsey.com/industries/consumer-packaged-goods/our-insights/feeling-good-the-future-of-the-1-5-trillion-wellness-market
[4] https://www.standard.co.uk/news/health/gps-trudy-harrison-dft-england-department-for-transport-b1020001.htmlwhen
[5] https://www.turing.ac.uk/blog/what-makes-us-happy
[6] https://www.gallup.com/workplace/349484/state-of-the-global-workplace.aspx?thank-you-report-form=1
[7] https://www.who.int/news/item/16-09-2021-who-ilo-almost-2-million-people-die-from-work-related-causes-each-year
[8] https://www2.deloitte.com/us/en/insights/topics/leadership/employee-wellness-in-the-corporate-workplace.html?id=us:2sm:3li:4diUS175466:5awa::MMDDYY::author&pkid=1008950
[9] https://www.mckinsey.com/business-functions/people-and-organizational-performance/our-insights/the-great-attrition-is-making-hiring-harder-are-you-searching-the-right-talent-pools
[10] https://www.mckinsey.com/business-functions/people-and-organizational-performance/our-insights/the-great-attrition-is-making-hiring-harder-are-you-searching-the-right-talent-pools
[11] https://www.betterworks.com/wp-content/uploads/2022/05/2022-PESurvey-Report.pdf
[12] https://www.metlife.com/employee-benefit-trends/2021-wellbeing-resilience-and-employee-benefits/?cid=q5s4f&utm_id=q5s4f&utm_source=vanity&utm_medium=vanity&utm_campaign=g_ebts_1q21_MetLife&utm_content=v_vanity_ebts2021corereport&promoid=q5s4f
[13] https://www.gallup.com/workplace/349484/state-of-the-global-workplace.aspx#ite-393248
[14] https://www.gallup.com/workplace/349484/state-of-the-global-workplace.aspx#ite-393257
[15] https://unsdg.un.org/resources/policy-brief-covid-19-and-need-action-mental-health
[16] https://www.nature.com/articles/s41598-021-89700-8
[17] https://www.westfieldhealth.com/resources/our-changing-attitudes-to-mental-health
[18] https://justentrepreneurs.co.uk/news/employee-wellbeing-new-research-reveals-exactly-what-employees-want-from-their-career

[19] https://www.who.int/news/item/27-08-2020-world-mental-health-day-an-opportunity-to-kick-start-a-massive-scale-up-in-investment-in-mental-health#:~:text=Mental percent20health percent20is percent20one percent20of,every percent2040 percent20seconds percent20by percent20suicide

[20] https://www.kcl-ipsos.com/research/projects/global-attitudes-to-mental-health

[21] https://www.imperial.ac.uk/news/221294/global-report-tracks-changing-health-behaviours/

[22] https://www.health.org.uk/publications/long-reads/public-perceptions-performance-policy-and-expectations

[23] https://headversity.com/the-cost-of-neglected-employee-mental-health-80-billion-and-counting/

[24] https://www2.deloitte.com/uk/en/pages/press-releases/articles/poor-mental-health-costs-uk-employers-up-to-pound-45-billion-a-year.html

[25] https://www2.deloitte.com/uk/en/pages/press-releases/articles/poor-mental-health-costs-uk-employers-up-to-pound-45-billion-a-year.html

[26] https://www.gallup.com/workplace/352952/employees-wellbeing-job-leave-find.aspx

[27] Great Expectations, Benefex, 2022

[28] https://hbr.org/2019/10/research-people-want-their-employers-to-talk-about-mental-health

[29] https://www.cnbc.com/2021/06/24/workers-are-quitting-their-jobs-to-prioritize-their-mental-health.html

[30] https://www.studyfinds.org/mental-health-quit-job/

[31] https://www.hsph.harvard.edu/nutritionsource/disease-prevention/

[32] https://psychcentral.com/health/mental-health-trends-to-watch-in-2022

[33] https://www.bacp.co.uk/news/news-from-bacp/2021/8-october-attitudes-towards-mental-health-are-changing-our-research-finds/

[34] https://www.westfieldhealth.com/docs/marketing/campaigns/changing-attitudes-to-mental-health/our-changing-attitudes-to-mental-health-report.pdf

[35] https://www.hellobenefex.com/resources/news/employees-turn-to-bosses-for-support-as-8-in-10-employers-report-more-staff-disclosing-mental-health-issues-and-feelings-of-loneliness/

[36] https://www.ipsos.com/en/four-five-say-mental-health-important-physical

[37] https://www.weforum.org/agenda/2018/04/5-charts-that-reveal-how-india-sees-mental-health/

[38] https://pubmed.ncbi.nlm.nih.gov/22757601/

[39] https://pubmed.ncbi.nlm.nih.gov/24118217/

[40] https://www.frontiersin.org/articles/10.3389/fpsyg.2021.627851/full#B52

[41] https://www.frontiersin.org/articles/10.3389/fpsyg.2021.627851/full

[42] https://www.mckinsey.com/industries/consumer-packaged-goods/our-insights/feeling-good-the-future-of-the-1-5-trillion-wellness-market

[43] https://oem.bmj.com/content/oemed/75/4/245.full.pdf

[44] https://www.washingtonpost.com/news/on-leadership/wp/2018/03/22/this-professor-says-the-workplace-is-the-fifth-leading-cause-of-death-in-the-u-s/

[45] https://www.thetimes.co.uk/article/three-ambulance-workers-dead-amid-claims-of-bullying-zwcwfwm7j

[46] https://www.nbcnews.com/news/us-news/uss-george-washington-sailors-detail-difficult-working-conditions-stri-rcna25882

[47] https://calmatters.org/environment/2022/06/california-firefighter-trauma-ptsd/

[48] https://hbsp.harvard.edu/product/721420-PDF-ENG

[49] https://nypost.com/2019/12/10/how-much-money-we-spend-each-year-on-trying-to-feel-less-stressed/

[50] https://www.studyfinds.org/self-care-americans-relaxed-40-minutes/

[51] https://www.openaccessgovernment.org/the-working-population-are-at-risk-of-job-burnout-mental-health-remote-working/136705/

[52] https://www.mckinsey.com/mhi/our-insights/addressing-employee-burnout-are-you-solving-the-right-problem

[53] https://www.businessinsider.com/nike-employee-survey-shows-dissatisfaction-global-technology-2022-5?r=US&IR=T

[54] https://www.cnbc.com/2021/06/22/dating-app-bumble-gives-workers-the-week-off-to-recover-from-burnout.html

[55] https://www.inc.com/christine-lagorio-chafkin/bumble-whitney-wolfe-herd-employee-wellness-time-off-burnout.html

[56] https://www.shrm.org/resourcesandtools/hr-topics/employee-relations/pages/toxic-workplace-culture-report.aspx

[57] https://www.researchgate.net/publication/43347440_Stress_personal_cha
racteristics_and_burnout_among_first_postgraduate_year_residents_A_n
ationwide_study_in_Taiwan

[58] https://www.mckinsey.com/mhi/our-insights/addressing-employee-burnout-are-you-solving-the-right-problem

[59] Dodge, R., Daly, A., Huyton, J., & Sanders, L. (2012). The challenge of defining wellbeing. International Journal of Wellbeing, 2(3), 222-235. doi:10.5502/ijw.v2i3.4

[60] https://www.ons.gov.uk/peoplepopulationandcommunity/wellbeing

[61] https://www.who.int/data/gho/data/major-themes/health-and-wellbeing

[62] https://www.weforum.org/agenda/2021/01/priority-workplaces-new-normal-wellbeing/

[63] https://www.iso.org/news/ref2677.html

[64] https://www.psychologytoday.com/gb/blog/click-here-happiness/201901/what-is-wellbeing-definition-types-and-wellbeing-skills

[65] https://hqlo.biomedcentral.com/articles/10.1186/s12955-020-01423-y

[66] https://www.frontiersin.org/articles/10.3389/fpubh.2022.855327/full

[67] http://www.healthscotland.scot/health-inequalities/fundamental-causes/income-inequality/income

[68] https://www.oecd.org/social/ministerial/OECD-RTM-Call-For-Proposals-2020.pdf?_ga=2.9460147.707617434.1655745685-784912388.1655745685

[69] https://www.abi.org.uk/globalassets/files/appg/the-financial-impact-of-the-pandemic_report.pdf

[70] https://www.ebri.org/publications/research-publications/issue-briefs/content/comparing-the-financial-wellbeing-of-baby-boom-generation-x-and-millennial-families-how-do-the-generations-stack-up

[71] https://business.yougov.com/content/39987-key-banking-insights-2021?mkt_tok=NDY0LVZISC05ODgAAAGCFejllYglBSYGBu5bmXz5XNj37MCHbyTasnH__oeQ7G3ft4Un4BiD8_7gWjtfvcwGOmdC66Oi wLadQe6bBa-aEsQYcHMg68I-rueNN5vgYApzpQ

[72] https://www.stepchange.org/media-centre/press-releases/credit-safety-nets-report.aspx

[73] https://www.wellandgood.com/financial-stress-discover-personal-loans/

[74] https://www.benefitscanada.com/benefits/health-wellness/pandemic-affecting-u-s-employees-financial-stress-productivity-survey/

[75] https://www.worldobesity.org/resources/resource-library/world-obesity-atlas-2022

[76] https://www.sciencenews.org/article/americans-are-sleeping-less-they-were-13-years-ago

[77] https://www.sciencedaily.com/releases/2013/04/130410082426.htm

[78] https://www.bloomberg.com/news/articles/2022-05-24/workers-in-office-feel-least-connected-countering-rto-claims

[79] https://www.apa.org/news/press/releases/2022/05/covid-19-increase-loneliness

[80] https://www.vox.com/future-perfect/21754625/covid-19-pandemic-generosity-charity-cash-transfers

[81] https://www.thelancet.com/journals/lanpub/article/PIIS2468-2667(22)00082-2/fulltext

[82] https://academic.oup.com/economicpolicy/article/37/109/139/6501443

[83] https://www.bath.ac.uk/announcements/new-paper-reveals-impact-of-first-lockdown-on-depression-and-anxiety-diagnosis/

[84] https://www.theguardian.com/world/2022/apr/21/covid-forces-china-to-face-mental-health-crisis-a-long-time-in-the-making

[85] https://celluloidjunkie.com/wire/going-to-the-cinema-improves-mental-health-of-nhs-hospital-patients/

[86] https://www.sciencedirect.com/science/article/abs/pii/S0005796703001037

[87] https://www.verywellmind.com/study-shows-more-frequent-travel-can-make-for-happier-life-5094820

[88] https://en.wikipedia.org/wiki/Framingham_Heart_Study

[89] https://psycnet.apa.org/doiLanding?doi=10.1037 percent2F0022-3514.83.5.1141

[90] https://oxford.universitypressscholarship.com/view/10.1093/acprof:oso/9780199686674.001.0001/acprof-9780199686674-chapter-5

[91] https://opencommons.uconn.edu/cgi/viewcontent.cgi?article=1777&context=srhonors_theses

[92] https://worldhappiness.report/ed/2022/exploring-the-biological-basis-for-happiness/#fn1

[93] https://genomemedicine.biomedcentral.com/articles/10.1186/s13073-020-00742-5

[94] https://www.ncbi.nlm.nih.gov/pmc/articles/PMC6181118/

[95] https://apps.who.int/iris/bitstream/handle/10665/112828/9789241506809_eng.pdf

[96] https://geneticliteracyproject.org/2022/08/22/did-you-follow-covid-lockdown-rules-whether-or-not-you-did-is-partially-driven-by-your-dna/

[97] https://www.thesun.co.uk/health/19542291/alcohol-genes-dna-beer-study/

[98] https://www.ons.gov.uk/peoplepopulationandcommunity/healthandsocialcare/causesofdeath/bulletins/alcoholrelateddeathsintheunitedkingdom/registeredin2020

[99] https://www.thelancet.com/journals/langas/article/PIIS2468-1253(21)00479-9/fulltext

[100] https://www.thelancet.com/journals/lancet/article/PIIS0140-6736(22)01438-6/fulltext

[101] https://www.aviva.com/newsroom/news-releases/2022/05/over-1-bn-in-individual-protection-claims-helped-more-than-53700-customers-and-families-in-2021/

[102] https://www.cdc.gov/cancer/dcpc/research/update-on-cancer-deaths/index.htm

[103] https://www.ncbi.nlm.nih.gov/books/NBK542737/

[104] https://www.cdc.gov/workplacehealthpromotion/initiatives/resource-center/index.html

[105] http://www.mentalhealthamerica.net/blog/manufacturing-retail-and-food-and-beverage-industries-rank-worst-workplace-mental-health

[106] https://theholistichealthcaregroup.com/2020/02/mental-health-in-the-construction-industry/

[107] https://www.william-russell.com/blog/countries-best-mental-healthcare/

[108] https://www.usnews.com/news/best-countries/articles/2016-09-14/the-10-most-depressed-countries

[109] https://unitedgmh.org/sites/default/files/2022-04/The percent20Return percent20on percent20the percent20Individual_Full percent20Report_2.pdf

[110] https://www.hellobenefex.com/resources/news/employees-turn-to-bosses-for-support-as-8-in-10-employers-report-more-staff-disclosing-mental-health-issues-and-feelings-of-loneliness/

[111] https://www.prnewswire.co.uk/news-releases/more-than-three-quarters-of-gen-z-employees-consider-job-move-seeking-better-benefits-and-wellbeing-support-according-to-perkbox-research-806318222.html

[112] https://www.forbes.com/sites/kristinstoller/2021/05/20/employees-are-more-vital-to-a-companys-success-than-shareholders-new-survey-finds/

[113] https://www.tlnt.com/a-bosss-day-survey-shows-us-trust-is-an-issue/

[114] https://www.bbc.co.uk/news/av/technology-52833547

[115] https://www2.deloitte.com/uk/en/pages/consulting/articles/working-during-lockdown-impact-of-covid-19-on-productivity-and-wellbeing.html

[116] https://www.wtwco.com/assets/covid-19/NA-COVID-19-ClientWebcast-April-22-Final.pdf

[117] https://hbr.org/2017/01/the-neuroscience-of-trust

[118] https://worldhappiness.report/ed/2013/

[119] https://worldhappiness.report/ed/2020/

[120] https://www.researchgate.net/publication/49615205_Trust_and_Wellbeing

[121] https://www.ncbi.nlm.nih.gov/pmc/articles/PMC6612929/

[122] https://www.inc.com/wanda-thibodeaux/the-1-thing-ceos-now-are-prioritizing-in-quest-for-personal-balance.html

[123] https://joshbersin.com/2022/07/new-research-shows-that-certain-hr-capabilities-drive-revenue-growth/

[124] https://www.peoplemanagement.co.uk/article/1751804/why-employers-paying-more-attention-wellbeing-2022

[125] Digital Health in the UK: National attitudes and behaviours research, ORCHA (2022)

[126] https://www.iqvia.com/-/media/iqvia/pdfs/institute-reports/digital-health-trends-2021/iqvia-institute-digital-health-trends-2021.pdf?_=1628089218603

[127] https://www.med-technews.com/news/Digital-in-Healthcare-News/report-shows-rise-in-search-for-digital-mental-health-apps/

[128] Evidence-Based Apps? A Review of Mental Health Mobile Applications in a Psychotherapy Context. Joyce H. L. Lui, David K. Marcus, and Christopher T. Barry Washington State University. Professional Psychology: Research and Practice © 2017 American Psychological Association 2017, Vol. 48, No. 3, 199–210

[129] https://www.forbes.com/sites/serenaoppenheim/2019/01/16/should-you-trust-an-app-with-your-mental-health/?sh=2870cbbd24b8

[130] https://www.forbes.com/sites/serenaoppenheim/2019/01/16/should-you-trust-an-app-with-your-mental-health/?sh=2870cbbd24b8

[131] https://www.wired.co.uk/article/mental-health-apps

[132] https://www.mobihealthnews.com/content/mental-health-apps-plentiful-few-provide-clinical-research

[133] https://www.frontiersin.org/articles/10.3389/fpsyt.2019.00831/full

[134] https://ebmh.bmj.com/content/18/4/97

[135] https://dailymontanan.com/2021/08/14/in-a-murky-sea-of-mental-health-apps-consumers-left-adrift/

[136] https://journals.plos.org/digitalhealth/article?id=10.1371/journal.pdig.0000002

[137] https://www.med-technews.com/news/Digital-in-Healthcare-News/report-shows-rise-in-search-for-digital-mental-health-apps/

[138] https://rorycellanjones.substack.com/p/health-apps-helpful-or-harmful?utm_campaign=Thought percent20leadership&utm_content=159423975&utm_medium=social&utm_source=linkedin&hss_channel=lcp-10190667

[139] https://www.sciencedirect.com/science/article/pii/S2214782918300460

[140] https://www.consumerreports.org/health-privacy/mental-health-apps-and-user-privacy-a7415198244/

[141] https://orchahealth.com/84-of-period-tracker-apps-share-data-with-third-parties/

[142] https://www.theguardian.com/world/2022/jun/28/why-us-woman-are-deleting-their-period-tracking-apps

[143] https://www.mckinsey.com/industries/healthcare-systems-and-services/our-insights/addressing-the-unprecedented-behavioral-health-challenges-facing-generation-z

[144] https://www.theguardian.com/society/2021/aug/29/strain-on-mental-health-care-leaves-8m-people-without-help-say-nhs-leaders

[145] https://pubmed.ncbi.nlm.nih.gov/29215315/

[146] https://reba.global/content/video-tutorial-matt-macri-waller-gethin-nadin-of-benefex-on-how-ai-is-changing-wellbeing

[147] https://www.axios.com/2022/05/02/mental-health-app-boom-raises-alarms

[148] https://www.hellobenefex.com/resources/reports/financial-wellbeing-insight/

[149] https://www.ipsos.com/en-uk/ftse-100-public-reporting-employee-wellness-engagement

[150] https://www.right.com/wps/wcm/connect/a2bd7426-4b2a-4af9-81ac-5211e83c72bb/the-wellness-imperative-creating-more-effective-

organizations-world-economic-forum-in-partnership-with-right-management.pdf?MOD=AJPERES

[151] https://www.personneltoday.com/hr/case-linking-employee-wellbeing-productivity/

[152]

https://assets.publishing.service.gov.uk/government/uploads/system/uploads/attachment_data/file/215455/dh_129656.pdf

[153] https://www.cipd.co.uk/Images/health-wellbeing-work-report-2021_tcm18-93541.pdf

[154]

https://www2.deloitte.com/content/dam/Deloitte/uk/Documents/consultancy/deloitte-uk-mental-health-report-2022.pdf

[155] https://www.glassdoor.com/research/employee-reviews-customer-satisfaction/

[156] https://blogs.lse.ac.uk/businessreview/2019/07/15/happy-employees-and-their-impact-on-firm-performance/

[157] https://news.harvard.edu/gazette/story/2019/04/workplace-wellness-programs-yield-unimpressive-results-in-short-term/

[158] https://www.cipd.co.uk/Images/health-wellbeing-work-report-2021_tcm18-93541.pdf

[159]

https://jamanetwork.com/journals/jama/fullarticle/2730614?guestAccessKey=f67976b4-63b8-4369-983f-196774f9404e&utm_source=For_The_Media&utm_medium=referral&utm_campaign=ftm_links&utm_content=tfl&utm_term=041619

[160] https://harris.uchicago.edu/news-events/news/new-research-finds-workplace-wellness-programs-deliver-little-no-impact

[161] https://www.hrzone.com/perform/people/employee-experience-why-less-is-more-when-it-comes-to-hr-policy

[162] https://onlinelibrary.wiley.com/doi/abs/10.1111/1748-8583.12000

[163]

https://assets.publishing.service.gov.uk/government/uploads/system/uploads/attachment_data/file/215463/dh_129657.pdf

[164] https://www.mckinsey.com/industries/healthcare-systems-and-services/our-insights/income-alone-may-be-insufficient-how-employers-can-help-advance-health-equity-in-the-workplace

[165] https://www.gov.uk/government/publications/covid-19-ethnicity-subgroup-interpreting-differential-health-outcomes-among-minority-ethnic-groups-in-wave-1-and-2-24-march-2021/covid-19-ethnicity-subgroup-interpreting-differential-health-outcomes-among-minority-ethnic-groups-in-wave-1-and-2-24-march-2021

[166] https://www.bls.gov/web/empsit/cpsee_e16.htm

[167] https://www.census.gov/library/stories/2021/07/how-pandemic-affected-black-and-white-households.html

[168] https://www.medicalnewstoday.com/articles/racial-inequalities-in-covid-19-the-impact-on-black-communities#Making-sense-of-incomplete-data

[169] https://www.cmaj.ca/content/194/26/E899

[170] https://www.mentalhealth.org.uk/a-to-z/w/women-and-mental-health

[171] https://www.bitc.org.uk/report/working-with-pride-issues-affecting-lgbt-people-in-the-workplace/

[172] https://www.stonewall.org.uk/lgbt-britain-health

[173] https://www.independent.co.uk/life-style/health-and-families/lgbt-mental-health-depression-symptoms-heterosexual-self-harm-child-teenager-adult-a8678261.html

[174] https://www.stonewall.org.uk/about-us/media-releases/stonewall-report-reveals-impact-discrimination-health-lgbt-people

[175] https://www.kff.org/coronavirus-covid-19/poll-finding/the-impact-of-the-covid-19-pandemic-on-lgbt-people/

[176] https://www.tuc.org.uk/sites/default/files/RacismintheUKlabourmarket.pdf

[177] https://www.independent.co.uk/life-style/racism-work-discrimination-gender-lgbt-sexuality-ageism-glassdoor-a9167256.html

[178] https://www.manchester.ac.uk/discover/news/racism-is-still-a-huge-problem/

[179] https://pediatrics.aappublications.org/content/early/2019/10/10/peds.2019-1187

[180] https://hbr.org/2019/10/research-people-want-their-employers-to-talk-about-mental-health

[181] https://www.kingsfund.org.uk/publications/health-people-ethnic-minority-groups-england

[182] https://theconversation.com/study-racism-shortens-lives-and-hurts-health-of-blacks-by-promoting-genes-that-lead-to-inflammation-and-illness-122027

[183] https://www.bbc.co.uk/news/uk-60208523

[184] https://www.healthaffairs.org/doi/10.1377/hlthaff.2021.01466

[185] https://onlinelibrary.wiley.com/doi/abs/10.1037/h0079479

[186] https://www.nationalgeographic.com/history/article/black-americans-see-health-care-system-infected-racism-new-poll-shows

[187] https://apple.news/ADduCXCOlQK6uec2zI-TMuQ

[188] https://www.parliament.uk/globalassets/documents/post/postpn276.pdf

[189] https://www.kingsfund.org.uk/publications/health-people-ethnic-minority-groups-england

[190] mortality from cancer, and dementia and Alzheimer's disease, is highest among white groups.

[191] https://apple.news/APRJNQtUSR3iLtb2NaZj32g

[192] https://www.mckinsey.com/featured-insights/diversity-and-inclusion/diversity-wins-how-inclusion-matters

[193] https://www.ncbi.nlm.nih.gov/books/NBK220636/

[194] https://www.ncbi.nlm.nih.gov/books/NBK220636/

[195] https://www.mckinsey.com/industries/healthcare-systems-and-services/our-insights/income-alone-may-be-insufficient-how-employers-can-help-advance-health-equity-in-the-workplace

[196] https://stories.butler.edu/sharing-gender-pronouns-in-employee-bios-email-signatures-helps-attract-lgbtq-applicants-study-finds/

[197] https://www.centreformentalhealth.org.uk/publications/mental-health-inequalities-factsheet

[198] https://www.centreformentalhealth.org.uk/publications/mental-health-inequalities-factsheet

[199] https://bmcpsychiatry.biomedcentral.com/articles/10.1186/s12888-020-02861-0

[200] https://www.mentalhealth.org.uk/a-to-z/w/women-and-mental-health

[201] https://www.mentalhealth.org.uk/a-to-z/b/black-asian-and-minority-ethnic-bame-communities

[202] http://www.stopstreetharassment.org/our-work/nationalstudy/2018-national-sexual-abuse-report/

[203] https://www.ncbi.nlm.nih.gov/pmc/articles/PMC5644356/

[204] https://www.ncbi.nlm.nih.gov/pmc/articles/PMC3227029/

[205] https://www.nbcnews.com/better/health/hidden-health-effects-sexual-harassment-ncna810416

[206] https://www.nasuwt.org.uk/advice/equalities/sexual-harassment-policy-checklist.html

[207] https://www.researchgate.net/publication/348247375_Transgender_Employees_Workplace_Impacts_on_Health_and_Wellbeing

[208] https://williamsinstitute.law.ucla.edu/wp-content/uploads/National-LGBT-Poverty-Oct-2019.pdf

[209] https://www.ustranssurvey.org/reports

[210] https://www.totaljobs.com/advice/trans-employee-experiences-survey-2021-research-conducted-by-totaljobs

[211] https://online.flippingbook.com/view/1021247/

[212] https://www.tandfonline.com/doi/full/10.1080/09585192.2021.2023895

[213] https://journals.plos.org/plosone/article?id=10.1371/journal.pone.0135225

[214] https://academic.oup.com/eurheartj/article-abstract/40/14/1124/5180493

[215] https://www.flexjobs.com/blog/post/flexjobs-2018-annual-survey-workers-believe-flexible-remote-job-can-help-save-money-reduce-stress-more/

[216] https://www.slideshare.net/PGi/state-of-telecommuting-2014-pgi-report/1

[217] https://www.food.gov.uk/research/research-projects/the-covid-19-consumer-research

[218] https://www.nextavenue.org/stigma-mental-illness-small-towns/

[219] https://hrexecutive.com/why-hr-needs-to-stop-the-clock-on-the-womens-recession/?eml=20210403&oly_enc_id=6577B4185945G7Z

[220] https://diversityq.com/remote-working-breeds-inclusivity-say-global-survey-respondents/

[221] https://www.cnbc.com/2021/06/22/remote-work-can-be-more-equitable-and-inclusive-to-lgbtq-employees.html

[222] https://amp-theguardian-com.cdn.ampproject.org/c/s/amp.theguardian.com/business/2022/aug/15/uk-workers-office-home

[223] https://www.amazon.com/Back-Human-Leaders-Connection-Isolation/dp/0738235032

[224] https://www.igloosoftware.com/state-of-the-digital-workplace/

[225] https://www.rsph.org.uk/about-us/news/survey-reveals-the-mental-and-physical-health-impacts-of-home-working-during-covid-19.html

[226] https://news.microsoft.com/en-gb/2021/02/15/research-reveals-how-we-really-feel-about-working-from-home/

[227] https://bmcpublichealth.biomedcentral.com/articles/10.1186/s12889-020-09875-z

[228] https://www.flexiform.co.uk/wellbeing-importance-office-design

[229] https://blog.frontiersin.org/2022/06/17/frontiers-virtual-reality-urban-design-mental-wellbeing-color-vegetation/amp/

[230] https://www.ciphr.com/advice/plants-in-the-office/

[231] https://www.microsoft.com/en-us/research/uploads/prod/2022/04/Microsoft-New-Future-of-Work-Report-2022.pdf

[232] https://www.tandfonline.com/doi/full/10.1080/09613218.2019.1710098

[233] https://www-vice-com.cdn.ampproject.org/c/s/www.vice.com/amp/en/article/pkpnng/the-research-on-how-nature-affects-mental-health-has-a-weird-problem

[234] https://sparq.stanford.edu/solutions/reface-space-keep-women-tech

[235] https://www.shrm.org/resourcesandtools/hr-topics/technology/pages/teleworkers-more-productive-even-when-sick.aspx

[236] https://www.linkedin.com/pulse/what-makes-people-want-return-office-whats-putting-off-siobhan-morrin/

[237] https://assets.publishing.service.gov.uk/government/uploads/system/uploads/attachment_data/file/772615/20150318_-_Physical_Environments_-_V3.0_FINAL.pdf

[238] http://www.healthscotland.scot/media/1725/employee-voice-and-mental-wellbeing-a-rapid-evidence-review.pdf

[239] https://www.tandfonline.com/doi/full/10.1080/09650792.2018.1436079

[240] https://www.researchgate.net/publication/349598237_Voice_More_and_Be_Happier_How_Employee_Voice_Influences_Psychological_Wellbeing_in_the_Workplace

[241] https://onlinelibrary.wiley.com/doi/10.1111/1467-8551.12471#bjom12471-bib-0061

[242] https://onlinelibrary.wiley.com/doi/10.1111/1467-8551.12471

[243] https://www.researchgate.net/publication/349598237_Voice_More_and_Be_Happier_How_Employee_Voice_Influences_Psychological_Wellbeing_in_the_Workplace

[244] https://www.gartner.com/smarterwithgartner/is-it-time-to-toss-out-your-old-employee-engagement-survey

[245] https://blessingwhite.com/wp-content/uploads/2018/11/Employee-Engagement-Research-Report-2013.pdf

[246] https://web.stanford.edu/dept/communication/faculty/krosnick/docs/2012/Anonymity JESP FINAL June 2012.pdf

[247] https://fortune.com/2022/06/30/young-professionals-slam-anonymous-workplace-surveys-viral-tik-tok/amp/

[248] https://www.roberthalf.com/salary-guide?utm_campaign=Press_Release&utm_medium=Link&utm_source=Press_Release

[249] https://www.oecd.org/statistics/oecd-releases-first-comprehensive-guidelines-on-measuring-subjective-wellbeing.htm

[250] https://academic.oup.com/edited-volume/42646/chapter-abstract/360565899?redirectedFrom=fulltext

[251] https://www.thelancet.com/journals/lancet/article/PII0140-6736(91)93068-K/fulltext

[252] https://journals.sagepub.com/doi/pdf/10.1177/0730888417697232

[253] https://journals.sagepub.com/doi/pdf/10.1177/0730888417697232

[254] https://pubmed.ncbi.nlm.nih.gov/26641482/

[255] https://doi.apa.org/doiLanding?doi=10.1037 percent2Fapl0000501

[256] https://www.scirp.org/journal/paperinformation.aspx?paperid=98229

[257] https://www.studocu.com/my/document/sunway-university/human-resource-management/the-overlooked-essentials-of-employee-wellbeing-mc-kinsey/15635824

[258] https://www.randstad.co.uk/s3fs-media/uk/public/2022-05/Randstad_REBR_UK_2022.pdf

[259] https://www.mckinsey.com/business-functions/people-and-organizational-performance/our-insights/gone-for-now-or-gone-for-good-how-to-play-the-new-talent-game-and-win-back-workers
[260] https://journals.sagepub.com/doi/abs/10.1177/0963721415628011
[261] https://www.scirp.org/html/4-2120312_42311.htm
[262] https://www.ncbi.nlm.nih.gov/pmc/articles/PMC8004082/
[263] https://wearewildgoose.com/uk/team-activities/flexible-working-survey-insights/
[264] https://pubmed.ncbi.nlm.nih.gov/33311716/
[265] https://www.ucl.ac.uk/news/2017/jul/being-zero-hours-contract-bad-your-health
[266] https://www.cam.ac.uk/research/news/zero-hours-contracts-are-tip-of-the-iceberg-of-damaging-shift-work-say-researchers
[267] https://worklifelaw.org/projects/stable-scheduling-study/report/
[268] https://www.ey.com/en_gl/news/2021/05/more-than-half-of-employees-globally-would-quit-their-jobs-if-not-provided-post-pandemic-flexibility-ey-survey-finds
[269] https://www-wsj-com.cdn.ampproject.org/c/s/www.wsj.com/amp/articles/workers-care-more-about-flexible-hours-than-remote-work-11643112004
[270] https://www.joblist.com/trends/the-elusive-work-life-balance
[271] https://employeebenefits.co.uk/staff-sacrifice-1949-salary-flexibility/
[272] https://www.mckinsey.com/business-functions/people-and-organizational-performance/our-insights/married-to-the-job-no-more-craving-flexibility-parents-are-quitting-to-get-it
[273] https://www.mckinsey.com/featured-insights/diversity-and-inclusion/women-in-the-workplace
[274] https://www.cisco.com/c/dam/m/en_us/solutions/global-hybrid-work-study/reports/cisco-global-hybrid-work-study-2022.pdf
[275] https://link.springer.com/article/10.1007/s10902-012-9345-3
[276] https://www.ncbi.nlm.nih.gov/pmc/articles/PMC7610217/
[277] https://www.glassdoor.com/blog/vacation-realities-2017/
[278] https://www.ustravel.org/sites/default/files/media_root/document/Paid percent20Time percent20Off percent20Trends percent20Fact percent20Sheet.pdf?utm_source=MagnetMail&utm_medium=email&utm_content=8 percent2E15 percent2E19 percent2DPress percent2DVacation percent20Days percent20Release&utm_campaign=pr
[279] https://www.thesun.co.uk/news/10734129/brits-arent-using-annual-leave/
[280] https://www.mirror.co.uk/news/uk-news/workers-failing-take-annual-leave-24636948
[281] https://www.independent.co.uk/news/uk/home-news/unclaimed-annual-leave-uk-holidays-b1892225.html
[282] https://www.kimbleapps.com/2018/05/no-vacation-nation-infographic/

[283] https://www.sciencedirect.com/science/article/pii/S0160-4120(21)00220-8

[284] https://www.ncbi.nlm.nih.gov/pmc/articles/PMC7610217/

[285] https://pubsonline.informs.org/doi/abs/10.1287/orsc.2015.0975

[286] https://neurosciencenews.com/vacation-mental-health-20898/

[287] https://scaffmag.com/2021/06/worlds-first-pilot-of-flexible-working-on-construction-sites-finds-wellbeing-soars/

[288] https://www.mckinsey.com/featured-insights/sustainable-inclusive-growth/future-of-america/american-opportunity-survey

[289] https://www.mckinsey.com/industries/real-estate/our-insights/americans-are-embracing-flexible-work-and-they-want-more-of-it?cid=other-soc-lkn-mip-mck-oth---&sid=7156895736&linkId=170524014

[290] https://www.shrm.org/resourcesandtools/hr-topics/technology/pages/teleworkers-more-productive-even-when-sick.aspx

[291] https://www.hiringpeople.co.uk/blog/rail-strike-fuels-google-searches-for-remote-jobs/

[292] https://www-wsj-com.cdn.ampproject.org/c/s/www.wsj.com/amp/articles/netherlands-poised-to-make-work-from-home-a-legal-right-11657206737

[293] https://apple.news/ANNuU_qyGQwmLidr4k0mmow

[294] https://iris.unica.it/retrieve/handle/11584/176541/157110/5431-16332-2-PB.pdf

[295] https://www.researchgate.net/publication/341775007_Empowering_Leadership_and_Psychological_Health_The_Mediating_Role_of_Psychological_Empowerment

[296] https://integraladvisors.com/wp-content/uploads/2013/02/State-Of-the-American-Manager.pdf

[297] https://www.mercer.com/our-thinking/career/global-talent-hr-trends.html

[298] https://www.managementtoday.co.uk/workplace-wellbeing-organisations-failing-employees/leadership-lessons/article/1577654

[299] https://graziadaily.co.uk/beauty-hair/wellness/mental-health-in-workplace/

[300] https://graziadaily.co.uk/beauty-hair/wellness/mental-health-in-workplace/

[301] https://www.peoplemanagement.co.uk/article/1744931/employees-scared-open-up-about-mental-health

[302] https://www.tandfonline.com/doi/abs/10.1080/09585192.2017.1423103

[303] https://www.researchgate.net/publication/308202797_Scarred_for_the_R

est_of_My_Career_Career-
Long_Effects_of_Abusive_Leadership_on_Professional_Athlete_Aggres
sion_and_Task_Performance

[304] https://www.elevatelimited.com/engage/events/learnings-from-
assessments-and-audits-integrated-with-worker-engagement/

[305] https://workplacebullying.org/2021-wbi-survey/

[306] https://www.mckinsey.com/business-functions/people-and-
organizational-performance/our-insights/gone-for-now-or-gone-for-good-
how-to-play-the-new-talent-game-and-win-back-workers

[307] https://www.catalyst.org/reports/empathy-work-strategy-crisis

[308] https://www.ncbi.nlm.nih.gov/pmc/articles/PMC3526833/

[309] https://core.ac.uk/download/pdf/13242652.pdf

[310] https://journals.sagepub.com/doi/abs/10.1177/0143831X19890678

[311] https://www.emerald.com/insight/content/doi/10.1108/EJMBE-03-
2020-0056/full/html

[312] https://www.ncbi.nlm.nih.gov/pmc/articles/PMC3439598/

[313] https://repositorio.iscte-
iul.pt/bitstream/10071/19740/4/master_virginia_ramos_pedro.pdf

[314] https://psycnet.apa.org/doiLanding?doi=10.1037
percent2Focp0000313

[315]

https://journals.plos.org/plosone/article?id=10.1371/journal.pone.019780
2

[316] https://invistainsights.com/wp-
content/uploads/Leadership_Impact_on_Employee_Wellbeing_Whitepap
er_1_21_847889890.pdf

[317] https://www.peoplemanagement.co.uk/article/1755631/two-thirds-
workers-not-share-mental-health-problems-employer-poll-finds

[318] https://www.peoplemanagement.co.uk/article/1755631/two-thirds-
workers-not-share-mental-health-problems-employer-poll-finds

[319] https://corporate-adviser.com/eight-out-of-10-hide-mental-health-
problems-at-work/

[320] https://www.peoplemanagement.co.uk/article/1742558/workers-call-
in-physically-sick-hide-mental-ill-health

[321] https://www.hrmagazine.co.uk/content/news/mental-health-named-
most-common-reason-for-employees-to-lie-about-sick-days/

[322] https://www.mind.org.uk/news-campaigns/news/the-final-taboo-
millions-of-employees-forced-to-lie-about-stress/

[323] https://www.mind.org.uk/news-campaigns/news/a-million-uk-adults-
who-had-problems-with-their-mental-health-for-the-first-time-during-
the-pandemic-have-not-spoken-to-anyone-about-it/

[324] https://www.theguardian.com/business/2021/aug/04/uk-workers-feel-
pressure-to-hide-mental-health-concerns-survey-finds

[325] https://www.mckinsey.com/business-functions/people-and-organizational-performance/our-insights/leadership-in-a-crisis-responding-to-the-coronavirus-outbreak-and-future-challenges

[326] https://bmjopen.bmj.com/content/8/6/e021795

[327] https://www.emerald.com/insight/content/doi/10.1108/MHSI-03-2022-0014/full/html

[328] https://www.personneltoday.com/hr/managers-must-improve-mental-health-support-during-coronavirus-crisis/

[329] https://www.rand.org/randeurope/research/projects/britains-healthiest-workplace.html

[330] https://www.vitality.co.uk/business/healthiest-workplace/

[331] https://www.federalreserve.gov/publications/files/2018-report-economic-wellbeing-us-households-201905.pdf

[332] https://www.fca.org.uk/publication/research/fawg-financial-wellbeing-workplace.pdf

[333] https://bmjleader.bmj.com/content/5/4/291

[334]
https://www.sciencedirect.com/science/article/pii/S0191886921007856

[335] https://www2.deloitte.com/us/en/insights/topics/leadership/employee-wellness-in-the-corporate-workplace.html?id=us:2sm:3li:4diUS175466:5awa::MMDDYY::author&pkid=1008950

[336] https://www2.deloitte.com/us/en/insights/topics/leadership/employee-wellness-in-the-corporate-workplace.html?id=us:2sm:3li:4diUS175466:5awa::MMDDYY::author&pkid=1008950

[337] https://www2.deloitte.com/us/en/insights/topics/leadership/employee-wellness-in-the-corporate-workplace.html?id=us:2sm:3li:4diUS175466:5awa::MMDDYY::author&pkid=1008950

[338] https://www.apa.org/news/press/releases/2015/02/money-stress

[339] https://www.apa.org/news/press/releases/2022/03/inflation-war-stress

[340] https://www.pwc.com/us/en/services/consulting/workforce-of-the-future/library/employee-financial-wellness-survey.html

[341] https://www.cnbc.com/2022/06/06/42percent-of-americans-say-money-has-a-negative-impact-on-mental-health.html

[342] https://www.sciencedaily.com/releases/2016/02/160222090652.htm

[343] https://www.seattletimes.com/seattle-news/health/study-iq-drops-with-worries-over-money/

[344] https://fortune-com.cdn.ampproject.org/c/s/fortune.com/2022/06/16/41-percent-of-employees-are-living-paycheck-to-paycheck/amp/

[345] https://www.aegon.co.uk/content/dam/ukpaw/documents/financial-wellbeing-CEBR-condensed.pdf

[346] https://www.zellis.com/resources/press-and-media/financial-wellbeing-2022/

[347] https://www.aviva.co.uk/business/business-perspectives/featured-articles-hub/jump-the-taboo-financial-wellbeing/

[348] https://www.aegon.co.uk/content/dam/ukpaw/documents/financial-wellbeing-CEBR-condensed.pdf

[349] https://www.jrf.org.uk/report/minimum-income-standard-uk-2021

[350] Local action on health inequalities: Health inequalities and the living wage, Public Health England and UCL Institute of Health Equity (2014)

[351]

https://www.livingwage.org.uk/sites/default/files/LW_LifeOnLowPayPandemic_Feb2020.pdf

[352] https://www.ncbi.nlm.nih.gov/pmc/articles/PMC1446793/

[353] https://onlinelibrary.wiley.com/doi/full/10.1002/hec.4490

[354] https://www.inc.com/minda-zetlin/paypal-wages-ndi-profits-growth-dan-schulman.html

[355] https://policyscotland.gla.ac.uk/wp-content/uploads/2020/05/LivingWageImpactforIndividuals.pdf

[356] https://www.canadalife.co.uk/news/redundancy-fears-causing-increase-in-presenteeism-during-lockdown/

[357] https://www.healthaffairs.org/doi/10.1377/hlthaff.2015.0965

[358]

https://www.tandfonline.com/doi/full/10.1080/02678373.2017.1356396

[359] https://www.brookings.edu/opinions/the-flu-is-awful-a-lack-of-sick-leave-is-worse/

[360] https://employeebenefits.co.uk/issues/april-online-2017/64-believe-employers-invest-in-benefits-that-staff-do-not-want-need-or-use/

[361] https://corporate-adviser.com/big-increase-in-demand-for-employee-benefits/

[362] https://corporate-adviser.com/big-increase-in-demand-for-employee-benefits/

[363]

https://www.tandfonline.com/doi/full/10.1080/13696998.2019.1581620

[364] https://dentistry.uic.edu/patients

[365] https://www.zurich.co.uk/media-centre/zurich-mental-health-claims-double-over-12-month-period

[366] https://www.employeebenefits.co.uk/poll-27-insurance-benefits-cancer/

[367] https://www.employeebenefits.co.uk/poll-27-insurance-benefits-cancer/

[368] https://www.dailymail.co.uk/news/article-9546403/More-one-four-income-protection-claims-triggered-mental-health-issues-2020-study-says.html

[369] https://www.moneymarketing.co.uk/news/royal-london-announces-record-claims-payment-in-2021/

370 https://www.aviva.com/newsroom/news-releases/2022/05/over-1-bn-in-individual-protection-claims-helped-more-than-53700-customers-and-families-in-2021/
371 https://www.independent-practitioner-today.co.uk/2022/06/mental-health-top-of-pay-help-claims/
372 https://www.aegon.co.uk/content/dam/ukpaw/documents/financial-wellbeing-CEBR-condensed.pdf
373 https://www.insurancebusinessmag.com/uk/news/breaking-news/covid19-pandemic-drives-sales-of-income-protection-policies-322760.aspx
374 https://ora.ox.ac.uk/objects/uuid:047dfae9-e1d3-4753-85b7-5664375d66bb/download_file?file_format=pdf&safe_filename=Experience_JoEP_R percent26R2_v2.pdf&type_of_work=Journal+article
375 https://www.the-exeter.com/news/two-thirds-of-uk-s-working-population-worried-about-a-loss-of-earnings-through-illness-including-covid-19-research-from-the-exeter-shows/
376 https://www.ftadviser.com/protection/2021/11/29/uk-adults-do-not-understand-protection-products-research-finds/
377 https://www.the-exeter.com/news/two-thirds-of-uk-s-working-population-worried-about-a-loss-of-earnings-through-illness-including-covid-19-research-from-the-exeter-shows/
378 https://www.yorkshirepost.co.uk/business/britain-faces-crisis-as-more-people-adopt-unhealthy-habits-in-response-to-rising-cost-of-living-says-benenden-3814159
379 https://www.greo.ca/Modules/EvidenceCentre/files/Capacci percent20et percent20al percent20(2017)_Are percent20consumers percent20more percent20willing percent20to percent20invest percent20in percent20luck_final.pdf
380 https://link.springer.com/article/10.1007/s10899-011-9282-9
381 https://www.icrg.org/sites/default/files/oec/pdfs/ncrg_fact_sheet_gambling_disorders.pdf
382 https://www.kflaph.ca/en/research-and-reports/gambling-and-gaming-health-impacts.aspx
383 https://www.ahajournals.org/doi/full/10.1161/01.CIR.0000048890.59383.8D
384 https://www.cancer.org/latest-news/exercise-linked-with-lower-risk-of-13-types-of-cancer.html
385 https://www.ncbi.nlm.nih.gov/pmc/articles/PMC1470658/
386 https://www.ncbi.nlm.nih.gov/pmc/articles/PMC2953272/
387 https://europepmc.org/article/med/20086603
388 https://www.thelancet.com/journals/lanpsy/article/PIIS2215-0366(18)30227-X/fulltext
389 https://www.ncbi.nlm.nih.gov/pmc/articles/PMC4498975/

[390] https://www.johnwbrickfoundation.org/move-your-mental-health-report/

[391] https://www.sciencedirect.com/science/article/abs/pii/S0165032715314221

[392] https://www.mdpi.com/1660-4601/17/18/6469/htm

[393] https://www.theguardian.com/lifeandstyle/2019/dec/02/one-step-at-a-time-exercise-mental-health

[394] https://link.springer.com/article/10.1007/s40279-015-0303-1

[395] https://www.annualreviews.org/doi/10.1146/annurev-med-060619-022943

[396] https://www.sciencedirect.com/science/article/pii/S1087079221001416

[397] http://www.nature.com/neuro/journal/v16/n2/full/nn.3303.html

[398] http://www.nature.com/nature/journal/v427/n6972/full/nature02223.html

[399] http://www.ncbi.nlm.nih.gov/pubmed/19910332

[400] https://www.cdc.gov/pcd/issues/2021/20_0573.htm

[401] https://www.sleepfoundation.org/sleep-hygiene/good-sleep-and-job-performance

[402] https://www.ncbi.nlm.nih.gov/pmc/articles/PMC1933584/

[403] https://academic.oup.com/occmed/article/67/5/377/3859790

[404] http://researchprofiles.herts.ac.uk/portal/files/12097546/Report.pdf

[405] https://www.ucl.ac.uk/news/2017/jul/being-zero-hours-contract-bad-your-health

[406] https://www.tuc.org.uk/news/zero-hour-workers-twice-likely-work-health-risk-night-shifts-tuc-analysis

[407] https://www.tuc.org.uk/news/two-thirds-zero-hours-workers-want-jobs-guaranteed-hours-tuc-polling-reveals

[408] https://www.modobio.com/these-statistics-on-wearables-help-us-better-understand-what-the-future-holds/

[409] https://www.mcmasteroptimalaging.org/full-article/es/activity-monitors-enhance-benefits-physical-activity-programs-adults-overweight-1591

[410] https://www.bmj.com/content/376/bmj-2021-068047

[411] https://www.ncbi.nlm.nih.gov/pmc/articles/PMC8826148/

[412] https://www.mrc-epid.cam.ac.uk/blog/2020/08/17/largest-study-wearable-devices-activity/

[413] https://www.ncbi.nlm.nih.gov/books/NBK220636/

[414] https://ifs.org.uk/docs/private_med.pdf

[415] https://www.nber.org/papers/w17190

[416] https://www.mckinsey.com/industries/healthcare-systems-and-services/our-insights/employers-look-to-expand-health-benefits-while-managing-medical-costs?cid=other-soc-lkn-mip-mck-oth---&sid=7116429323&linkId=170216749

417

http://jamanetwork.com/journals/jamanetworkopen/fullarticle/10.1001/ja manetworkopen.2022.16349?utm_source=For_The_Media&utm_mediu m=referral&utm_campaign=ftm_links&utm_term=060922

[418] https://bmchealthservres.biomedcentral.com/articles/10.1186/s12913-020-4967-3

419

https://www.researchgate.net/publication/228209697_The_Effectiveness _of_Health_Screening

[420] EAP Effectiveness and ROI. Attridge, M., Amaral, T., Bjornson, T., Goplerud, E., Herlihy, P., McPherson, T., Paul R., Routledge, S., Sharar, D., Stephenson, D., & Teems, L. (2009). EAP effectiveness and ROI. EASNA Research Notes, 1(3), 1-5. Available online from http://www.easna.org

[421] https://www.shrm.org/resourcesandtools/hr-topics/benefits/pages/health-benefits-foster-retention.aspx

[422] https://www.shrm.org/resourcesandtools/hr-topics/benefits/pages/health-benefits-foster-retention.aspx

[423] https://healthcareandprotection.com/affordable-guided-care-policies-driving-pmi-boom-sawyer/

[424] https://healthcareandprotection.com/private-healthcare-spending-soars-as-long-term-lack-of-nhs-funding-bites-ippr/

[425] https://www.abi.org.uk/globalassets/files/subject/public/health/smf---insuring-a-return-winter-2021---final-version.pdf

[426] https://healthcareandprotection-com.cdn.ampproject.org/c/s/healthcareandprotection.com/pmi-and-pay-rises-the-most-desired-employee-benefits-canada-life/amp/

[427] https://www.cambridge.org/core/journals/the-british-journal-of-psychiatry/article/mental-health-literacy/5563369643662EC541F33D1DD307AD35

[428] https://www.ncbi.nlm.nih.gov/pmc/articles/PMC1492599/

[429] https://www.ncbi.nlm.nih.gov/pmc/articles/PMC2668931/

430

https://eprints.soton.ac.uk/418650/1/HEJ_17_0250.R1_Final_version_20 17_12_01_.pdf

[431] https://www.ncbi.nlm.nih.gov/pmc/articles/PMC4577469/

[432] https://www.ncbi.nlm.nih.gov/pmc/articles/PMC5680908/

[433] https://www2.deloitte.com/us/en/insights/industry/health-care/consumer-health-trends.html

[434] https://www.ncbi.nlm.nih.gov/pmc/articles/PMC5743920/

[435] https://www.vice.com/en/article/z3ekqx/we-asked-people-how-the-pandemic-has-changed-their-approach-to-health-and-wellness

[436] https://ec.europa.eu/eurostat/web/products-eurostat-news/-/edn-20220406-1

[437] https://www.rethink.org/news-and-stories/news/2021/03/demand-for-mental-health-advice-soars-in-year-after-first-lockdown/

[438] https://www.forbes.com/sites/johnkoetsier/2020/09/26/global-online-content-consumption-doubled-in-2020/

[439] https://www.edelman.com/sites/g/files/aatuss191/files/2022-01/2022 percent20Edelman percent20Trust percent20Barometer percent20FINAL_Jan25.pdf

[440] https://www.microsoft.com/en-us/research/uploads/prod/2022/04/Microsoft-New-Future-of-Work-Report-2022.pdf

[441] https://www.mindsharepartners.org/mentalhealthatworkreport

[442] https://www.science.org/content/article/parents-emotional-trauma-may-change-their-children-s-biology-studies-mice-show-how

[443]

https://www.science.org/doi/10.1126/science.343.6169.361?adobe_mc=MCMID percent3D40632800142560007463190267046148702678 percent7CMCORGID percent3D242B6472541199F70A4C98A6 percent2540AdobeOrg percent7CTS percent3D1655453608&_ga=2.132229390.1025615040.1655453607-1951691582.1655453607

[444] https://www2.deloitte.com/global/en/pages/about-deloitte/articles/genzmillennialsurvey.html

[445] https://www.ncbi.nlm.nih.gov/pmc/articles/PMC4911781/

[446] https://www.frontiersin.org/articles/10.3389/fpsyg.2019.00284/full

[447] https://www.linkedin.com/pulse/neglected-middle-child-mental-health-bruce-isdale/

[448] https://www.ncbi.nlm.nih.gov/pmc/articles/PMC3150158/

[449] https://www.nytimes.com/2017/06/12/well/live/having-friends-is-good-for-you.html

[450] http://www.health.harvard.edu/newsletter_article/the-health-benefits-of-strong-relationships

[451] https://www.exeter.ac.uk/news/research/title_801978_en.html

[452] https://link.springer.com/article/10.3758/s13428-011-0091-y

[453] https://www.accenture.com/_acnmedia/PDF-152/Accenture-Gaming-Article.pdf

[454] https://academic.oup.com/jcmc/article/20/4/381/4067557

[455] https://eprints.whiterose.ac.uk/133834/1/CHB_D_17_01556R1.pdf

[456] http://gamestudies.org/1901/articles/lee

[457] https://www.statista.com/statistics/1033742/worldwide-microsoft-teams-daily-and-monthly-users/

[458] https://www.uctoday.com/collaboration/microsoft-teams-statistics-the-ultimate-ucaas-hub/

[459] https://www.accenture.com/us-en/insights/strategy/organizational-culture?c=acn_glb_omni-connectedmediarelations_13017967&n=mrl_0522

[460] https://www.personneltoday.com/hr/survey-engage-with-frontline-workers-or-risk-losing-them/

[461] https://www.bloomberg.com/news/articles/2022-05-24/workers-in-office-feel-least-connected-countering-rto-claims

[462] https://www.frontiersin.org/articles/10.3389/fpsyg.2020.552867/full

[463] https://www.neighbourly.com/blog/employee-volunteering-creates-a-happier-workforce-research-finds

[464] https://www.lse.ac.uk/News/Latest-news-from-LSE/2021/e-May-21/Volunteering-in-the-NHS-Covid-19-Volunteer-Responders-Programme-significantly-increased-volunteers-overall-life-satisfaction

[465] https://bmjopen.bmj.com/content/6/8/e011327

[466] https://www.uea.ac.uk/news/-/article/volunteering-linked-to-improved-life-satisfaction-happiness-and-quality-of-life

[467] https://journals.sagepub.com/doi/abs/10.1177/135910539900400301

[468] https://www.ncbi.nlm.nih.gov/pmc/articles/PMC5508200/

[469] https://www.ncbi.nlm.nih.gov/pmc/articles/PMC1622872/

[470] https://www.ncbi.nlm.nih.gov/pmc/articles/PMC1622872/

[471] https://www.nature.com/articles/nclimate2449

[472] https://www.psychologicalscience.org/news/giving-rather-than-receiving-leads-to-lasting-happiness-study.html

[473] https://ifs.org.uk/publications/14799

[474] https://opentextbc.ca/socialpsychology/chapter/understanding-altruism-self-and-other-concerns/

[475] https://www.kcl.ac.uk/news/exposure-to-air-pollution-linked-with-increased-mental-health-service-use-new-study-finds

[476] https://www.mckinsey.com/business-functions/sustainability/our-insights/delivering-the-climate-technologies-needed-for-net-zero

[477] https://www.nature.com/articles/s41598-020-71916-9

[478] https://www.recyclingbins.co.uk/blog/survey-says-that-being-green-makes-us-happier/

[479] https://www.rug.nl/gmw/news/sustainable-behavior-makes-people-happy?lang=en

[480] https://iopscience.iop.org/article/10.1088/1748-9326/abc4ae/meta

[481] https://sdgs.un.org/goals

[482] https://www.unleash.ai/learning-and-development/learning-to-be-well/

[483] https://www,ecowatch.com/air-pollution-childrens-mental-health-2640650546.html

[484] https://www.corporateknights.com/health-and-lifestyle/does-working-for-a-sustainable-company-make-you-happier/

[485] https://www.sciencedirect.com/science/article/abs/pii/S1462901122000776

[486] https://www.naturalnews.com/2017-12-17-does-being-green-make-you-happy-research-suggests-engaging-in-eco-friendly-behavior-makes-us-feel-good-about-ourselves.html

[487] http://www.dvirc.org/energy-efficient-buildings-increase-worker-productivity-health/

[488] https://www.aon.com/unitedkingdom/employee-benefits/resources/benefits-and-trends/default.jsp

[489] https://heartbeat.peakon.com/reports/employee-expectations-2020/

[490] https://www.gartner.com/en/articles/employees-seek-personal-value-and-purpose-at-work-be-prepared-to-deliver?utm_medium=social&utm_source=linkedin&utm_campaign=SM_GB_YOY_GTR_SOC_SF1_SM-SWG&utm_content=&sf256916116=1

[491] https://hbr.org/2018/11/9-out-of-10-people-are-willing-to-earn-less-money-to-do-more-meaningful-work

[492] https://www.keystepmedia.com/shop/12-leadership-competency-primers/#.YrGONi8w27d

[493] https://www.webmd.com/balance/features/sense-purpose-health

[494] http://www.ncbi.nlm.nih.gov/pubmed/22359156

[495] http://www.ncbi.nlm.nih.gov/pubmed/23597331

[496] https://www.fastcompany.com/3041738/millennials-want-to-work-at-organizations-that-focus-on-purpose-not-just-p

[497] https://workplaceinsight.net/majority-of-office-workers-discontented-with-workplace-environment/

[498] https://www.mercer.com/our-thinking/career/global-talent-hr-trends.html

[499] https://www.pwc.com/gx/en/issues/workforce/hopes-and-fears-2022.html

[500] https://www.washingtonpost.com/business/2020/05/27/millennial-recession-covid/

[501] https://iea.org.uk/media/67-per-cent-of-young-brits-want-a-socialist-economic-system-finds-new-poll/

[502] https://news.gallup.com/poll/240725/democrats-positive-socialism-capitalism.aspx

[503] https://www.trtworld.com/magazine/a-majority-of-british-youth-blame-capitalism-for-climate-change-and-racism-48206

[504] https://www.agilitypr.com/pr-news/public-relations/why-we-buy-from-brands-that-take-a-stand-we-care-about-and-ditch-those-that-dont/

[505] https://www.ft.com/content/d328ba92-5af1-46d2-b3a4-05f15c9ba964

[506] https://thriveglobal.com/stories/recycling-is-good-for-the-environment-but-did-you-know-it-can-also-improve-your-mental-health/

[507] https://www.emerald.com/insight/content/doi/10.1108/MD-06-2019-0713/full/html

[508] http://thewellbeingpulse.com/bank-on-your-people/

[509] https://jamanetwork.com/journals/jamanetworkopen/fullarticle/2734064

[510] https://www.ncbi.nlm.nih.gov/pmc/articles/PMC3827458/

[511] https://www.mentalhealth.org.uk/blog/employment-vital-maintaining-good-mental-health

[512] https://www.fastcompany.com/90306556/most-millennials-would-take-a-pay-cut-to-work-at-a-sustainable-company

[513] https://www.tandfonline.com/doi/abs/10.1080/0267257X.2019.1569549?journalCode=rjmm20&

[514] https://www.ncbi.nlm.nih.gov/pmc/articles/PMC3827458/

[515] https://www.psychreg.org/wp-admin/post-new.php

[516] https://www.tandfonline.com/doi/abs/10.1080/13607861003713216

[517] https://wsp.wharton.upenn.edu/book/beating-burnout-at-work/

[518] https://www.apa.org/monitor/2022/01/special-burnout-stress

[519] https://www.stress.org.uk/wp-content/uploads/2022/03/THE-IMPACT-OF-WORKPLACE-STRESS-2022.pdf

[520] https://f.hubspotusercontent30.net/hubfs/7677235/The percent20State percent20of percent20Burnout percent20in percent20Tech percent20-percent202022 percent20Edition.pdf

[521] https://sigmapubs.onlinelibrary.wiley.com/doi/abs/10.1111/jnu.12642

[522] https://www.frontiersin.org/articles/10.3389/fpsyg.2020.623587/full

[523] https://research.birmingham.ac.uk/en/publications/does-psychological-capital-and-social-support-impact-engagement-a-2

[524] https://www.semanticscholar.org/paper/Fostering-psychosocial-wellness-in-oncology-nurses percent3A-Medland-Howard-Ruben/9152e6990eecb3e3dd9ecb5d4827aa4775f1ac4b

[525] https://link.springer.com/article/10.1023/A:1005324405249

[526] https://www.frontiersin.org/articles/10.3389/fpsyg.2021.625506/full

[527] https://journals.sagepub.com/doi/abs/10.1177/10986111211036007

[528] https://www.gallup.com/workplace/236213/why-need-best-friends-work.aspx

[529] https://wearewildgoose.com/uk/news/friends-happiness-in-the-workplace-survey/

[530] https://online.olivet.edu/news/research-friends-work

[531] https://www.nbcnews.com/better/lifestyle/here-s-no-1-reason-why-employees-quit-their-jobs-ncna1020031

[532] https://www.cfo.com/human-capital/employee-retention/2022/07/employee-recognition-turnover-attrition-labor-market-gallup-weekly-stat/?blaid=3289842

[533] https://yougov.co.uk/topics/consumer/articles-reports/2020/06/01/do-key-workers-feel-appreciated-work-during-covid-

[534] https://www.psychologytoday.com/us/blog/comfort-gratitude/202006/the-positive-impact-gratitude-mental-health

[535] https://www.hellobenefex.com/resources/reports/psychology-of-recognition/

[536] https://www.researchgate.net/publication/343417770_The_Anxiety-Buffer_Hypothesis_in_the_Time_of_COVID-19_When_Self-Esteem_Protects_From_the_Impact_of_Loneliness_and_Fear_on_Anxiety_and_Depression

537
https://www.researchgate.net/publication/281779489_Does_Employee_R
ecognition_Affect_Positive_Psychological_Functioning_and_Wellbeing
[538] https://www.hsmsearch.com/unappreciated-emloyees-mental-health-
issues
[539] https://www.multivu.com/players/English/8294451-cigna-us-
loneliness-survey/docs/IndexReport_1524069371598-173525450.pdf
540
https://www.researchgate.net/publication/286153549_The_association_of
_loneliness_at_the_workplace_with_organisational_variables
[541] https://www.apa.org/news/press/releases/2012/03/wellbeing
[542] https://firstup.io/blog/the-impact-of-communication-on-mental-health-
and-why-return-to-work-is-the-moment-for-change/
[543] https://core.ac.uk/download/43560548.pdf
[544] https://www.mckinsey.com/business-functions/organization/our-
insights/what-employees-are-saying-about-the-future-of-remote-work
[545] https:/hbr.org/2021/10/how-to-get-employees-to-actually-participate-
in-wellbeing-programs?utm_campaign=Feed
percent3A+harvardbusiness+ percent28HBR.org
percent29&utm_medium=feed&utm_source=feedburner
[546] https://www.treefrogmarketing.com/9-reasons-customers-arent-
reading-emails/
[547] http://www.nngroup.com/articles/how-little-do-users-read/
[548] https://www.visualcapitalist.com/media-consumption-covid-19/
[549] https://www.visualcapitalist.com/media-consumption-covid-19/
[550] https://www.edelman.com/sites/g/files/aatuss191/files/2022-01/2022
percent20Edelman percent20Trust percent20Barometer
percent20FINAL_Jan25.pdf
551
https://www.aafp.org/pubs/fpm/issues/2018/0300/p31.html#fpm2018030
0p31-b1
[552] https://www.onefpa.org/journal/Pages/OCT19-The-Sentimental-
Savings-Study.aspx
553
https://assets.publishing.service.gov.uk/government/uploads/system/uplo
ads/attachment_data/file/214406/WP109.pdf
[554] https://www.bi.team/wp-content/uploads/2020/09/BIT-Scottish-
Widows-Nudging-for-retirement-report-18-Sep.pdf
[555] https://www.retirementlivingstandards.org.uk
[556] https://journals.sagepub.com/doi/10.1177/0011000016633507
[557] https://bmjopen.bmj.com/content/6/7/e010641
[558] https://www2.deloitte.com/us/en/insights/topics/leadership/employee-
wellness-in-the-corporate-workplace.html
[559] https://employee-experience.unmind.com/#/
[560] https://www.ncbi.nlm.nih.gov/pmc/articles/PMC2921311/

[561] https://www.unleash.ai/future-of-work/hybrid-work-reduces-attrition-by-35/?utm_medium=Social&utm_source=LinkedIn#Echobox=1658844751-2

[562] https://www.frontiersin.org/articles/10.3389/fpubh.2020.00103/full

[563] https://link.springer.com/article/10.1007/s12144-019-00550-0

[564] https://www.routledge.com/Shaping-the-Future-of-Work-A-Handbook-for-Action-and-a-New-Social-Contract/Kochan-Dyer/p/book/9780367504700?gclid=Cj0KCQjw3v6SBhCsARIsACyrRAlWhG_v-U_3mpQpEoPxnYGENyfvkuL0ddWWQfBnqq2OBUW8vvfTlSIaAhYuEALw_wcB

[565] https://warwick.ac.uk/newsandevents/pressreleases/new_study_shows/

[566] https://app.fridaypulse.com/en/help-center/happiness-at-work/what-an-oxford-research-study-teaches-us-about-happiness-in-the-workplace

[567] http://citeseerx.ist.psu.edu/viewdoc/download?doi=10.1.1.456.1948&rep=rep1&type=pdf

[568] https://news.gallup.com/poll/394025/world-unhappier-stressed-ever.aspx

[569] https://business.linkedin.com/content/dam/me/business/en-us/talent-solutions-lodestone/body/pdf/global_talent_trends_2022.pdf

[570] https://www.linkedin.com/business/talent/blog/talent-strategy/more-roles-focused-on-culture-wellbeing-flex-work